A SENSE OF STYLE

A SENSE
of STYLE

STUDIES IN THE ART OF FICTION
IN ENGLISH-SPEAKING CANADA

W. J. Keith

ECW PRESS

CANADIAN CATALOGUING IN PUBLICATION DATA

Keith, W.J. (William John), 1934–

A sense of style.

Includes index.
ISBN 1–55022–092–6 (bound). – ISBN 1–55022–094–2 (pbk.)

1. Canadian fiction (English) – 20th century – History and
criticism.* 2. Novelists, Canadian (English) – 20th century –
Criticism and interpretation. 3. Style, literary.   I. Title.

PS8187.K45 1989   C813'.5'09   C89–094668–X
PR9192.5.K45 1989

This book has been published with the assistance of a grant from the
Canadian Federation for the Humanities, using funds provided by
the Social Sciences and Humanities Research Council of Canada.
Additional grants have been provided by the Ontario Arts Council
and The Canada Council.

Imaging by ECW Production Services, Sydenham, Ontario.
Printed by The Porcupine's Quill, Erin, Ontario.

Distributed by University of Toronto Press
5201 Dufferin Street, Downsview, Ontario M3H 5T8

Published by ECW PRESS
307 Coxwell Avenue, Toronto, Ontario M4L 3B5

CONTENTS

There are no absolutes in literature, that can be applied without reference to personal taste and judgement.

— *Robertson Davies*

We all have styles. The poet is the one who is aware of his style.

— *Hugh Hood*

I don't begin with a theory. If I did, I'd be lost.

— *Mavis Gallant*

With literary criticism, I really feel that it ought to be graspable.

— *Margaret Atwood*

PREFACE

Over the past twenty years or so, the period in which I have been acutely interested in the critical discussion of Canadian literature, successive waves of fashion and ideology have passed over the subject. At the beginning, one still encountered what I am tempted to call, after Touchstone in *As You Like It*, the poor-thing-but-mine-own school: "the literature is thin, a bit embarrassing, but it's ours and we must make the best of it." Then, of course, came nationalism and the thematic approach: "this material helps us to understand who we are and where we came from, a function so important that matters of evaluation and discrimination are irrelevant." Since then, we have witnessed a bewildering array of theories and pedantries — structuralism, post-structuralism, deconstruction, post-modernism, etc. — plus applied ideological approaches, of which the Marxist and the feminist are perhaps the most conspicuous. My own response to these developments combines elements of gratitude and irritation. We have all benefited from the best criticism arising out of each of these approaches, but the worst examples — jargon-ridden, pedantically arid, and (alas) numerically considerable — have not only unnecessarily obfuscated a subject which ought to be of broad appeal and concern, but have even brought it into disrepute. The literary-critical centre, we might say, has not held. Between the uninformed chitchat that passes for reviewing in newspapers and popular magazines, and the mandarin pretentiousness of too many learned journals, literary criticism as a civilized humane discipline threatens to become an extinct species.

Perhaps everywhere, but certainly in Canada, literary criticism needs, I believe, to go "back to basics," to return to its traditional function of providing help in the profitable reading and enjoyment of literature as a serious and richly rewarding cultural pursuit. Literature should be read not as a patriotic duty nor as a sociopolitical therapy, nor as a convenient springboard for aesthetic abstractions, but as an activity that nurtures the intellect, the imagination, and the emotions — and does so by providing increased pleasure and satisfaction through a sensitivity to language and an appreciation of subtlety and nuance.

In the following pages I have tried, as far as possible, to avoid any rigid critical methodology, though I am hardly as naïve as to suppose that my own way of reading is not deeply affected by the approach in which I was trained: English "practical criticism" of mid-century. But that, in comparison with what came after, was a liberatingly flexible approach, which at its best eschewed preconceived assumptions. I fully believe that, in learning how to read perceptively, we should proceed with caution by beginning with the words on the page and then moving out towards their relevances, rather than invoking a generalized theory (however impressively supported by selective quotation from the eminent) and then "applying" it to whatever text comes within range. I have tried, then, to consider the novelists discussed here with an open mind — or as close to an open mind as the average human being is capable of possessing. I have not — at least, not consciously — tried to force any approach on to these authors, but have asked instead: what are they doing? what emphases throw light upon their best qualities? And particularly: what is special about them, as individual writers, that distinguishes them from their fellows?

This is a book, then, that advocates not a single critical approach but a number of critical approaches, each suitable for the individual author or work under consideration. Hugh MacLennan once claimed that he had to be conservative in order to be revolutionary (E. Cameron 272), and this book is, in some respects, old-fashioned for a similar motive. It pins its faith on what some will regard as an antiquated interest in "style" and "close reading" in an endeavour to isolate what Robertson Davies's Saraceni in *What's Bred in the Bone* describes as the "something individual" (239) that exists in every significant work of art. It focuses on the experience of reading, the imaginative challenge involved in thoughtful and discriminating reading; although not a contribution to "reader-response theory," it is ultimately concerned with the way — or, rather, the ways — in which readers read fiction. It is intended as a stimulating guide for those who *enjoy* taking the art of fiction, and art in general, seriously.

Most of the preliminary details that need to be aired will be discussed in the introduction chapter, but a few general issues can more conveniently be treated here. Because I have occasion to quote in most chapters from interviews in which authors discuss their own work, it may well be assumed that I have fallen with almost indecent alacrity into the "intentional fallacy," often considered the most elementary and fatal of critical traps. I wish therefore to state at the outset that I have made every effort to avoid the pitfalls on this particular critical path. There is in fact nothing culpable in itself about establishing authorial intention; the fallacy arises only if we proceed to make a possibly unjustified assumption that this intention has been successfully realized. A writer's aims can frequently provide useful clues about how a work may be judged. This evidence, like any other, can be employed either well or badly; I have tried to use it judiciously and responsibly.

A second cause of possible misconception may also be confronted here. Because I profess to be interested in "style," there may be some readers who will expect me to have immersed myself in computer-statistics on such matters as sentence length, syntactical order, and the relative incidence of clausal constructions. I must therefore insist that, while I have investigated the results of such procedures, I have come to the conclusion that this kind of information is virtually useless for my practical purpose. The mere existence of isolatable stylistic characteristics, especially those not readily detectable by careful and sensitive reading, is of minor interest. What matters is *how* they are used and what effects they achieve. I know of no computer analysis that can respond to the rhythmic subtleties and tonal nuances that so often carry an essential part of a passage's meaning, or can register the larger cumulative effects of which individual grammatical units form a subordinate part. Well-planned computer programmes are doubtless valuable for various scholarly purposes, but they have little to offer when one is grappling with the elaborate effects of sentences upon the minds and emotions of individual readers.

I realize only too well that the separate chapters devoted to specific novelists in the pages to follow barely scratch the surface of what might properly be written. Each chapter, indeed, could well be expanded into a book-length study. My aim is not comprehensiveness but a kind of literary-critical signposting, an attempt to set inquisitive readers on to a promising track — to encourage them to ask the most

9

pressing questions about the works they read (questions, I have to say, that rarely seem to get articulated in the standard handbooks). This being so, I have not hesitated to make qualifying judgements about some of the works under scrutiny. In any healthy literary-critical situation, this would be taken for granted, but in the rather cosy — not to say, incestuous — world of Canadian writing, this is not yet the norm. Two points need to be made. First, I would not have devoted detailed attention to any of these writers if I did not believe that they had something of value to offer; critical strictures on parts of their work should therefore have the effect of throwing the importance of the rest into bolder relief. Second (a less obvious point), in some cases the approach taken has highlighted weaknesses, whereas in others it has skirted and so downplayed them. This, under the circumstances, was inevitable. It may therefore be wise, for the record, to acknowledge a few reservations. I am well aware that, say, the weakly unconvincing presentation of Ardith Aeriola in Howard O'Hagan's *Tay John* is a serious (though not fatal) blemish; that the climactic revelation about Mrs. Broom in *Hetty Dorval* is ludicrously out of place and harks back to a dead literary convention that Ethel Wilson ought to have outgrown; that Hugh Hood's *The Scenic Art* fails to attain the standard of the other novels in the first half of his *New Age* series. These and certain other judgements seem to me to be obvious, but to have made them in the body of my text would have obscured the lines of my main argument. I mention this here because, like some of the more prominent qualifications registered in other chapters, they need to be made if in Canadian literary culture we are ever going to aspire to the condition of what T.S. Eliot called the common pursuit of true judgement.

Finally, it is necessary to insist that the writers I have chosen to discuss represent a selection among many. The absence of a name does not imply that I necessarily consider that writer unimportant or unworthy. The selection itself was governed by a number of factors. First, I wished to concentrate on authors who had produced a substantial body of work. Writers generally considered to have produced only one really notable book — Sinclair Ross with *As for Me and My House*, Ernest Buckler with *The Mountain and the Valley*, Sheila Watson with *The Double Hook* are among those who spring to mind — present special problems and do not invite the particular kind of discussion I have attempted here. True, Howard O'Hagan might be considered to belong to this category, but I include him for three reasons: first, because it seemed necessary to counter the prevailing assumption that serious Canadian fiction in English began with *As for Me and My House* and MacLennan's *Barometer Rising*; second, because the special qualities of *Tay John* are becoming increasingly recognized as significant; third, because O'Hagan's treatment of story seems to be crucial for an understanding of certain special features relating to Canadian fiction. Similarly, although W.O. Mitchell is also best known — I think rightly — for one book, *Who Has Seen the Wind*, he has written a great deal that has attracted extraordinarily little critical commentary; the case is unusual, and seemed to demand further investigation. On the other hand, while MacLennan and Morley Callaghan have received a good deal of attention, Ethel Wilson's contribution has been less widely recognized, and abundantly repays study. As for other omissions, I have already written at some length about certain writers, notably Frederick Philip Grove and Rudy Wiebe, and see no reason to repeat my points here. Others again — Mordecai Richler and Robert Kroetsch are perhaps the most prominent — have attracted their full share of critical scrutiny, and to this I have nothing of significance to add. By contrast, the ten I am about to discuss raise pressing literary-critical issues which — perhaps because they are essentially *literary* issues — have been curiously neglected, despite the amount of commentary devoted to certain individuals. For this reason, it seems to me that they invite additional discussion.

Finally, although I am interested in what distinguishes one writer from another, I would like to insist that there are continuing concerns that run through the book and help to unify it, even if sections appear self-sufficient. I am aware that many readers will consult it for particular chapters, and there is obviously nothing wrong with that, but I believe that individual studies read better within the context provided by the whole.

The chapter on Howard O'Hagan makes use, in altered form, of some material due to appear in a forthcoming gathering of essays to be published in *Essays on Canadian Writing*; similarly, my discussion of Atwood's *The Handmaid's Tale* incorporates certain passages from "Apocalyptic Imaginations: Notes on Atwood's *The Handmaid's Tale* and Findley's *Not Wanted on the Voyage*" (*Essays on Canadian Writing* 35 [1987]: 123–34). Elsewhere, especially in the chapter on Jack Hodgins, I have occasionally introduced phrases and even sentences first coined in earlier essays and reviews. With these minor exceptions, all the material appears here for the first time.

Most of this book was written while I was on sabbatical leave, for which I thank my college, my department, and my university. I would also like to thank Robert Lecker for patient answers to niggling queries while the typescript was being produced, and, as always, my wife Hiroko for excusing my absorption and absentmindedness while the book was being planned and written.

CHAPTER 1

Introduction

"They have style, each his own, and without style . . . how dull."
These are Ethel Wilson's words in a discussion of her favourite
novelists (*Stories* 184), and they may be usefully compared with a
comment by Alice Munro recalling the impact of Wilson's writing
upon her own emerging literary consciousness:

> I was *enormously* excited by her work [*The Equations of Love* is
> mentioned specifically] because the style was such an enormous
> pleasure in itself. . . . It was important to me that a Canadian
> writer was using so elegant a style. You know I don't mean style
> in the superficial sense, but that a point of view so complex and
> ironic was possible in Canadian literature. (Struthers "Real
> Material" 18)

Similar references to "style" recur continually in the critical comments of our most prominent writers of fiction. Here, for example, is
Robertson Davies in *A Voice from the Attic*:

> It may be stated as a law of criticism that any book which has
> anything of worth to say will impress a receptive reader by the
> style in which it is written. This is not to say that it will be written
> in a great style, or an easy and accomplished style, but that it will
> be written in a style which compels attention and impresses by
> its aptness. (75)

And Mavis Gallant, in an essay entitled "What Is Style?," goes further, informing us, among other things, that "Style is inseparable from structure, part of the conformation of whatever the author has to say," and that "Style cannot be copied, except by the untalented" (*Paris Notebooks* 177, 179).

This enthusiasm for style is not, however, shared by all writers. Margaret Laurence, for example, was always uneasy with the word. In an interview with Robert Kroetsch first published in 1970, she speaks of "a word that I hate — style. It always seems like such a pretentious word to me. I really prefer the words *form* and *voice* in the novel" (Kroetsch 52). And at about the same time, in the lecture "Gadgetry or Growing," she observed: "I have never thought of forms and means of expression (I refuse to use the odious word *style*) as having any meaning in themselves" (81). One suspects a terminological vagueness here; after all, "form" and "voice" are themselves very different concepts, and "style" as understood by Munro, Davies, and Gallant seems far removed from either. Since Laurence is also on record as referring to "the 'fine' oratorical writing which I have come to dislike more and more" ("Ten Years" 29), it is reasonable to assume that she is objecting to a false notion of style as extraneous overlay, not to its broader and more legitimate sense.

An immediate requirement, then, is more precise definition. The *Oxford English Dictionary* contains no less than twenty-eight subdivisions in its entry, though most of these are concrete nouns bearing no relation to our present purpose. I use the word in this book in accordance with *OED*'s thirteenth definition: "The manner of expression characteristic of a particular writer . . . a writer's mode of expression considered in regard to clearness, effectiveness, beauty, and the like." I dissociate myself entirely from the fourteenth definition (which I take to be closer to Laurence's understanding of the term): "Those features of literary composition which belong to form and expression rather than to the substance of the thought expressed. Often used for: Good or fine style." Gallant virtually paraphrases this in her characteristically stylish account of "what style is *not*: it is not a last-minute addition to prose, a charming and universal slipcover, a coat of paint used to mask the failings of a structure" (*Paris Notebooks* 176–77). On the contrary, a writer's style is inseparable from the meaning that it both conveys and embodies; Laurence is right to question whether "forms and means of expression" have "any meaning in themselves." Contained within style in this inclusive sense are various aspects of form and technique, of genre (especially the artful blending of genres), of moral attitude, of adherence to or divergence from convention — indeed, of everything that together makes up an artist's individual vision. Style, in Hugh Hood's phraseology, is the "signature" without which no creator's work, human or divine, is "genuine." Or, as Davies writes of Laurence, with a simplicity which proves in itself that ornateness and intricacy are unnecessary artistic qualities: "The style is in the grain" (*Well-Tempered Critic* 240).

Because style constitutes so central a part of their stock-in-trade, it is hardly surprising that Canadian writers, like those of every other country, make frequent reference to the importance of words and the artistic arrangement of words when discussing their own work and that of their fellow practitioners. Thus Margaret Atwood, asked by Geoff Hancock what she considered her strengths as a writer, pointed to the way, at her best, she "can get the words to stretch and do something together that they don't do alone. Expand the possibilities of the language" (Hancock 267). The emphasis seems natural. When we turn to Canadian literary critics, however, the case is sadly different. By directing their energies towards other matters (dominant themes, generic classifications, archetypal patterns, etc.), they generally neglect stylistic considerations — to such an extent that John Metcalf has in desperation gone so far as to remark: "Critics in Canada don't have a horror of elegance. They don't even know it's there" (*Kicking* 7). This may well be an exaggeration — and in any case elegance and style are by no means interchangeable — but the outburst draws attention to an imbalance that needs to be rectified. My own view is that literary commentators nervously skirt the subject because they instinctively recognize stylistic analysis to be more demanding and revealing than other scholarly practices that are supposedly more objective. As Paul West once shrewdly commented: "Safe stuff, ideas; not risky, like style" ("Canadian Fiction" 265).

But there is another, deeply embedded reason for suspicion: the belief that a preoccupation with style is inappropriate for a young, rough, and energetic culture. Style, so the argument runs, belongs to an over-sophisticated, probably effete "high art" and places a priority upon smoothness, polish, and even Metcalf's "elegance," qualities allegedly alien to "the Canadian experience." And at this point phrases like "colonial mentality" and "imperial domination" are likely to follow. Such a line of reasoning is understandable, sometimes justified, but ultimately, I am convinced, false. It reflects the typical unease of a young country responding to the oppressive literary influence of an older one. But there are positive aspects of this relationship which suggest, not that the concept of style should be resisted, but that distinctive Canadian styles need to be recognized as developing in response to the impact of unique geographical and social factors on the inherited tradition of literature in English. Style emerges in company with maturity and confidence, and defines itself as soon as any discrete body of work becomes recognizably distinctive. My object here is to indicate certain tendencies — not rigid determinants but available possibilities — that seem to affect individual Canadian styles before going on to examine the stylistic variety achieved by ten important writers of fiction.

At this point it may be useful to quote some stimulating remarks by Barbara Godard, originally written to introduce a discussion of what she calls Atwood's "folk narratives":

> Attempts to create a national literature in Canada have developed on [the] interface of metropolis and hinterland, of written and oral literary models, a most frequent literary device being the "Battle of the Books" which pits high European cultural models against the oral narrative of North American experience, as in the work of Robert Kroetsch or of Antonine Maillet, where the Odyssey and Don Quixote are repeated in the vernacular. In their writing folklore breaches the walls and facilitates the entry of the speech or dialects of North American peoples into the high literary tradition . . . . (59)

There are various aspects of this assertion that need, I think, to be qualified. First, the resuscitation of tired traditional methods by a healthy injection of energy from extra-literary sources has been a time-honoured and continuing process throughout English literary history, from Shakespeare's rural imagery and idiom through Wordsworth's "language really used by men" down to our own time (James Joyce, we recall, produced a vernacular *Odyssey* decades before Kroetsch). Second, it is surely a little late in the day to see "the speech or dialects of North American peoples" as an upstart challenge to set linguistic conventions; the "high literary tradition" long ago

16

absorbed an infusion of North American speech-characteristics into its life-blood. Nonetheless, in directing our attention towards the tension between "written and oral literary models," Godard is feeling her way to an important insight that can illumine our understanding of what is potentially distinctive about Canadian fiction. Stated at its simplest, our fictional tradition is much closer to oral origins than is its English counterpart. In my next chapter, for instance, I describe Howard O'Hagan listening to tales of the wilderness told over camp-fires at a time before fiction in English-speaking Canada had developed in any definite and recognizable form; yet this was also the time when Joyce was putting the finishing touches to *Ulysses.* We are clearly involved here with radically different time-schemes, and it would be surprising indeed if these circumstances did not have notable stylistic repercussions.

This example of temporal relativity is significant because of its impact upon assumptions about the nature of story and the deceptive grey area that separates true from tall tales. Such concerns may seem at first to take us a long way from stylistic considerations, but, within the Canadian context, they are crucial because they indicate distinctive kinds of narrative situation which in their turn demand new voices and therefore new literary styles. Historically, most of the earliest records of Canada were explorers' accounts, the best-known of which appeared in London at the turn of the eighteenth and nineteenth centuries. These created an interest because they coincided with a taste for primitivism (Ossian, the old ballads, Robert Burns, magnificent exercises in pastiche like "The Ancient Mariner") occurring as a rebound from what was seen as the excessively sophisticated elegance and artifice of the age of Pope. The material that came from the extreme hinterland of Canada to the English metropolitan centre at that time, though technically classified as non-fiction (the work of Hearne, Mackenzie, etc.), was in fact story — first-hand accounts of exploration into unknown country, of dangers faced and obstacles overcome, of unusual flora and fauna, unimaginable weather-conditions, strange human beings with unexpected customs. And within these accounts were embedded other stories, tales within tales, rumours recorded, traditions transcribed. These narratives possessed all the qualities of sanctioned story with the additional interest that the mysteries they contained were (or at least purported to be) true.

The process continued with the early settlements. Often isolated for many weeks or months at a time, the inhabitants of this hinterland were themselves eager for stories when travellers arrived. Many individuals lived on their own and hungered after the latest news when their solitary paths crossed those of others. Tales were naturally exchanged, communicated by word of mouth; moreover, they often altered with the telling, and some story-tellers proved more skillful — perhaps more inventive — than others. Occasionally, literature from elsewhere, usually the United Kingdom or the United States, was brought by more literate immigrants into the wilderness and backwoods. This often provided solace, sometimes intellectual sustenance, but it clearly belonged to a different category from the local yarn. In rare instances, the two came together in the writings of one person, the best-known instance being Susanna Moodie, who brought "high culture" with her into the bush, continued to write marketable stories in the refined tradition into which she had been born, but also produced her own inimitable versions of the personal story that sometimes approached surprisingly close to the status of the tall tale.

So much for story. In order to show the parallel importance of voice in the intricate compound we call style, I would like to juxtapose with Godard's comments some equally stimulating remarks by the playwright John Gray recounting his experiences with travelling dramatic groups in rural Ontario:

> Playing on stages where you had to kick the cowpies aside while crossing the boards, I noticed that Canadians don't much like listening in on other people's conversations. They think it's impolite. This plays havoc with the basic convention of theatre itself, so what do you do? Well, you drop the fourth wall and you simply talk to the audience. They tend to relax a bit because they are in an arena whose aesthetic they understand: the arena of the story-teller. (6)

I have no wish, of course, to insinuate that these local audiences were representative; obviously, educated Canadian readers have long assimilated all the conventions of literary discourse. But Gray's idea of "the arena of the story-teller" may still have much to teach us. This was a group that responded to the intimate tale told by a personal story-teller, a situation in which the voice recounting the story is as important as the story itself. We catch a glimpse of how, through

18

personal idiom, individual rhythms, local vocabulary, appropriate dialect, Godard's "folklore" can be converted into "high literary tradition." It may well be that the remarkable upsurge in first-person narration within Canadian fiction during the last quarter of a century, often in most complex and experimental forms, is partly explained by our temporal and spatial proximity to "the arena of the [oral] story-teller." Hence Rudy Wiebe's famous question that rings through the story-telling of our time, "Where is the voice coming from ?" — a timely reminder of the power of oral tradition in a first-person story that is itself a notable example of high art.

Needless to say, I hope, in this emphasis on the personal voice I am not attempting to privilege first-person novels over more traditional fiction employing third-person narration. I am merely pointing out that a large number of the finest Canadian novels take advantage of this form, and that this may well reflect the relative closeness of Canadian experience not merely to a predominantly oral situation but to one in which authenticity and trustworthiness (or the illusion of these) were favoured qualities. Such a predilection was often strengthened, of course, by Puritan attitudes that mistrusted fiction as telling "the thing which is not" and possibly suggested the production of first-person novels that imitated the sanctioned form of confessional autobiography. The convergence of style, story, and voice that we encounter here offers unparalleled opportunities to the writer of fiction that are in no way qualified by the somewhat narrow historical factors that helped to develop them.

Voice is necessarily more obvious when protagonists tell their own stories, but it is present, albeit more subtly, in works employing omniscient narration. In such cases, indeed, "style" comes close to being identified with the voice of the individual novelist. This is most evident in a stylistically conspicuous writer like Davies in the Salterton trilogy, less so in writers like Munro or Hood or Jack Hodgins (though careful readers will soon pick up their characteristic stylistic features). Moreover, writers using omniscient narration can create dramatic contrasts between their own style and those of the characters whose speech-patterns they reproduce. Thus the woman on the bus in the twelfth chapter of *Swamp Angel* is especially memorable because her voice is so diametrically opposed to Ethel Wilson's own. Yet the distinction between third- and first-person narration is not in practice as drastic as we might expect, since writers often choose

19

spokesmen to whom they can assign their own stylistic traits. Matt Goderich could have written many of Hood's short stories just as Del Jordan could have written many of the stories that make up Munro's *Dance of the Happy Shades*. Where, then, is the voice coming from? As discriminating readers we must, of course, distinguish between speaker and novelist, just as it is generally wise in third-person fiction to follow Wayne Booth and differentiate between the implied author and the flesh-and-blood fiction-writer. But even more necessary — and I stress the point because in Canadian criticism it is too often neglected — is the capacity to recognize the manifold effects that a writer's basic attitude and cast of mind can have upon the material that is being presented. Here a committed attention to style becomes inescapable.

In one of the supreme traditional examples of "high art," *King Lear*, the Earl of Kent, disguised as a servant and offering his services to the king, remarks in a bluff, ingratiating, self-deprecatory way that he can "mar a curious tale in telling it" (I.iv.35). Here, if anywhere, is acknowledgement that style, voice, and story-telling go hand in hand. The qualities we look for in an effective speaking voice, whether that voice comes from O'Hagan's Jack Denham, Laurence's Hagar Shipley, Davies's Dunstan Ramsay, Munro's Del Jordan, or the protagonist in Atwood's *Surfacing*, may be more colloquial, less formal, than we expect in conventional third-person prose, yet "style" remains a vital factor. And, of course, these narratives belong no less to story because they are offered as forms of autobiography. When Hodgins, referring in an interview to his debt to Laurence, praised her language because "It's about *us*! It's the way *we* talk!" (Hancock 54), he was paying tribute to a distinctively Canadian style. It is time that Canadian criticism paid more attention to stylistic matters, not only in themselves but taking into consideration their integral relation, through voice, to story.

Here, however, we encounter a paradox, best expressed perhaps by John Metcalf — and it is significant that I now find myself turning once again to a practitioner for an instance of the artistry involved in fiction. He is arguing that stories should move their readers emotionally and so extend the boundaries of their emotional world:

But that emotional impact will not be felt until the reader has responded with great skill and knowledge to all the nuances of a highly complex performance. *Reading a story is a purely literary activity.*

The reader's final emotional response, however, is *not* literary but it can only be felt by someone with a refined knowledge of and honed skill in the rules of the game . . . . [G]enuine *depth* of emotional response can only be achieved by those willing and able to immerse themselves in amazing artificiality — in language, in literary device, in rhetoric. The "real," in other words, is only available to us through an embrace of the unreal and artificial. ("Curate" 52)

Story, fiction, tale-telling all *imply* artifice. Those who listened, like O'Hagan himself, to the tales told by his wilderness men judged them by their convincingness, their claims to authority, but also — however unwitting the impulse may have been — by their artistry. And this is true not merely of stories about the mysterious and apparently inexplicable, but of narratives that we are accustomed to label as "realistic" or even "naturalistic." George Woodcock has properly insisted on this point while praising the achievement of Mavis Gallant. "Absolute plausibility, though not mimesis as such, I take to be one of the principal goals of fiction. . . . And absolute plausibility demands absolute artifice" (*World* 93).

An extreme emphasis on artifice, or story for story's sake, as in the case of the outer fringes of post-modernism, can lead to pointlessness. Once one has insisted that all is story, there is little else to say and nowhere to go. But the current renewed interest in story, though it almost invariably underrates the element of artifice in earlier writings, has performed an immense service in alerting us to the presence of artistry in places where it is too often overlooked. The more we recognize the artistry underlying literature, the greater will be the satisfaction we derive from reading. Hugh Hood has articulated what he considers the ideal approach to his own fiction: "Reading [my stories], you ought to get a sharp sense of me, twiddling away behind them, turning a dial one degree here, doing a spot of fine-tuning there, laughing quietly to myself and enjoying the procedure a lot" (*Trusting* 37). Appreciation of the art that reveals art is therefore offered as one of the main "pleasures of the text." The subsequent chapters will range widely over different kinds of fiction, suggest different approaches, and raise various literary-critical problems, but they are united in their continued emphasis on the interlocking elements of story, voice, and the artifice that creates and controls them — in other words, with each author's sense of style.

CHAPTER 2

Howard O'Hagan

In the summer of 1920 Howard O'Hagan, while still an undergraduate, made the acquaintance of an eccentric wilderness man named (at least in his writings) "Old" MacNamara. Many years earlier, MacNamara had built a cabin near Lucerne on Yellowhead Lake, an area on the border between Alberta and British Columbia that was destined to become O'Hagan's fertile region of imagination and story; when the railroad and railroaders came, however, MacNamara constructed another retreat on the Grantbrook, further away from the interferences of a threatening civilization. During the summer in question, having performed odd jobs for the town doctor, who happened to be O'Hagan's father, he got to know the youth, and in September, when he went out to the Grantbrook cabin "to get his winter's meat" (*Wilderness* 12), he invited the young O'Hagan to accompany him. On the second evening, "over a feast of caribou steak, bannock, and tea" (13), MacNamara began talking, and told O'Hagan the story of "the Thing That Walked like a Man" (15), his personal experience of a shadowy and unexplained presence that provides the subject for a disturbing ghost-story. A few days later, he "unburdened himself . . . of what he called 'the strangest hunt' of his life" (18), a frightening encounter with a wolverine.

I have drawn my evidence in the previous paragraph from O'Hagan's account, "The Black Ghost," in *Wilderness Men* (1958). This is a tale about tale-telling that purports to be non-fiction —

O'Hagan assures us in the Foreword, "I was the 'doctor's son' who went with 'Old' MacNamara up the ghostly Grantbrook" (6) — but I cannot ignore the fact that, however accurately O'Hagan reproduced the authentic circumstances, I am already relying on "literature" for my account of the supposedly autobiographical incident. I must perforce do so in want of any other version. But *Wilderness Men* is a decidedly tricky text, a *mélange* that appears (doubtless deliberately) to violate our norms of categorization. Many of the subjects of these narratives are well-known to North American wilderness history — Almighty Voice, the mad trapper Albert Johnson, Grey Owl — but others, notably "Old" MacNamara and a similar character called Montana Pete, belong to O'Hagan's own autobiographical experience — which seems already to have acquired the status of a personal mythology.[1] The Foreword implies that the book is to be classified as non-fiction, though the title-page of the 1978 reprint reads, perhaps significantly, "Tales by Howard O'Hagan." "Tales," to be sure, can be true, yet the word irresistibly suggests fiction, and O'Hagan varies between a discursive style characteristic of the popular historian and a narrative mode more often associated with the yarn-spinner. Here and throughout his writings O'Hagan both challenges and exploits our habitual vagueness about the implications of "story" and "tale."

We can be certain, at any rate, that the experience of listening to MacNamara and other reminiscent "loners" had a dramatic effect upon O'Hagan's consciousness and therefore upon his subsequent literary career. To complicate matters, however, the written accounts appeared between thirty and forty years after the events described, and almost twenty years after the publication of *Tay John* (1939), where his experiments in tale-telling found their subtlest and most artistically satisfying form. Yet, despite their apparently late publication date, these particular stories provide clues concerning his earlier practice; their form appears to have been fixed close to the time when O'Hagan first heard them. I suspect that they were written up for journalistic purposes from earlier notes, and so represent a comparatively early stage in his literary apprenticeship. They deserve attention because I am convinced that these experiences were crucial in introducing O'Hagan to a literary form that can reasonably be described as endemic to North America.

The form in question comprises stories poised intriguingly between fiction and non-fiction. The phrase "Tales of Hearsay" (the title of a collection by Joseph Conrad we know O'Hagan to have read) is as accurate a designation as any. They are — or, at least, purport to be — oral yarns told round a camp-fire or in some communal setting, or perhaps by one trapper to another as they meet on a remote trail. There is usually something surprising or unusual about them; they may be mysterious, even inexplicable, yet the possibility of their being true is almost always present. They are received, at any rate, with something close to Coleridge's willing suspension of disbelief. The exception here is the tall tale deliberately designed to expose the gullible; O'Hagan offers a splendid example in which a water ouzel hit a rock with its beak in order to create a spark to warm the foot it was standing on (182–83). Because wilderness men themselves often have a secret past (Albert Johnson, for instance, in "The Man Who Chose to Die"), they are always interested in stories of others who are not what they seem — hence, no doubt, O'Hagan's inclusion of the "Grey Owl" chapter. Also, since even in modern times they live in areas where communication and "entertainment" are often non-existent, a tale represents (though they would never describe it in this way) an art form cherished for its own sake, for the imaginative power that it embodies. Therefore such tales (including, in *Tay John*, "Jackie's Tale" [77] and Blackie's Tale) are widely enjoyed and savoured, their contents accepted as perhaps fact, perhaps fiction. Above all, they are judged by their quality; it is well known that tales "grow," improve with retelling, even if their factual, historical authenticity is thereby impaired. And somewhere, as O'Hagan soon came to realize, a raw tale can cross the boundary from merely this-is-what-happened to become a sophisticated work of art.

As a result, O'Hagan became interested not merely in the tales themselves but in the process of their telling. In "Shwat — The End of Tzouhalem," for instance, in which he revives the career of a renegade Indian of the mid-nineteenth century whose robber-band harried the northwest Pacific coast, O'Hagan is less concerned with clarifying the historical record than with the way in which the memory of Tzouhalem has been passed down in Indian lore, by the tale-tellers, from generation to generation: "Old men of the Cowichan tribe, who have had the story from their fathers, mothers, aunts or uncles, still tell . . . " (159). And he ends with a "mythic" account of Tzouhalem's body rising into a sitting position within the dugout canoe in which it had been laid out, and pointing towards his dwelling in the mountains. But O'Hagan adds, characteristically:

> To doubt that this happened — that Tzouhalem's corpse rose and gestured — would be to doubt the word of Johnny Bear, an eighty-year-old Cowichan of Duncan, short, solidly built, with bristling white mustache and a voice that resounds like a foghorn. He had the story direct from his father, whose cousin was in the dugout conveying the body homeward. (174)

O'Hagan is here drawing attention to the difference between white and Indian attitudes and stories, and the consequent literary conventions that derive from them. This, then, is ultimately a story about how stories grow.

I am suggesting, therefore, that O'Hagan's all-important contribution to fiction lies in his gradual mastery of techniques that could transform yarn into serious art. Two main elements contribute to this result. The first, which he learned early, derives from his realization that the circumstances of the telling are as important as the tale itself — or, rather, that the circumstances are an intrinsic part of the tale. After MacNamara's story of "the Thing," O'Hagan writes:

> There in the forest night, with the wind sighing and the river murmuring, his tale had not seemed incredible and the old man with white long hair, staring into the campfire as he spoke, was only a sorcerer reading the story in the coals. MacNamara was making his own contribution to the lore of the 'man-beast' that walks the mountains, in North America as in Asia. (16–17)

MacNamara's tale is encircled by and contained within O'Hagan's, the latter complicating the situation and, as it were, transforming it into a subtler form of narrative. Moreover, while the story of the wolverine is not presented in any detailed atmospheric context, O'Hagan is careful to inform us that MacNamara tells the story in the precise area in which it had taken place almost a year before. The geographical location becomes an essential part of O'Hagan's conscious artistic effect. A related circumstance occurs in *Tay John*, where one of the incidents is located in the "very bar" (166) in which Jack Denham is telling his story to anyone who will listen.

O'Hagan invariably draws attention to his story-tellers and insists on their importance. Of Montana Pete he writes: "Stories told around the campfire were his library, and his experiences were his reference shelf" (1958 ed. 242). In *Tay John* Denham, himself in the process of telling a tale, "talking, stretching his story the length of Edmonton" (77), offers his own comment on tale-tellers:

> . . . your backwoodsman is a thorough gossip. Left alone he gossips to himself. He lives too much with silence to value it unduly. He pays for a meal, for a night's lodging, with a tale. His social function is to hand on what he has heard, with the twist his fancy has been able to add. . . . What he has not seen he deduces, and what he cannot understand he explains.
>
> Each valley where a cabin has been built has its lore kept alive by the unceasing movement of human lips and tongues. (114)

Appropriately, we get our final glimpse of Tay John, the last "tale" within the novel, from the viewpoint of Blackie, a trapper who "spoke in amazement . . . of what he had seen, of the things he had heard"; among the stories he "garnered with his furs" was one of "wolverines that could outwit a man" (259), so he is obviously of the tribe of "Old" MacNamara. Similarly, in *The School-Marm Tree*, the guides who lead tourists through the mountains were "seldom without words. They gossiped more than women ever gossiped. They gossiped about incidents on the trail, horses, or other guides in the outfit who were absent" (170). All these gossips are ultimately recognized by O'Hagan as, at least potentially, literary artists. As he remarked in an interview, "some of the best writers never put pen to paper. They were natural story-tellers" (Geddes 92). "Old" MacNamara in *Wilderness Men* clearly belongs to this group; he is described as "an artist in words" (12) and as one who "seemed eager for the release of speech" (13).

But — and this brings me to the second element that becomes essential for O'Hagan's art — in relating MacNamara's stories O'Hagan fails to reproduce one vital ingredient: the tale-teller's own rhythms and turns of phrase. MacNamara's experiences are given in indirect speech as if, at the time when O'Hagan drafted this story (the date is uncertain), he lacked the total confidence in his narrator to allow him to tell the story in his own way. Impressive as "The Black Ghost" is, we miss the ultimate revelation of MacNamara's terror that could only have been communicated through his unique personal idiom.

"Montana Pete Goes Courting," a chapter that appears only in the 1958 edition of *Wilderness Men*, becomes of particular interest at this point. Another trapper from Yellowhead Lake, Pete is specifically compared and contrasted with MacNamara. The date is 1934, in which year he is visited by his old friend Fred Brewster, an Argentinian newspaperman, and O'Hagan. (O'Hagan is invisible in the chapter itself, but once again admits to being present in the Foreword.) The bizarre scene in the cabin is memorably described with an appropriate mixture of humour, pathos, and grotesquerie; Pete's initiation into the mystery of foreign languages is related ("Then you can say the same things in Spanish as we do in English?" [1958 ed. 229]), and, because he suffered from prostasis, we are informed how the stories are punctuated by his continually relieving himself into Hudson's Bay Company tobacco tins. So far, the situation is similar to that in "The Black Ghost" with the emphasis split between tales and teller, but in this chapter we see O'Hagan experimenting (not always successfully) with various aspects of narration. Pete tells three stories, though one, a brief Indian fable he had heard from one of his Indian friends, need not concern us here. The second (which O'Hagan tells first and in his own words before the cabin-setting has been described) is a fairly straightforward story about Montana Pete's search for a lost horse. The third, which accounts for the chapter-title, records a personal encounter with an Indian woman and later with her husband, and is of interest because here O'Hagan makes a conscious — even self-conscious — effort to tell it by reproducing Pete's own speech. "His words, as his hearers would remember them, were ..." (1958 ed. 231): so runs the introductory formula. And at the end: "The words, of course, in the foregoing tale are not exactly those of Montana Pete, but they give the effect of what he said" (1958 ed. 242).

The precise date when O'Hagan wrote "Montana Pete Goes Courting" is not clear. Presumably, he took some detached notes in 1934 (assuming that the circumstances as related are authentic). At some point, however, and it is reasonable to assume that this was soon after publication in 1958, O'Hagan split up the chapter, discarded the Indian fable, rewrote the opening tale as a much longer and more complex short story, "The White Horse," and extracted the third tale so that it could stand on its own as "The Tepee." Both stories appeared in *The Woman Who Got On at Jasper Station* in 1963 (and the whole chapter was dropped from the Talonbooks reprint of *Wilderness Men* in 1978). The alterations here provide an essential clue to O'Hagan's stylistic development — "The White Horse" in terms of content and structure, "The Tepee" in terms of vocabulary and verbal effect.

In its original version, the former is a simple anecdote in which Montana Pete, as an old man, goes to seek his aged horse that has strayed from the vicinity of his cabin. He eventually finds it frozen to death, and sadly leaves its body for the wolves. For no compelling reason, Pete had named the horse Bedford after an English surveyor for whom he had once worked. This is no more than an undeveloped detail in the original anecdote, but in "The White Horse" naming has become a principal subject. Despite the new title, the death of the horse is no longer the main concern. Now the central figure, who in this version is called Nick Durban, sets out like Montana Pete to look for Bedford in "the High Valley," but unlike Pete he begins brooding on the name — and upon names and naming in general:

> It was called the High Valley for some reason that Nick Durban could never understand for it was no more than a sloping tangle of jack-pine and down-timber.
>
> Yet, on the whole, poor though the name might be, he was glad that it had one. It was more home-like and warmer to have names about. In the valley only the creek was named and one mountain, called Black Mountain. All the hills were nameless. Even the pass which Nick crossed several times a year, leading into town and the railroad, was without a proper name. (*Woman* 56)

The meditative strain here is new, and significant. Later, Nick discusses the matter with his friend Olaf the Swede, who "had said that in the old country all such places had names, but he did not see how, in these foothills a pass, especially a low, gentle pass, that had no name, would acquire one" (56). Within this context the story of the naming of the horse after the surveyor takes on a little more meaning.

This meaning is developed considerably in the subsequent enlarging of the original version. The discovery of the dead horse reminds Nick of his own age and mortality. On going back to his cabin, he rereads the "In Memoriam" and "Lost and Found" notices in old newspapers that he uses to keep out drafts, and is moved by "the idea of posting a reward to indicate you had lost what was important" (61). With great difficulty he paints a sign announcing the loss of the horse and nails it to a tree where trapper friends, including Olaf, would be sure to see it. Some weeks later, on passing the notice, Nick reads the tracks of previous travellers and follows one set towards "the pass without a name" (61). There he finds that Olaf, in response to his own notice, has erected a sign christening the place "Bedford Pass."

The narrative has evolved, then, into a probing story about the way in which individuals and animals — and, by extension, even stories — are remembered. Nick has performed a creator's part in giving Bedford his name; now Olaf has commemorated the incident. The name itself, we note, has already become ambiguous: does it memorialize the Englishman or the horse? Yet Nick doesn't become sentimental. He knows that the origins of names are soon forgotten, but also that they nurture and perpetuate developing myths:

> Afterwards, the time would come when no one would remember. It would be a name, as the High Valley was a name. . . . Then the name would sink into the earth and become part of it.
>
> Nick, the first man to cross Bedford Pass, pointed his snowshoes down hill to town and the railroad were Olaf had gone before him. Bedford was now a name. The wolves would not have him. He would outlast flesh and bone and hide and hair. He would endure so long as men climbed rivers to their source and spoke into the wind the pass's name they travelled. (64–65)

It seems clear that O'Hagan finds value in the narratives of wilderness men who preserve memories of significant events and adventures that would otherwise be lost. At the same time, he realizes that "literature" demands more than a mere record of actions. When O'Hagan's yarns grow into stories they take on a philosophical cast, and this is generally achieved through the development of a story-teller — like Nick Durban, or Denham in *Tay John* — who meditates upon the implications of the tale.

O'Hagan knows that words are important because memory is dependent upon them in a predominantly oral culture; he also knows that the words and rhythms employed by tale-tellers are integral parts of the experience that they communicate. At his best, he is extraordinarily skillful in providing a deliberate, informed style for his tale-tellers that is in no way pretentious or fancy yet proves to be delicately

30

varied and modulated. The opening paragraph of "The Tepee" provides a characteristic instance:

> I went into that valley, tributary to the Athabaska, to look at the timber. It was not big timber. Timber does not grow big on the Arctic slope of the Rockies. It was big enough though, and clean, the branches beginning high up, tall, lean, black lodgepole pines, with the hard look of hunger on them — hundreds of them, thousands of them, rank after rank by the river, column after column coming down to it. (9)[2]

One notices the repetition of "timber" and "big" in the opening lines, the geographical precision ("tributary to the Athabaska," "the Arctic slope of the Rockies"), the description following the movement of the timberman's eye, his colloquial emphasis ("big enough though"), the special meaning of "clean" and the way the word leads by way of the rhyming sound to "lean," which in turn suggests the toughly fanciful "hard look of hunger." Then "hunger" leads in terms of sound into "hundreds of them," expanded but rhythmically repeated in "thousands of them," and then the phrases pile up ("rank after rank, . . . column after column") mirroring the sense, though the sentence ends on a dying fall, simply, without fuss.

By the next paragraph, without surrendering his firm wilderness-man status, the narrator can introduce a sensitive, almost poetic imaginative effect when he presents himself as walking "carefully as a child who searches for God in an empty church" (9), a phrase introduced into the revised version. A little later, he describes his first sight of the Indian woman on her pinto: "She sat him close as a burr, holding with a high hand the lines of her rawhide bridle" (10). It is not just the idiomatic use of "sit" as a transitive verb or the unusual simile that is remarkable here, not even the sharp, staccato rhythms. The alliteration ("holding . . . high hand") is conspicuous but it blends into a complex assonance ("high . . . lines . . . rawhide bridle"), and the last word echoes alliteratively back to "burr." Needless to say, I am not implying that O'Hagan deliberately planned the intricate sound-patterning here, but there can be no doubt that he moulded the sentence with a scrupulous insistence that the sound should be a perfect medium for the sense. He knows that he must evolve a supple vocabulary to make the necessary distinctions that his subject-matter requires. At times he can combine colloquial rhythms with an extra-

31

ordinarily mannered, euphonious style. For instance: "I heard the river throbbing in the dark. At first a gentle flow of streaming waters. Then an endless advance and an endless receding of ripples over shallows and the beat of the conflict filled the night" (12–13). The subtle development of meaning from "throbbing" through "gentle flow of streaming waters" to the "endless advance" balanced by the "endless receding," the tripping grace of "ripples over shallows," and the harsh explosive combination of words in "beat of the conflict" is exquisite — a word one would not expect to apply to the speech of a rugged wilderness man but I know of no other that better expresses the effect that O'Hagan achieves here. This is O'Hagan's personal and unique "style," perfectly adapted to the needs of his fictive vision.

Effective as this style is, however, it can lead O'Hagan into difficulties. One can see, I think, why he decided to detach the story from Montana Pete. Pete is twice described as "illiterate" (*Wilderness* 1958 ed. 242, 243), and the language of the story certainly seems too elaborate, too sophisticated, for the unlettered old man. O'Hagan was obviously uneasy about the *Wilderness Men* version, hence his insistence, already quoted, that the words "are not exactly those of Montana Pete." Although he was losing the atmospheric context of the tale in Pete's cabin on the Little Hay, the disembodied, unidentified voice avoided any risk of verbal inappropriateness. Changes like this may seem slight, but in the act of making them O'Hagan reveals the extent and the direction of his maturation from talented journalist to literary artist. Now that we recognize them, we are in a better position as readers to consider the larger question of voice in O'Hagan's wilderness fiction.

Throughout his work, but especially in *Tay John*, O'Hagan emphasizes the articulateness and eloquence — albeit rough eloquence — of his oral story-tellers. This verbal ability is, of course, very different from the correct but often bloodless speech of those educated at the metropolitan centres. Thus Denham's language in *Tay John* is different from the Aldersons' or Dobble's or Father Rorty's, and in *The School-Marm Tree* the essential contrast between Clay and Peter is partly communicated by their speech rhythms. In an interview O'Hagan praised what he called "the peasant quality of language" (Roberts 44), and much of the effectiveness of his speakers is compatible with this assertion. One obvious point involves imagery drawn from the wilderness itself. When on the first page of "The Black Ghost" MacNamara's eyes are described as "cold and pale as twin chips of glacier ice" (*Wilderness* 9), O'Hagan is using the kind of simile that MacNamara might employ himself, and the same is true of descriptions of trees "thick as prime marten fur" (15) and the black ghost itself "unassailable as a mountainside" (16). Later the old man, trying to articulate his desperation during his battle of wits with the wolverine, describes himself — in one of the few places where his actual words are relayed to us — as "fit to gnaw the bark off a spruce tree" (18). Similarly, when Jake kills Clem in "Trees Are Lonely Company," his fingers, "strong as spruce roots, were around the other's throat" and he felt Clem's pulse "beating against his fingertips like a marten's heart, but slower" (*Woman* 27). Examples could extend almost indefinitely, but one important instance in *Tay John* needs to be noted. In the frequently quoted passage in which Denham speaks of his story as existing independently of himself, he observes:

... every story only waits, like a mountain in an untravelled land, for someone to come close. ... You mine it, as you take ore from the mountain ... — and when you have finished, the story remains, ... unfathomable, like the heart of the mountain. (166–67)

It is hardly surprising that the garrulous Jack Denham should be the tale-teller who has most to say on the subject. He is initially described as one "whose speech and life were close to events" (76), and the imaginations of his auditors are said to be "cradled in a web of words" (77). These phrases catch as well as any the combination of eloquence and down-to-earth directness that is a feature of O'Hagan's story-tellers and of the narrative voice itself. Denham remarks of Tay John's story that it "found its root in the memories of men, and its form, and a sequence to its incidents in their speech" (113–14). The story itself, then, is inextricable from the words in which it is couched, and in an important passage Denham draws attention to what might almost be called the autochthonous quality of the words he uses:

It was early autumn, then, before the snow began to fly. — (There's an expression for you, born in the country, born from the imaginations of men and their feeling for the right word, the

33

only word, to mirror clearly what they see! Those with few words must know how to use them.) (91)

Had he not drawn attention to the word, it is doubtful if most readers would have noticed anything special about it, but the reminder nudges us into attending to style as well as to meaning. This is, indeed, a usage that O'Hagan is fond of; one finds it cropping up again and again in his prose — twice later in *Tay John* (260, 263), in the opening sentence of "Trees Are Lonely Company" (*Woman* 19), in "Ito Fujika, the Trapper" (*Woman* 82), and in one of Clay's speeches in *The School-Marm Tree* (218). Other words are also noted as regionally appropriate. A little later in *Tay John*, "outside" is praised as "a good word" (258) for describing a wilderness man leaving his lonely country for the risks of civilization, and O'Hagan offers a similar example in "I Look Upward and See the Mountain" when he glosses "avalanche" as "an apt word, concise, born from the routine of a mountain people" (*Wilderness* 180).

Having registered this insistence, within the text itself, on the significance of verbal texture and the all-important "feeling for the right word," we may now embark, cautiously, on an examination of the narrative style of *Tay John*. The opening words present a problem: "The time of this in its beginning, in men's time, is 1880 . . . " (11). Margery Fee has described this opening as "narrative by an omniscient and oracular voice that distinguishes itself from the human in the first sentence" (12–13), but this is not quite accurate, since the phrase "in men's time" merely acknowledges another time (mythic time? geological time? eternity?) that human beings cannot adequately measure. The voice is certainly "omniscient" but it is not consistently "oracular." With the exception of "in men's time," a phrase subtly as well as conspicuously inserted to alert us to the limitations (but, I would insist, not the falsity) of any human viewpoint, the narrator begins by imitating the mode of the white historian, but soon evolves — perhaps "blends" would be the better word — into that of the conventional story-teller to present the account of Red Rorty and his mission to the Shuswaps.

The story of Red Rorty is a story about words, and we gather immediately that his message is remarkable more for its loudness than for its truth. Before his "conversion," he is always shouting, and often "he would shout when there was nothing to shout for" (14). Once he has become, in Arnold E. Davidson's words, "as drunk on religion as he ever was on whiskey" ("Silencing" 31), he sees himself as a modern Paul of Tarsus spreading "the Word" to the Shuswaps. In preaching the coming of Christ, he is recognizable as a John the Baptist figure (albeit a suspect one), and the Indian response, somewhat enigmatic in context, is that "no man had spoken with such a great voice before" (24). But his actions are more violent than his words; when he rapes the wife of an absent hunter, they revenge the wrong by shooting him with arrows, burning him alive, and finally forcing a stone between his jaws because "he was a great liar, and the word has choked him" (28). Davidson is justified in remarking that "[t]he parodic Paul who became a parodic John the Baptist now becomes a parodic Saint Sebastian" ("Silencing" 31), but wrong, in my view, to see the parody as undermining and destroying the validity of a Christian or any religious viewpoint. The narrative voice here insists on our registering the biblical parallels, but invites us to hold the sacred and the profane in suspension.

In the next chapter, a further suspension is achieved. The omniscient narrator has entered the Indian world with Red Rorty, but after Rorty's death remains with the Shuswaps and takes over an Indian perspective. The story of the appearance of Tay John (presumed son of Rorty) from the grave of his mother who had died while pregnant is not only told as if it were an Indian myth but is in fact a transcription of an authentic Indian myth taken over, with due acknowledgements, from Diamond Jenness's *Indians of Canada* (197–99). The white reader will not accept the story as literally true but is invited to respond to the imaginative challenge of myth. The aloof historical voice, the crisp narrative voice, the mysterious mythic voice are all united by the same omniscient mode. Certain stylistic changes can be isolated; as Burke Cullen has noted, in an as yet unpublished paper, the sentences grow shorter and simpler as we move away from historic generalization, while abstractions are replaced by a greater emphasis on physical imagery. By means of the narrative method white and Indian assumptions and viewpoints are balanced one with the other, and the balance is maintained through O'Hagan's stylistic skill.

As half-breed, of course, Tay John is torn — eventually torn apart — by the power-struggle between white and Indian. The balancing narrative method continues until his departure from the Shuswaps.

In Part II the omniscient historian of the opening returns for a few pages, but is soon forced to give way to the personal and therefore fallible (but not necessarily unreliable) version of an individual narrator. In leaving his tribe, Tay John has not only dissociated himself from the world of myth but has entered the world of wilderness men for whom personal story, yarn, even tall tale, become the only possible means of expression. And so for the first time we are introduced to Jack Denham, a carefully chosen inquirer-interpreter for this particular story. As remittance-man, whose rumoured but never substantiated past includes "a great white house in the north of Ireland, in the county of Tyrone" (75), Denham is at once credibly equipped with an articulateness, a tendency towards imaginative blarney, and not least an independent "otherness" (as an immigrant severed from his own past, he is a curiously suitable interpreter for a novel through which Indian legend is communicated to white readers). O'Hagan has subtly created Denham like himself but different. O'Hagan's own grandfather was from Tyrone, and Denham shares various qualities with his creator, including verbal eloquence and a penchant for philosophical meditation as well as a weakness for whisky. Denham's speech can follow on from O'Hagan's omniscient narration with little strain; the tone becomes more colloquial, more gruff, more clipped:

> Do you see what I mean? (the tale continued.) An adventure. A real one. Blood in it. (78)

Henceforth, though he quotes many other speakers and tale-tellers, the dominating voice is Denham's.

It is the voice of Jack Denham that conducts us through the impressive series of modal shifts and varied perspectives that constitute the rest of the book. Without a unifying stylistic norm — henceforth we know, in Wiebe's phrase, where the voice is coming from — the novel could easily fall apart. As it is we are confronted with a series of literary forms remarkably compatible with Northrop Frye's theory of modes as they evolve through literary history — from myth through a version of epic (Tay John's "heroic" fight with the grizzly), through varieties of romance (the ballad-like story of the severed hand, the romance-triangle involving Tay John and the Aldersons, the medieval allusions [142], and the surely deliberate if sardonic use of Arthur as the husband's name), through the mimetic mode (the world of work, railroads, and the North West Mounted Police) to the level of irony (the roughhouse and the absurd farce of Dobble's Aphrodine Girdle), all this culminating in what Frye calls the "return of irony to myth" (62) as Tay John seemingly descends, according to Blackie's tale, to the earth from whence he came. Denham's obsession with probing the mystery of Tay John (obviously influenced to a considerable though not damaging extent by Conrad's Marlow in *Lord Jim*) leads him to collect evidence — albeit "without a finding" (159) — from a series of spokesmen, including the trader Colin McLeod, the witnesses of the police "hearing," Dobble, Sergeant Flaherty as reported through Inspector Wiggins, and Blackie the trapper from the "north country" (260). Such reports vary from credible eye-witness accounts to official record to Blackie's curious blending of tall tale and myth at the end of the book. O'Hagan's ability, through Denham, to hold these diverse elements in balance is an extraordinary artistic achievement.

O'Hagan succeeds, it is clear, through the power of his words and the solidity of this structural balance. "Those with few words must know how to use them" (91). Because of his habitual attitudes to words and stories, I am unable to accept Davidson's assertion of "the general rule advanced in *Tay John* that the word on any level, from the cartographical to the cosmological, is suspect" ("Being" 138). Nor am I satisfied by the radically "deconstructive" readings of the novel recently offered by Davidson and Fee. These interpretations are based upon the premise — so far as I can see, an unsubstantiated premise — that each shift of narrative mode in the novel "under-mines" or "dismantles" or "subverts" or "erases" what has gone before. I do not find any basis for this assumption within the text which, I would argue, comprises an anthology of narrative conventions and literary-philosophical allusions, none of which is favoured over any other. Similarly, while religious parallels are continually available, including the Shuswaps' exodus into the desert, Tay John as (failed) Messiah, Father Rorty's personal crucifixion, and the numerous symbolic journeys in search of vision, I do not see the versions presented as undercutting or denying the stories they recall. That irony and parody are employed at various points is indisputable, but I cannot accept that Red Rorty's religious confusion somehow negates St. Paul's theology, or that his brother's self-generated cruci-fixion renders Christ's any less sublime. Davidson's baldest statement of his position reads as follows: "From beginning to end, then, *Tay John* turns on Biblical parallels but it employs those parallels to undo the model on which it is based. With such erasure of the original Book, *Tay John* is finally grounded in nothing" ("Silencing" 35). If that were true, the book itself — and, presumably, literature as a whole — becomes meaningless. But the premise is false. The "original Book" cannot be "erased" without destroying the intertextual reference upon which O'Hagan depends. Whether author or reader accepts the Judeo-Christian stories as literal truth or symbolic truth or neither is irrelevant to the indisputable fact of their mythic resonance. Nor can we "erase" the opening myth, the Shuswap version of Tay John's "birth," since this is the only version we are offered within the text itself. While we are at liberty, as "superior" readers, to reject it as accurate history, we have no alternative but to accept it on the level of indigenous myth. Much the same applies to Blackie's tale, a prime example of the wilderness man's unlikely yarn that may well be true. While I would agree that O'Hagan is skeptical of absolutes, or at least doubtful that human beings can make contact with them, there can be no doubt that he possessed not merely a firm respect for words and story but also a profound sense of "mystery" behind the visible universe.

Such a sense of mystery does not blend well with authorial omniscience, and this may well explain why, as O'Hagan told Gary Geddes, he came to a critical point during the writing of the novel when he was "aware that he could go no further with the omniscient point of view." He goes on to claim that the impasse was resolved when he "heard the voice of a local marine editor named Jack Denham talking to him, telling him about Tay John . . . " (Geddes 87). O'Hagan being O'Hagan, this may itself be a literary example of a tall tale, but by transporting Denham from California to the Canadian Rockies he makes him one with characters like "Old" MacNamara and Montana Pete. At this point we can witness a prime example of oral tale at the very instant of metamorphosis into written literature.

Still, it would be a mistake to classify Denham, in deference to Jamesian technical complexities, as an "unreliable" narrator. Granted, his tale is told in an Edmonton bar, but Davidson is not justified in seeing this fact as detrimental to his credibility ("Being" 138; "Silencing" 37). This may be an unusual setting for a serious novel, but it is as appropriate a locale for wilderness story as

MacNamara's telling his yarn about the wolverine over his camp-fire. Like Conrad's Marlow, Denham assembles his narrative by recounting his own experience and then by amassing and recording information and stories told by others. In themselves, these stories are fragments of varying reliability; Denham combines them into his own story, "Jackie's Tale" (77). In a passage already quoted, he describes, frankly and openly, the methods of the backwoodsman tale-teller which are also his own: "What he has not seen he deduces, and what he cannot understand he explains" (114). As readers we measure his words and (surely) come to admire both his backwoods wisdom and his verbal skill. Within the text (and, since he is an invented character, that is all one can say), he convinces his hearers that he uses words not to deceive but to come as close to understanding another man's life as is possible in human terms. He achieves this through the means available to him in the wilderness of western Canada. And through Denham, O'Hagan succeeds in exalting wilderness story to the level of high art.

CHAPTER 3

Ethel Wilson

In order to explain the remarkable contribution of Ethel Wilson to the literature of British Columbia and of Canada as a whole, it is necessary to begin with a reconsideration of some well-known biographical facts. She was born in South Africa of parents with strong links to British life and culture, but, after being orphaned by the age of ten, was brought to Vancouver in 1898, where she lived with her maternal grandmother in circumstances presented in only minimally fictionalized form in *The Innocent Traveller*. At that time, Vancouver, incorporated only twelve years before, was enjoying an ambiguous prosperity, in part as an indirect result of the Klondike Gold Rush. Wilson's relatives were part of the English "establishment" in the process of impressing its stamp upon this area of British Columbia; however, Vancouver could hardly have been called a sedate English settlement at that time, since it was also a lively seaport, a haven for on-shore sailors, potential prospectors, and loggers on furlough.[1] The heyday of "Gastown" lay only a decade in the past, as did the age of railway development "in men's time" described by O'Hagan on the opening page of *Tay John*. All in all, the ethos of Vancouver at this period in its history, if literary presentation had ever been considered, would have favoured O'Hagan's "rough-edged chronicle of a personal destiny" told in a bar-room (*Tay John* 166) over the elegance and assurance so characteristic of Wilson's work.

Theoretically, then, Wilson ought to be an anomaly, an "English" sensibility working in unpropitious surroundings and circumstances. There ought to be something alien, unassimilated, about her literary production, at best an idiosyncratic talent writing fiction that, though physically belonging to western Canada, resides spiritually elsewhere. On the contrary, however, Wilson's work belongs firmly and indisputably to British Columbia, and catches an important aspect of the province that has never been expressed so completely and so skillfully. Indeed, she became so "naturalized" that, at the close of her career as a novelist, she could write in a literary memoir: "my locale in a sustained piece of writing (that is, in a book) has to be British Columbia" (*Stories* 104). The young immigrant had by this time become the mature interpreter of a geographical and social region that she had made her own; this was rendered possible by her capacity to combine the functions of distanced observation and sympathetic intimacy — a capacity reflected, as we shall see, in her remarkable artistic technique.

Her literary assumptions and preferences are clear enough. To Desmond Pacey, in a passage I have already quoted in my introduction, she wrote of her favourite novelists: "They have style, each his own, and without style ... how dull." And, more generally: "If you ask me to look at what I most like — I like the English sentence; clear, un-lush, and un-loaded. ... It is like architecture, it should have a function and be very beautiful" (*Stories* 184). Similarly, the narrative voice in " 'To keep the memory of so worthy a friend' " emphasizes the "beauty and felicity in the words and cadences" of Heminge and Condell (*Mrs. Golightly* 95), and Aunt Maury in *Love and Salt Water* praises George Vancouver's "good plain rational seaman's English" (171). Wilson's list of favourite writers includes, forecastably, Austen, Woolf, Forster, Cary, and also (perhaps less obviously) Fielding, Dickens, Joyce, Proust, Maugham, Compton-Burnett, and even Kingsley Amis. She dislikes Hemingway and Kerouac, but approves of Fitzgerald (because "he writes beautifully") and also of Bellow. Rather oddly, she calls Willa Cather "a fine writer" but admits to having read only one of her books many years before (Stouck 55). The emphasis on style will come as no surprise to anyone who has read her prose with attention. Appropriately, her first stories for adults appeared in an English magazine, and the fact that she has not yet been fully accepted as a major Canadian novelist may well stem from a "nationalist" suspicion that she is too English in her basic

41

literary instincts. Yet, as I have noted, her fiction is irrevocably connected with the landscape and people of British Columbia. Her great contribution to Canadian literature, I believe, is that, into a fiction that set a premium on the rugged and the vigorous, she succeeded in acclimatizing a serene and elegant poise.

The technique that embodies this poise has clearly been learned elsewhere, deriving in the main from British fiction of the nineteenth and early twentieth centuries. Her habitual stance — which, as I shall show later, is integral to her world-view — requires omniscience (*Hetty Dorval*, her first published novel written in the first person, is technically a "sport" never repeated), and one gets a strong sense of the assurance and solidity of a Victorian narrative voice behind the writing. Also Victorian, of course, though Wilson uses it in her own uniquely effective way, is the device of authorial intrusion. George Eliot seems an obvious influence here, though her name does not appear in Wilson's discussion of favourite authors; however Wilson's biographer, Mary McAlpine, notes that her husband had introduced her to Eliot, who subsequently became "[o]ne of her favourite writers" (*Other Side* 66, 107), and it is worth noting that Rachel is to be found reading *Adam Bede* in the eighteenth chapter of *The Innocent Traveller*. Yet, qualifying her high Victorian fictional inheritance, there are also strong intimations of some of Wilson's modernist contemporaries (her contemporaries, that is to say, as living woman if not as publishing novelist). *Hetty Dorval* irresistibly recalls James in its narrative technique. More crucial, though by no means easy to pin down, is a hint of Woolf, and more than a hint of Forster, whose thoughtfully witty comedy, tone of compassionate confidence, and especially an unobtrusive sense of form, seem to me a conspicuous presence behind Wilson's work. That Forster is the one notable, early twentieth-century British novelist who did not look upon authorial intrusion as an unforgivable crime is also relevant here.

I have written all this not to imply that Wilson is derivative — obviously, she is not — but to insist that her artistic roots, like her ancestral roots, belong elsewhere. In a curious but compelling way, her fiction embodies a memorable balance between the placid tone of her "English" prose and the not uncommon cruelty and violence of her "Canadian" subject-matter. It is customary to assume that writers inevitably conform to the determinants of their time and place, that part of human history in which they flourish and the requirements of that part of the earth's surface in which they find themselves. But Wilson is, at least to some extent, an exception to this rule. The geographical determinant is certainly strong, but she resisted many of the more conspicuous pressures of the period of literary history in which she wrote. This is probably because she embarked on her career as a novelist so late in life. George Woodcock, while acknowledging "her antennae tremulously open to every kind of perception," notes her "patrician assurance" and, deriving his remarks from personal acquaintance as well as familiarity with her writing, observes shrewdly that she "retained . . . an Edwardian sensibility" while at the same time developing "a contemporary ironic intelligence" (*World* 121, 122). In this insight may be found the essential clue to Wilson's qualities as a novelist. In the course of this chapter I want to establish two main points: first, that her basic way of looking at the world blended completely with her narrative strategies (which may seem old-fashioned in the current literary milieu but were artistically appropriate and totally right for her); second, that her importance and significance for Canadian literature stem from the fact that she serves as a reminder that imported traditions of serenity, clear narrative outlines, and a style that combines beauty and function can be just as effective, successful, and ultimately "Canadian" as the rougher native forms developed by O'Hagan.

It is impossible to read at length in Wilson's fiction without becoming aware of her preoccupation with the writings of John Donne, whom she describes as "my daily miracle and lasting delight" (*Stories* 125). She is, of course, especially fond of the famous passage from the seventeenth Meditation: "No man is an Iland, intire of it selfe; . . . I am involved in Mankinde." This provides the first of three epigraphs from Donne at the opening of *Hetty Dorval*; the same quotation had appeared in a Red Cross handbook she compiled during the War, and she uses it again in the forty-fourth chapter of *Swamp Angel*. Moreover, the sentiments if not the words are prominent throughout her work. The celebration of the family in *The Innocent Traveller* (which ends with another extended Donne quotation) is an acknowledgement that individuals inevitably form part of a group that is larger than themselves. In "Tuesday and Wednesday" Mort's involvement in mankind takes the form of his friendship with Hansen the high-rigger, which proves fatal; Lilly in "Lilly's Story" finds a sustaining role in life through the struggle to bring up her daughter, while Mr.

Sprockett learns "how taut yet tenuous are the filaments that bind our beings" (*Equations* 257) just as his life is about to impinge on that of "Mrs. Walter Hughes." In *Love and Salt Water*, where a subtle, unidentified allusion to Donne's poem "The Good Morrow" occurs (155), we are told that "[t]he circle of life is extraordinary" (133), and when Johnny almost drowns as a result of her carelessness Ellen Cuppy realizes her involvement in mankind with a vengeance. Mr. Willy's attempt to live islanded "in a vacuum" (*Mrs. Golightly* 197–98, 199) in the late short story "The Window" is recognized as both impossible and undesirable.

But in Wilson, as in Donne himself, the sense of interconnectedness is not confined to human relationships, but extends to embrace the whole physical universe. Thus virtually all Wilson's protagonists, at some time or another, experience a profound sense of otherness in the presence of wild creatures. Such scenes range from the breathtakingly beautiful (Hetty and Frankie watching the skein of migrating geese in *Hetty Dorval*), through Topaz's amusing yet poignant brush with pan and panic in the highly Forsterian seventeenth chapter of *The Innocent Traveller*, to the complicated series of events in the sixth chapter of "Lilly's Story" where a robin tries to carry off a garter-snake, is in its turn stalked by a kitten, which attracts the attention of a bald eagle, which is attacked in its turn by a gull and a crow. Nature in Wilson alternates between the Wordsworthian and the Darwinian/Tennysonian. Response to the night sky can be equally equivocal. The Northern Lights make their appearance in *The Innocent Traveller* (ch. 11), in *Swamp Angel* (ch. 20), and in "The Window"; in each case they are presented as awesomely beautiful but just as awesomely remote. To Topaz, they are "a threat or a promise," to the Grandmother "a foretaste of Heaven and Hell," for they seem to say: " 'I am independent of you, uncontrolled by you, indifferent to you, and you know nothing at all about Me' " (*Innocent* 99). The world of nature is frequently presented as sustaining and alien at the same time.

Though one gets the impression that Wilson, like Topaz, had "an indigenous faith in God" (89) — she once described herself as "a Christian, and not a good enough one, and not entirely conventionally a Christian" ("Series" 6) — she never provides anything approaching facile consolation. We encounter throughout her work an acknowledgement of the dark side of life, its unfairness and its suffering; "It's not fair" is, indeed, a phrase that recurs constantly

44

through her fiction. As Mary McAlpine has observed, "she had that sense of the unexpected and dangerous" ("On Ethel Wilson" 243). She can at one point in time celebrate "the rapture of that beautiful unexpected moment" (*Mrs. Golightly* 10), yet at another confront "the most crushing indiscriminate and callous blows of life and fate" (*Equations* 256). Death is a familiar visitant in most of her work, and frequently appears with shocking suddenness. Natural violence (the storms in "From Flores" and *Love and Salt Water*), individual violence ("Fog," "Hurry, Hurry," the attempted attack in "The Window"), the violence of war (experienced directly by several characters in *Love and Salt Water* and by Maggie before the opening of *Swamp Angel* when her first husband is killed in action) are all close to the surface of her writing.

At the same time, while this may be the message we derive from her subject-matter, the tone of her prose conveys something very different. A life-affirming resilience is to be found in the vast majority of her protagonists. *The Innocent Traveller*, despite its succession of deaths, inevitable perhaps in a chronicle extending over almost a century, is a profoundly positive book. Topaz's life teeters on the edge of tragedy when her love for William Sandbach is not reciprocated, but her natural buoyancy soon restores her. "Lilly's Story," *Swamp Angel*, and *Love and Salt Water* all focus on the process of reconcilement and recovery; Lilly, Maggie Lloyd, and Ellen Cuppy respectively build new lives over the chasms of deprivation and sorrow. In the formal sense, Wilson's books are all comedies celebrating continuity and coherence — not divine comedies, to be sure, but aspiring towards a sustaining spiritual dimension. The intensely religious life and attitudes of the Grandmother in *The Innocent Traveller* are offered with an awed reverence; we may not share them, but we cannot help respecting the humanity and goodness that emanate from them. Mort and Myrt's "angels" in "Tuesday and Wednesday" are somewhat whimsical and certainly ineffective, but they point to a larger perspective, coyly hinting at a higher reality beyond the earthy materialism of the main characters. In *Swamp Angel* Maggie's three-day "retreat" by the Similkameen River, where she "lifted her heart in desolation and in prayer" but ultimately felt "a lifting of her spirit to God" is likened to "the respite that perhaps comes to the soul after death" (39–40). It is a religious though not sectarian experience communicated in religious vocabulary (but notice that "perhaps") and it is upheld within the novel by the earned wisdom of Nell Severance, who offers a characteristically poised *credo*: "I believe in faith. I believe in God . . . and in man, to some extent at least" (103). Ellen Cuppy, reflecting on "the nature of reality" at two o'clock in the morning, finds a "design of great beauty" in the patterns created by perpetually altering kaleidoscopic shapes of light and darkness on her bedroom ceiling (*Love* 67–68), patterns which are reflected in the shifting circumstances of her own life.

Throughout Wilson's fiction, the immediate world of the senses is always surrounded by hints of a higher world that cannot be fully comprehended, is often not to be trusted, but is undoubtedly beyond and behind existence as we know it. As I have argued elsewhere ("Overview"), her work is dominated by the sense of sight which, as in Wordsworth's "Ode on Intimations of Immortality," can rise to that exalted sense of irradiated understanding that we call "vision." Even in *Love and Salt Water*, the "design of great beauty" implies a design-accommodating world that ultimately makes sense, that manifests both form and meaning. The form and meaning are, however, generally more evident to ourselves as readers than to the participants, since we are privileged with a broader view — even an overview — that can appreciate the context of an individual moment within a larger pattern. And at this point omniscience as an artistic procedure is seen to be crucial; Wilson's authorial stance presupposes and to some extent embodies the sense of an imperfectly recognized but still palpable divine purpose. For the remainder of this chapter I shall endeavour to demonstrate how the technical control conspicuous in her fiction is perfectly attuned to her world-view.

If we look back to *Hetty Dorval* (1947) after familiarity with Wilson's later work, we see that, accomplished as it is, it lacks the assurance and virtuosity that became her hallmark. The plot, involving New-World "innocence" confronting Old-World "experience," obviously owes much to James (or at the very least to an awareness of James, since Wilson denies being "a James reader" [*Stories* 168]); it is not therefore surprising that the technique is also Jamesian. Wilson has set herself an artistic challenge that inevitably recalls *What Maisie Knew*: the sophisticated Hetty is presented to us from the viewpoint of the impressionable British Columbian teenager Frankie Burnaby, and Wilson must convey to readers indirectly meanings and subtle implications of which Frankie is unaware. Wilson is not, however, so rigorous as James; as in such classic Victorian first-person narratives as *David Copperfield* and *Great Expectations*, an older narrator is recreating incidents from earlier years. At the end of the first chapter, for example, after a skillful introduction of both the setting and Frankie's initial interest in "Mrs. Dorval," we are startled by a time-shift and baldly informed of the subsequent death by drowning of Frankie's companion. We recognize the effect as one that Wilson is fond of employing; it derives, surely, from well-known instances in Woolf and Forster. But these other instances, in Wilson and elsewhere, are omniscient effects portraying the plight of human beings in the temporal world, matters which are decidedly peripheral to Frankie's concerns in this first novel.

The second chapter provides an intriguing instance of the problems Wilson encounters in first-person narration. Frankie is describing the natural phenomenon for which Lytton is famous:

> [W]hat gives Lytton its especial character . . . is that just beside the town the clear turbulent Thompson River joins the vaster opaque Fraser. . . .
>
> Ever since I could remember, it was my joy and the joy of all of us to stand on this strong iron bridge and look down at the line where the expanse of emerald and sapphire dancing water joins and is quite lost in the sullen Fraser. It is a marriage, where, as often in marriage, one overcomes the other, and one is lost in the other. (6–7)

Most of this, particularly the descriptive details omitted here, sounds like omniscient narration and not like Frankie Burnaby at all. In the sentence about marriage we recognize the attitudes and cadences as Wilson's, not Frankie's, about whose marriage — if indeed she ever married — we can know nothing since no mention is made of it in the book. Oddly enough, the same scene is replayed with variations in *Swamp Angel* (ch. 12), where Maggie Lloyd, after having deserted her impossible second husband, travels up the Fraser Valley and is urged to look down from the bridge in the same way. Since marriage and domination are at the forefront of Maggie's mind, the sentence from *Hetty Dorval* would have been wholly appropriate. In fact, however, Wilson has by this time taken on the subtle indirection of a major imaginative artist, and in *Swamp Angel* the point is made supremely without the word "marriage" being mentioned at all. Here in *Hetty Dorval* we can see, I believe, a writer whose literary vision required the opportunity for a generalizing omniscient comment that intruded against her conscious will.

The advance in narrative assurance when we turn to *The Innocent Traveller* (1949) is astonishing.[2] Wilson has abandoned the first person — for ever, so far as full-length fiction is concerned — and at once a sense of liberation and extended artistic possiblity becomes evident. *The Innocent Traveller*, in fact, is a triumph of technical artistry from start to finish. It is amazing that Canadian critics have, for the most part, failed to recognize the masterpiece it undoubtedly is — until one realizes that its qualities will not reveal themselves to any thematic or nationalistic approach, and that the neglect is compatible with a consistent failure to respond to a consummate sense of style.

Stylistic assurance is evident from the first paragraph. In the opening sentences — "Far away at the end of the table sat Father, the kind, handsome and provident man. At this end sat Mother . . . " — the personal and the omniscient have already been fused. The plain "Father" and "Mother," without articles, may initially suggest a first-person speaker, but we soon recognize a more formalized "family voice" appropriate to a book Wilson herself described as "a family chronicle" (*Stories* 87), and are thus prepared to follow the fortunes of the Edgeworth family, in England and Canada, over a period of almost a century. The viewpoint is further complicated by the end of the paragraph when reference to "the last and fatal child" implies omniscience or at the very least a family chronicler distanced in time. A specific form of omniscience is soon developed, of course, in the brilliant sequence in which the young Topaz slides down beneath the table and "crawls on" beneath the dinner guests, observing the assembled company, including Matthew Arnold, at boot level. An extraordinary flexibility of narrative viewpoint is involved here. At first, we seem limited to a severely circumscribed perspective — a toddler's view of "a world of shoes" (4) — but as Topaz gazes at boots and shoes and slippers Wilson grants us a capsule description of their wearers' careers and destinies so that we see the whole family *sub specie aeternitatis.*

By the second chapter, Wilson is able to allow herself her first authorial intrusion: "You and I, who pick our way unsurely amongst the appalling wreckage of our time" (9). Since she makes no secret of the fact that she is partly recording and partly inventing the earlier history of her own family, this personal voice can readily be assimilated into the "family voice," but we become accustomed as we read to an authoritative omniscient consciousness moving freely and effortlessly across time and space as well as in and out of individual minds. It can engineer drastic temporal shifts — "(said Great-Aunt Topaz with authority nearly one hundred years later)" (11) — and we soon realize that the authorial voice, the family voice, and the voice of Topaz are all subtly interrelated and interconnected.

Nowhere is this flexible interconnectedness more evident than in the long eleventh chapter in which the Grandmother, Rachel, and Topaz cross Canada by train to their new home in Vancouver. Wilson can, for instance, interrupt the action to interpose three parenthetic paragraphs containing the thoughts of a great-grandson "about half a century later" (104). She can also contrast what they see from the window and what they cannot see "beyond the northern horizon" (105) — which we recognize now as the terrain of O'Hagan and his wilderness men. More subtly, she can tell us what the new immigrants cannot see because they are blinkered by their English preconceptions:

> The scene upon which the mother and daughter looked had great beauty. They did not recognize it as great beauty because they had always acquiesced in what they saw, not distinguishing beauty unless it presented itself in familiar, obvious, and inescapable form; but there was something strange and old and new in this scene which pleased them. (107)

(Topaz is absent because, interestingly enough, she has roamed into the men's smoking room where she becomes the gullible victim of a traditional "tall tale" about the "Rolling Prairie . . . caused by thousands and millions of bison . . . rolling over and over and causing these humps and hollows — some years ago, of course" [110] — an interesting juxtaposition of the "English" and "Canadian" literary modes.)

Omniscience also allows Wilson to move freely from one character to another. In its simplest form, this merely means that she can include, within a story centred on Topaz, such incidents as Mrs. Porter's response to her husband's desertion (ch. 5) or the father's proposing to two different women in quick succession when over ninety (ch. 9). More complicated effects also become possible, the most important being the presentation of Topaz's doomed romance. Again privileged by omniscience, readers can hear the inner thoughts of *both* participants alongside their formal conversation (ch. 7). A similar effect is achieved in the "Family Prayer" chapter when, as Dr. Carboy is praying, we hear the inner responses of Rose, Topaz, and the Grandmother.

The flexibility of omniscient narration is all the more necessary in a novel that celebrates both a family and an individual. A related flexibility is apparent in the distinctions established between, say, the characteristic speech rhythms of Topaz and the Grandmother, or between the relative formality of the narrative voice and Topaz's irrepressible idiolect that continually punctuates it. We register Topaz's perpetual talking because she continually interrupts the narrator with literally parenthetical comments. The result is a stylistic delight. On the other hand, the fastidious precision of Wilson's own verbal choices can be savoured — in such phrases as "blessed obliviousness" (70) that so perfectly sums up Topaz, "gentle domination" (102) applied to the Grandmother, or "innocent ghoulish pleasure" (140) for the Rev. Pratt's revivalist enthusiasm. Wilson believes in "pure" English but not to the exclusion of original and unconventional usage. She can therefore lace her prose with dialect words ("sneaped" [7] and "jannock" [232]), with the occasional neologism ("watchdoggery" [65]), and with an equivocal response to slang (212, 214).

But the supreme example of this flexibility is to be found in the presentation of Topaz's own language. This is unmistakable, and brilliantly sustained. Early in the novel, while she is still only a small child, we are told (in one of those radical time-shifts) of "her special genius for repetition" (8). But the time-shift is unnecessary in this case since she has already demonstrated her capacity: "it goes woosh," she told Matthew Arnold of the revolutionary plumbing, "Woosh, woosh!" (2). This verbal characteristic continues to the end ("Let me go immediately . . . immediately" [275]), and combines with her fondness for overemphasis (her speeches are littered with italics) and for parenthesis, since so much of her life is parenthetical. There are, moreover, her characteristic phrases, "to be sure," "I'm sure," "I do declare," culminating in her magnificently comic but apt death-

50

scene: "I'm going to die, I do declare!" (275). She may now be "a memory, a gossamer," but she will not be sneaped (God, we feel, might even be sneaped by Topaz). *The Innocent Traveller* is a tribute to one who had an unremarkable life but led it with a vitality and irrepressible curiosity that deserves celebration.

Finally, while the book at first reads like a conventional family history, it is boldly original (as well as influentially "Canadian") in its blending of fiction, history, memoir, traditional anecdote, even gossip. As far removed as Wilson's art generally seems from O'Hagan's, there are connections in their common determination to preserve the oral history of their respective "tribes." Wilson has acknowledged in her author's note that the book is "part truth and part invention." Many of the incidents ring true, sounding precisely like family anecdotes handed down from one generation to another; others are doubtless "improved," adapted, transformed from other contexts, perhaps even fabricated in the interests of a continuing and well-shaped narrative. (Mary McAlpine has recently provided instances in *The Other Side of Silence*.) Wilson emphasizes the representativeness of her story: "the history of families like the Hastings family is to some extent the history of the city of Vancouver" (158), and Topaz insists at one point: "In this new country it is very important that we should not lose track of family history. Tradition tends to die" (168). This last statement has complex ramifications. Topaz is in the process of proposing a madcap scheme for a grand reunion of the whole Hastings clan "on the beach at Hastings, or in Normandy, or even here" (168). She has in fact no proof that her ancestors came to England with William the Conqueror; her vulnerable enthusiasm ("It stands to reason! Look at the name!") is gently squelched by the Grandmother who recommends substantiating the claim first — and that is the last we hear of the matter. But Topaz is correct in principle if not in practice: tradition *does* tend to die, and the idea of creating a family myth that would encase genuine traditions in a dubious fiction is not all that far removed from Wilson's own practice.

Wilson referred to "Tuesday and Wednesday," the first of two novellas juxtaposed as *The Equations of Love* (1952), as her "own choice of work" among her fictions (*Stories* 88), and this may well be because she enjoyed the flaunting of omniscient technique that this story makes possible. Mort and Myrt are continually overlooked: by their "angels," Wilson's curious presentation here of their fitful moral conscience; by the author, who must articulate what her often ignorant protagonists cannot express for themselves; and finally by ourselves as readers. I suspect that Wilson sees an aesthetic challenge in mastering Mort and Myrt's colloquial speech, one which she would never use herself. At all events, the novella opens with an elaborate description of a sunrise in Vancouver which is "unobserved by anybody" (3) — except, of course, the omniscient narrator — and goes on to exploit aspects of omniscience already discussed in the context of *The Innocent Traveller*, and a few more besides. As in the previous book, we are continually told of what the characters do not and often cannot know. Myrt "did not see that [her] room was dingy" (8); she misinterprets the situation of the woman with alligator shoes on the bus, and the omniscient narrator is there to set us (but not Myrt) right (10); she "forgot" (but Wilson informs us) that she had recently described Mort to her employer as "lazy" whereas now he is offered as considerate and a "superior type of husband" (11–12). The same treatment is applied to Mort later. More crucially, a complex effect is achieved when we learn about Mort's death before Myrt, and even witness his last hours while knowing, alone with the narrator, that they are indeed his last. Later, when Victoria May Tritt tells her white lie (which, incidentally, is an improved "tale of hearsay" developing along the lines laid out by O'Hagan), only narrator and readers are in a position to compare it (and the inaccurate version provided by the police) with what actually happened.

Stylistically, the novella is remarkable for a unique experiment on Wilson's part. With some notable exceptions, she takes pains to adapt her vocabulary (the slack use of "nice," for example) to that of her subjects. The exceptions draw attention to the point — the formal opening description already mentioned, and the dramatic change of style in the last few pages when Wilson, following Victoria May homewards, suddenly withdraws from her subject's idiom ("Oh, she thought mournfully, my hat-with-the-veil will be rooned") to a distanced narrative complexity: "As she hurried along the dark wet pavements, life and time continued as usual everywhere under heaven with practised ease their ceaseless fluid manipulations and arrangements of circumstance and influence and spiked chance . . . " (127). Only at this point, perhaps, do we become fully conscious of the linguistic limitation to which Wilson has confined herself for most of the story. And one of the effects here, hitherto uncommon, now becomes a favourite Wilson technique, what the post-Flaubertian French designate as *style indirect libre*, the adroitly managed shift in mid-sentence, without the convention of quotation-marks, from authorial prose to direct speech. The effect is well illustrated by this early passage:

> For very irrational reasons [Myrt] would end the day disliking Mort, even when she hadn't seen him all day; because, perhaps, the butcher had said that so upstanding a man as Mort deserved the best steak in the shop, or because Aunty Emblem in her luscious fashion had said that *there* was a man, if you like! Or even because his socks had gone at the toe, or because he was darn lazy, which he was, or for no reason at all. Then she knew herself wasted on this louse. (8–9)

The passage begins formally (Myrt lacks the irony to employ the phrase "irrational reasons"), but then blends into the reported speech of the butcher, something close to the intonations of Mrs. Emblem, and then Myrt's own vocabulary so obviously distinct from Wilson's: "darn lazy," "louse." The technique enables Wilson to maintain a controlled detachment where necessary but also to identify with the emotions and attitudes as well as the speech of her characters according to the requirements of the story. She uses it frequently through the rest of her writing career.

The rich ambiguities of "Lilly's Story" begin with the title. The novella is Lilly's story in the obvious sense that it records in linear sequence the series of actions and challenges that constitute her life, but also because Lilly herself invents the background to that life. This, then, is a story about the creation of story. Wilson's interest in lying that comes to the surface in "Tuesday and Wednesday" (where Mort and Myrt are continually fabricating stories to deceive their employers, and where Victoria May's white lie proves redemptive) is further developed here, since Lilly's accounts of herself are a tissue of lies, though initiated for a legitimate, even moral purpose. This purpose is, of course, Lilly's resolve to bring up her illegitimate child to the best of her ability. The theme we immediately recognize as quintessentially Victorian (Elizabeth Gaskell's *Ruth*, George Moore's *Esther Waters*), but the "style" is just as quintessentially twentieth-

53

century, not least on account of its moral attitude — not just sympathy for her plight but approval of the single-minded determination with which she faces it, a stance that manages to be compassionate while avoiding sociological earnestness. We come to admire Lilly's "easy ruthlessness" (195) — the possible pun on Gaskell's title may be part of the point — and her canny blend of selfishness and sacrifice. Wilson is able to create subtle artistic effects by juxtaposing her own omniscience with Lilly's "innocent ignorance ("I hadn't what you'd call an edjcation myself" [271]), and so revealing that Lilly's wily, sinewy cunning can be justified as one of the equations of love.

We follow Lilly's fortunes from the shabby and dubious world of cheap restaurants and police interviews, through her sheltered sojourn as maid to the cultured and well-to-do Butlers, to an honourable and responsible position as housekeeper in a hospital. To Mrs. Butler she is "this common common girl" (201), an accurate but incomplete assessment that Lilly herself would never challenge. Looking down at her sleeping baby, she can say with justifiable satisfaction: "She's a lady, that's what she is. She's not common" (187). Through her authorial omniscience, however, Wilson is able to show her *un*commonness as well. She can articulate the basic and decent instincts which Lilly could never express in words or even in thoughts. Lilly is totally lacking in "style"; that she goes to the Beauty Shop to be "styled" (250) so that she may later achieve her final metamorphosis as Mrs. J.B. Sprockett is Wilson's indirect way of making the point. But style is necessary on Wilson's part if she is to account convincingly for Lilly's growth from the "pale slut" (145) who flees from Yow's criminality into the "very lovely woman" (271) who captivates Mr. Sprockett.

The section recounting her decision to leave the Butlers provides a convenient example. Lilly has suddenly realized that, if she stays, Eleanor will be typed as the daughter of the Butlers' maid. Wilson needs her own sophistication and language to present the situation in all its social, emotional, and above all personal complexity: "And Lilly, who had left the house that afternoon with her usual equability, . . . and had watched the hunt of bird and beast and reptile, came back to the house alert, alarmed, hunted, and committed to a plan from which she would not turn aside" (196). "Equability" is beyond Lilly's vocabulary, but the precise word is needed in context. Similarly, Lilly would not have been able, at a conscious level, to connect her own state with that of the animals she had been observing, a connection conveyed so deftly and unobtrusively by Wilson's "hunt...hunted." At the same time, we need the convincing movement of Lilly's own thoughts for full acceptance, and Wilson provides them:

> Seven years of Eleanor growing into [her] life. Seven years of Eleanor becoming a lady and like folks, and now a revelation that Eleanor's life would be phony, she thought, not real. It's a good start for her though, she reflected, and now goodbye, we're going. I know a lot more'n I did, and if I'm not a lady, my girl is, and she's going to be, and I'll have done it. For me, I've just got to watch and study to be quiet so she'll never be ashamed. (196)

Though unostentatious, this is surely a beautifully achieved passage. At first Wilson's language (the rhetorical repetition, and use of "revelation") exists side by side with Lilly's ("like folks," "phony"). Later, we move into Lilly's unspoken meditation. Her balancing of the pros and cons is realized in the rhythms as well as in the meaning. A modesty ("I've just got to watch") is balanced by an excusable pride ("I'll have done it"). Finally, in a remarkably audacious stroke, Wilson allows her the famous phrase, "study to be quiet." Lilly will have picked this up, we decide on reflection, from a lesson in church containing 1 Thessalonians 4.11 (though Wilson as fishing enthusiast might well be more familiar with it in Walton's *Compleat Angler*). In such a phrase, narrator and protagonist are aptly united.

With the publication of *The Equations of Love*, Wilson came to full maturity as a technically resourceful writer of fiction. The relation between omniscience and first-person perspective had been mastered, the means of blending formal and colloquial perfected. In *Swamp Angel* (1954), often regarded as her finest single work, she returns to more articulate central characters with a new depth and understanding and an even more assured stylistic control. In no other novel does she move with such apparent ease through so wide a range of voices, from the Chinese-English of the Quongs and the Italian-English of Alberto (both presented faithfully and endearingly without a trace of condescension), through Vardoe's vulgarity, Corder's homespun chattiness, and the breathless garrulity of the woman in the bus, to

55

Maggie Lloyd's crystal-clear directness and Nell Severance's experienced serenity. The novel is divided in emphasis between the active, outdoors-minded, future-directed Maggie and the almost inert, contemplative, past-obsessed Nell. Both can express their own attitudes, but need to be seen by readers in comparison with each other. The balance of artifice is the supreme effect here. Each represents, as it were, an extreme instance within which the novel finds its central focus, and once again Wilson needs her omniscient stance to mediate between the two worlds. One of the most impressive qualities in the novel is the ease with which Wilson can simultaneously recount her linear plot and move back and forth between Nell's life in Vancouver and Maggie's at Three Loon Lake.

Swamp Angel is a consummate exercise in patterned experience. The novel becomes a demonstration of artistic dexterity that manifests itself in many forms. Most conspicuous perhaps is the structural principle by which Maggie and Nell meet only once, briefly, in the course of the action, yet are dependent upon each other's qualities; here is Wilson's subtlest example of Donne's "no man is an Iland" theme. We also notice not merely recurrent imagery but linked families of images: the Chinese boys relate to Maggie's yellow Chinese bowl, which in turn is linked with the "awful-looking bowl" (137) in which she serves reviving soup to Mr. Cunningham and the set of earthenware bowls that Cunningham sends in gratitude; another group explores a subtle interconnection between fishing, swimming, solitariness, and the limpid quality of water. Like Nell, Wilson is suspicious of "[a]ll this nowadays of symbol symbol symbol . . . destroying reality" (79), but deftly introduces natural images — the migrating birds at the opening, faun and kitten and eagle and osprey in the middle, the wary fish of the last paragraph — that suggest meanings greater than themselves. Above all, this artistry is evident in Wilson's language, always noticeable in the way phrase echoes or balances phrase, the habitual use of words startling in their unexpected rightness. In particular, Wilson shows here a wonderful rhetorical command of the parenthesis. The narrator continually controls by interrupting in asides that have the curious effect of setting the whole temporal aspect of the book against a backdrop of eternal process. Thus, on her journey towards a geographical as well as metaphorical Hope, Maggie is presented as "free of care or remembrance as if she had just been born (as perhaps she had, after much anguish)" (34); more sombrely, when she is out swimming on the lake, imagining herself as evading the most inhibiting of life's obstacles, she "could never sink, she thinks (but she could)" (100). In such instances the omniscient voice takes on the role of providential nurturing and warning.

Love and Salt Water (1956) is not only Wilson's last novel but her least known work of fiction. This is a pity because, though not perhaps so rich and resonant as her earlier books in the exploration of human nature, it is the clearest and sparest in its communication of her world-view. All the technical artistry already illustrated is here, but it is used in the presentation of a darker but ultimately balanced vision. *Love and Salt Water* is as quintessentially British Columbian as her other books, though it is dominated by seascapes rather than landscapes (the Wilsons, we are told by Woodcock [*World* 121] always lived in apartments that looked out over the sea), but the setting, though vividly and realistically rendered, is closer to allegory than any of her other full-length fictions. The title is indicative: love in all its manifestations is pitted against the inexorable fact of the biblical image of chaos, Conrad's "destructive element," and Arnold's "unplumb'd salt, estranging sea."

Looking back over Wilson's writing after encountering this novel, we realize how preoccupied she is with death by water. The exceptions are *The Innocent Traveller* and "Lilly's Story," but the reason for these exceptions reinforces the basic point. Aunt Topaz, in a well-known passage, is compared to "those 'water-gliders' which we see in summer running about on the top of pleasant weed-fringed pools, ... unaware of the dreadful deeps below them"; only occasionally, we are told, had her foot "slipped below the surface of her pool" (103). Similarly, Lilly refrains from seeking "below the surface" (202). Their avoidance of the extreme of passion saves them from acute distress and suffering. Elsewhere, actions involving various equations and "encroachments of love" (*Love* 82) are almost invariably associated with drowning. In *Hetty Dorval* Ernestine wades into the Fraser River in a loving attempt to save her dog, and drowns. In "Tuesday and Wednesday" Mort, in a befuddled state though still conscious of the complexity of moral duty, attempts to save Hansen and is drowned with him. In *Swamp Angel* Vera tries to drown herself but fails in this as in everything else (though in an early version of the book she succeeded); in addition, Mr. Cunningham almost dies on the lake, while Maggie, as I have just noted, thinks she could never sink but Wilson (as well as Providence) knows better. In the short story "From Flores," fisherman, young lover, and Indian child all drown. And here in *Love and Salt Water*, the "sea-boy" is swept overboard, Johnny almost drowns, and Ellen is disfigured in the boating accident.

The natural world, land or water, though often beautiful, can be dangerous; indeed, "most things," the omniscient narrator tells us here, "are dangerous. Nothing is safe" (72). Wilson's vision in this novel is clearly at its bleakest. The shadow of human war is particularly evident. It had been present before but muted; Topaz reads the casualty lists in the First World War, while Maggie Lloyd loses a husband in the Second. But for Topaz "the numbers were not people but numbers" (216), and the emphasis in *Swamp Angel* is not on Maggie's sufferings but on her capacity to surmount them. This is also true of *Love and Salt Water*, but the suffering is closer to hand. Ellen sees death at close range during the raids on London; her first fiancé suffered as a prisoner of war; the husband of one of her friends lost an arm in the conflict. And these unnecessary tragedies are augmented by others: the death of Ellen's mother while she is still young, her sister's mongoloid child and the threat of deafness hanging over Johnny, the boating accident and her own consequent sufferings, both moral and physical.

I would argue, however, that *Love and Salt Water* does not contradict the serenity that emanates from her other work; rather, it draws attention to the contrasts as well as to the balance and mystery that dominate human life. Wilson's omniscient narration is essential to her fiction because it draws attention to the larger perspective. Beyond human experience lies mystery, but Wilson is confident that, were we to view the larger pattern, an ultimate meaning and purpose would become evident. She offers brief glimpses of this pattern from an at least partly elevated viewpoint. Time after time, omniscience enables Wilson to point out a factor of which the participants are unaware. When Ellen breaks off her engagement to Huw Peake, she is criticized by other characters for her treatment of a man who had suffered in the war, but Wilson can assure us that his bitterness and ill-temper are integral parts of his character. While she lets us know that the whole incident involving the boating accident was unnecessary, since the professional reasons for the parents' going away came to nothing, she also tells us — what none of the protagonists knows — that the attempt of George Gordon's first wife to initiate a reconciliation and so endanger Ellen's engagement mercifully came too late. In Wilson's work, the dice of chance are not always loaded, as they are in Thomas Hardy, against human happiness. The climax is a case in point. Had Johnny died, the moral burden on Ellen would have been intolerable (in an alternative manuscript version, in which Johnny is not revived, Ellen promptly forces her way back into the water, and her body is never found).[3] As it is, her disfiguring — which is not, as she first fears, an impediment to her marriage with George — can be interpreted as a balancing punishment for her moral lapse in foolishly taking Johnny into danger.

It may seem odd to conclude a discussion of *Love and Salt Water* with a seemingly extreme moral interpretation. I have done so because it returns us to Wilson's traditionalist and specifically Victorian inheritance, and reminds us that she was in fact a profoundly committed moral artist. Her books continually centre upon actions and their consequences, especially (in line with the Donne quotation) consequences to others. Yet the direction of Wilson's moral sympathy was by no means "Victorian" in the popular sense of that term; we never doubt for a moment that Maggie was right to walk out on her husband, and the concern in "Lilly's Story" is not with the fact of an illegitimate birth but with Lilly's moral hardihood in transforming a social lapse into a human achievement. Wilson is particularly fond of creating situations in which precise discriminations have to be made between a justified regard for the interests of self and a culpable selfishness. Moreover, precise moral discriminations require infinitely subtle artistic equivalents. Wilson recognized the importance of art in exploring the human dimension of moral arguments and especially of finding the most appropriate artistic tools for any specific task. What she offered to the emerging Canadian literary tradition (which was not always accepted or even perceived, though Laurence, Munro, and Hodgins are on record as acknowledging her encouragement) was the insistence that artistic rigour, precision, poise, and attention to the minutest details of style and language are indispensable. She grew up in a Canada wary of the seductions of art (as sections of *The Innocent Traveller* make clear). I strongly suspect that the character of Hetty Dorval, the sophisticate from outside with artistic sensitivity and an unquestionable sense of style but also with a dubious moral self-centredness, was conceived as a subtle correlative of the attitude of the artist in her time and place. In her finest work, Wilson explored moral self-centredness, and condemned it where necessary (Hetty overstepped the bounds whereas Lilly and Maggie, specialists in the art of living, did not).[4] But she always championed the cause of true art. Her greatest contribution was the example of her own fiction — generous in sympathy, radiant in tone, but strongly self-disciplined in the technical and stylistic niceties — an example that was much needed, and perhaps still is.

CHAPTER 4

W.O. Mitchell

W.O. Mitchell's first (and in the most readers' opinions his best) book, *Who Has Seen the Wind*, was first published in 1947; his second, *Jake and the Kid*, did not appear until 1961. These bibliographical facts are, however, profoundly misleading, since *Jake and the Kid* represented a collection of short stories (some subsequently adapted for radio and TV), many of which predate *Who Has Seen the Wind*. Indeed, only the last three of the thirteen collected stories are later in date than the story of Brian Sean MacMurray O'Connal. The truth of the matter is that the contents of both books developed simultaneously, and the short stories might not have seen the light of day in volume form if publication had not coincided with the television adaptations. As for *Who Has Seen the Wind*, two excerpts were published as early as 1945 and in a chronological listing are sandwiched between Jake and the Kid stories. As Michael Peterman has written, in one of the surprisingly few general introductions to Mitchell's work, "the important relationships in *Who Has Seen the Wind* had their beginnings in the interaction of the Kid and Jake Trumper" ("Mitchell" 10). Moreover, the basic elements in Mitchell's fiction may be found in his first published story, "But as Yesterday," which appeared in *Queen's Quarterly* in the summer of 1942. These include a close relationship between a young boy and an elderly person, the making of a toy for their mutual enjoyment, a preoccupation with the tyranny of clock-time, the reproduction of colloquial prairie vernacular, and a deeply human tone that can easily verge on sentimentality. As early as "Elbow Room," his third publication and the second Jake and the Kid story (published in *Maclean's* on 15 September 1942), his main prairie-images besides the wind — gopher, meadowlark, and coyote — are already assembled.

These historical facts draw attention to the first major problem that confronts any critical approach to Mitchell's work. *Who Has Seen the Wind* is, as I hope to demonstrate shortly, a masterpiece; the Jake and the Kid stories, by contrast, are a series of cosy, sentimental, "cute" sketches that never rise out of the harmless but ultimately trivial category of "pop" entertainment. Both are intensely regional, but unlike the novel *Jake and the Kid* never transcends the regional (as, Mitchell insists, all serious literature must do [Barclay 54]). This is because it belongs essentially to the level of the contemporaneous song about those dear hearts and gentle people who live and love in our home town. There is no genuine tension, since we know that the hired man and the kid will always emerge triumphant. (Even when the kid loses his dog in the first story — an incident recalling the end of Part 2 of *Who Has Seen the Wind* — it is replaced by a "brother that's just like 'im" [14].) Each episode becomes formulaic, like a comic strip. The series was conceived in war-time, which excuses some of the rather treacly patriotism as morale-boosting though not as art, but it continued long after the war and catered to an undiscriminating, even philistine audience. Mitchell seems to have been unable to sever himself from what was a successful and financially rewarding venture, but the circumstances may well have inhibited his development as a serious artist. Interestingly enough, he acknowledged the connection by informing Patricia Barclay that in the later Jake series he concentrated on other "inhabitants of the mythical community of Crocus," including Daddy Johnson [*Jake* 176] who became Daddy Sherry in *The Kite*, with the express intention of providing himself with " 'semi-polished material' from which he could draw future novels" (54–55). Only in *Who Has Seen the Wind* did he fully extricate himself from the seductions of mass-media popular standards.

Jake and the Kid, then, requires no detailed consideration here, though one story deserves brief discussion. This is "The Liar Hunter," which is plotted around the phenomenon of the tall tale. It is easily the subtlest and most satisfying of the stories because the tale itself is an illustration of the very theme that organizes it. Mr. Godfrey, the liar hunter in question, is a folklorist in search of "the creative liar" (93) who will add to his local-history collection of tall tales. After Godfrey has alienated his fiancée's father, Old Gatenby, who is annoyed by the historian's note-taking during his tall-tale-telling, Jake attempts to go one better by outdoing Gatenby and telling the tallest of tall tales. Just as Godfrey is about to leave town with his engagement in ruins, he explains the importance of tall tales to Jake, the kid, and Molly, his almost ex-fiancée. He doesn't offer the traditional explanation, summarized by Margery Fee as a means of teaching "the inexperienced and naive not to believe everything they hear" (14); instead, he emphasizes their "democratic" origins ("Not the history of great and famous men . . . but of the lumberjacks and section men, hotel keepers and teachers and ranchers and farmers. The people who really count"), their therapeutic effect on the teller ("These men lie about the things that hurt them most"), and their status as a "defence of exaggeration" (100–01). Eventually, Godfrey is able to become a "creative liar" himself, make use of his collection of tall tales, and win back his fiancée. The story is amusing in its folksy way, not least because (ironically) it makes a valid comment on a generally popular art form of which most of the Jake and the Kid stories represent sentimentalized, bastardized versions. In fact, many of Mitchell's finest effects originate out of the tall-tale tradition. It is not accidental that one of the best interviews with Mitchell, by Donald Cameron, begins with a discussion of tall tales that specifically alludes to many of the examples and discussions already presented in "The Liar Hunter."

If we turn now to *Who Has Seen the Wind* in the light of this discussion, we may see in high relief some aspects of the novel that might otherwise pass unnoticed. Because it belongs to the genre of the *Bildungsroman*, it consists of a series of separate stories linked by their association with a common central figure. These stories, we then find, vary dramatically in their kinds. For example, the seventeenth chapter, concentrating on the skates given to Brian as a Christmas present, is in its sentimental tone and "happy ending" compatible with most of the Jake and the Kid stories, while others, including the account of the Ben and his still in the church basement (ch. 14) and that of Saint Sammy, Bent Candy, and the Lord speaking out of the whirlwind (ch. 28), have obvious connections with the tradition of the tall tale.

These are examples of tales that have a bearing on the narrative methods discussed earlier, but there are other kinds of story represented as well. I refer to various disturbing stories of prejudice and injustice (Brian's "lie" on his first day at school [ch. 10], the events centred on the Wongs' birthday party [ch. 18]), and a classic version of the "tables turned" comic routine in the defeat of Mrs. Abercrombie (ch. 30). What is remarkable about *Who Has Seen the Wind* is its capacity to combine and unify so many totally discrepant ingredients. Part of this success may be explained by the fact of combination itself, the sense of a convincing multiplicity of attitudes that connects with our sense of the bewildering variety of experiences that we encounter in "real life." The constant intercalation of the "mystical" and the ordinary may well be more characteristic of everyday experience than are the conventions of realistic fiction. If *Who Has Seen the Wind* can be designated "realist" in any sense, it is because of its refusal to offer a single-minded, consistent, and therefore over-contrived picture of life in a small prairie-town. The scene involving the skates may be accepted here, since such sentimental incidents are part of the reality we know, whereas within *Jake and the Kid* it would seem artificial and perfunctory, one more sweetmeat in an excessively sugary dessert. Similarly, the story of Bent Candy's barn is effective in context by virtue of its tonal incongruity. Had it appeared in a company of tall tales (in the middle of Robert Kroetsch's *What the Crow Said*, for example), it would constitute just "more of the same." An informed reading of the section will recognize its tall-tale origins, admire the appropriateness of such an incident within the prairie context out of which so many tall tales emerged, and applaud Mitchell's artistry in containing it within his larger and tonally varied narrative.

The anatomy-type form employed here, bringing together so many different kinds of tale, would not cohere unless other unifying qualities were involved. All these are inevitably interrelated, so that it is virtually impossible to discuss one without considering the others. There are, however, two supremely important, and separable, constituents of this unity: first, a unifying philosophical attitude or world-view; second, a reconciling stylistic effect which binds the individual elements together. I shall endeavour to discuss each in turn.

Perhaps aware of a possible problem in unifying his diverse material, Mitchell attempts to assist his readers by appending a prefatory explanation intended to emphasize consistency of theme: "Many interpreters of the Bible believe the wind to be symbolic of Godhood. . . . This is the story of a boy and the wind." Which means that it is also the story of a boy and his developing awareness of God. Mitchell is here associating himself with a persistent intellectual and linguistic tradition that is reasonably well-known but may be briefly summarized here. Words like "wind," "breath," "spirit," "inspiration," "soul," are commonly related in idea and through language. The Christian Bible begins with the words "In the beginning God created the heaven and the earth. And the earth was without form, and void; and darkness was upon the face of the deep. And the Spirit of God moved upon the face of the waters" (Gen. 1.1–2 A.V.). And, a little later: "And the Lord God formed man of the dust of the ground, and breathed into his nostrils the breath of life; and man became a living soul" (Gen. 2.7). Here "God," "Spirit," "breath," and "soul" are all linked. Other relevant quotations from the Old Testament include God speaking out of the whirlwind in Job (alluded to, as already indicated, in the tall tale of Bent Candy's barn), the verses from Psalm 103 employed by Mitchell as an epigraph, and the passage from the Valley of Dry Bones chapter in Ezekiel: " . . . Prophesy unto the wind, son of man, and say to the wind, Thus saith the Lord GOD: Come from the four winds, O breath, and breathe upon these slain, that they may live" (Ezek. 37.9).

In the New Testament, these interconnections are carried further, especially with reference to the Holy Spirit. At the Incarnation the angel announces to Mary: "The Holy Ghost shall come upon thee, and the power of the Highest shall overshadow thee" (Luke 1.35). At the time of the baptism in Jordan, Jesus "saw the heavens opened, and the Spirit like a dove descending upon him: And there came a voice from heaven, saying, Thou art my beloved Son, in whom I am well pleased" (Mark 1.10–11). And at Pentecost,

> . . . suddenly there came a sound from heaven as of a rushing mighty wind, and it filled all the house where they were sitting.
>
> And there appeared unto them cloven tongues like as of fire, and it sat upon each of them.
>
> And they were all filled with the Holy Ghost, and began to

speak with other tongues, as the Spirit gave them utterance. (Acts 2.2–4)

In traditional symbolism and iconography, the Holy Spirit is represented in the form of a dove, and this explains why Brian's initiation into the mysticism of birth (and death) comes through his watching the nesting pigeons, which are ornithologically doves.

The special "feeling" experienced by Brian in the prairie wind relates to the biblical wind imagery just documented and to the use made of such imagery by poets in the British tradition. John Milton, realizing the inappropriateness of invoking the Classical muse for "inspiration" when writing his Christian epic *Paradise Lost*, substitutes the Holy Spirit, and succeeds in linking poetically and imagistically many of the texts already quoted:

> thou from the first
> Wast present, and, with mighty wings outspread,
> Dovelike sat'st brooding on the vast Abyss,
> And mad'st it pregnant. (1.19–22)

Wordsworth, writing an epic about the human mind, depends on natural inspiration, the real wind blowing across the English Lake District, and goes on to invoke a "correspondent breeze" within the heart (*Prelude* [1850] 1.35) equivalent to Milton's "Paradise within thee, happier far" (12.587), the presence of the Holy Spirit within the believing Christian. *Who Has Seen the Wind* implicitly alludes to these key texts and others in making its point. Thus the meadowlark whose song pervades the novel is a North American prairie equivalent to Shelley's skylark which is itself (like his west wind) a symbol of both aspiration and inspiration. And at the comic level, Mitchell slyly and punningly draws on the same congeries of imagery in the scene in which the Ben's still explodes during the church service. Here a secular form of spirit interrupts an act of Christian worship badly in need of resuscitation, in a kind of profane Pentecost. When a scene superficially removed from the "serious" side of the novel can be linked to it through the unifying fact of words, symbols, and the ideas they promulgate, the unifying power of Mitchell's art may be better appreciated. (The detail of the grandmother's "gas" — or wind — and her "belshing," taken up by the young Brian into his imaginative concept of God, is another example.)

The employment of the key words already discussed — "wind," "breath," "spirit," etc. — inevitably becomes part of Mitchell's "style" in its narrower, specifically verbal sense. Moreover, his approach in *Who Has Seen the Wind* differs from that in *Jake and the Kid* by being omniscient instead of first-person. The short stories are all told exclusively in the Kid's idiom. In *Who Has Seen the Wind*, by contrast, ordinary colloquial conversation (whether of children or adults) is interspersed with more formal "overview" passages that enable Mitchell, like Wilson, to insert a sense of mystical coherence into the narrative. The novel begins, for example, with an eloquent evocation of prairie in which "the unfailing visitation of wind" gives "life" to the long grasses (3). From a panoramic view of "the least common denominator of nature, . . . Saskatchewan prairie," Mitchell pans on to the small detail of a boy's tricycle, and so to the tricycle's owner, Brian O'Connal. This alternation of panorama and close-up recurs throughout the novel, and depends, of course, on the omniscient perspective. The structure is highly controlled, each section (as every commentator notes) ending with a death that leads Brian further into understanding and maturity though away from the Wordsworthian intimations of immortality that characterize childhood. Brian himself is presented as an imaginative and intelligent child with a youthful vision reflected in vivid imagistic language and expressed through indirect speech in Mitchell's prose. Instances include a bee's "licorice all-sorts stripes" and its "cellophane of folded wings" (8), and "a fox-red caterpillar making a procession of itself over a crack" (11), both originating in the almost microscopically close perspective of a small child. At the same time, certain moments of mystical insight, like the central incident where Brian is entranced by the dewdrops on the spirea bush (107–08), are communicated in a style which employs the full resources of adult speech beyond a child's capacity.

Mitchell has therefore created an ideal form through which to explore the relation between a palpable but undefinable spiritual reality and the intimate details of an individual human life. At the same time, it is an excellent way of creating a bridge between the profoundly serious and the entertainingly popular. Balance is, indeed, a key to the success of *Who Has Seen the Wind*. Its presentation of prairie life includes both communal cohesiveness and personal loneliness. The human society of the town can be both warmly supportive and cruelly bigoted. Prairie itself can be both sustaining and "awful" (128), the meadowlark's song balanced by the gopher's cry. All this culminates in the artistic *tour de force* of the final two pages or so, where an intense lyricism coexists with a notably *un*sentimental view of the life-process. Like the extract from O'Hagan's "The Tepee" analysed earlier (pp. 31–32 above), this passage is just as verbally complex, though creating a very different effect. O'Hagan evokes the "rough-edged" toughness of the wilderness man's life; Mitchell leads up to a mature philosophic acceptance of human life and death within the larger scheme of things. The same verbal resources — rhythmic variety, alliteration, assonance, even rhyme — are employed to create an elevated sense of understanding: "He looked up at rime-white wires, following them from pole to pole to the prairie's rim" (299); "High above the prairie, platter-flat, the wind wings on" (300). But it is not merely a matter of sound and vocabulary. The novel's opening echoes its close just as the vowels and consonants echo each other in the sentences just quoted. The ant that, in a macabre image, makes its "long pilgrimage down the backbone spools" of the skeleton of Brian's dog (300) recalls Brian's first infant thoughts recorded in the book when he sat "imagining himself an ant in a dark cave" (4). And, of course, the wind lifts the topsoil in the first paragraph and in the last — with the added subtlety that, in noticing that obvious connection, we also notice the balanced repetition of "skeleton" in the opening and closing sentences, the symbols of immortality and mortality supremely fused. This is the confident eloquence of major art.

Who Has Seen the Wind, then, was an extraordinary first novel. It almost immediately attained the status of a popular classic, and it was also accepted as a work of artistic importance, despite what appears to be a characteristic (and in many cases justifiable) suspicion in academic circles of the commercial success. This suspicion has, however, been strengthened over the years by the realization that Mitchell has never quite equalled this initial achievement. In my discussion of his later novels, I shall try to indicate why, in my opinion, this (comparative) failure is indeed connected with the inevitable tension of our time between the artistic success and the best-seller.

The Kite (1962) has generally been neglected by academic critics, and I had better state at once that, although it lacks the mystical dimension of *Who Has Seen the Wind*, it seems to me an excellent comic novel. Its neglect may be explained, at least in part, by its unusual form, which is easily overlooked and so not understood. W.H. New, for example, goes astray when he assumes that David Lang the narrator must be at the centre of the novel and so concludes that, "[s]tructurally and thematically, Daddy Sherry is a minor figure" (179). This is not in fact so; Daddy *is* at the centre of the novel's structure. A clue is provided within the text itself by Jack Dagliesh: " 'all of us at one time or another have had something to do with Daddy that's — well especially between ourselves and — and Daddy' " (109). This remark explains the inset stories that occur throughout the book. The first is Keith's story of the trapeze and the berry-picking (ch. 5), and this is succeeded by Dr. Richardson's saga of the goose-hunt (ch. 7), Dagliesh's story of Daddy and the oil-shares (ch. 9), the Rev. Donald Finlay's account of Daddy's almost-marriage (ch. 12), Helen Maclean's disclosure of her relationship to Daddy (ch. 13), and Belva Tinsley's uproarious tale of Daddy and the flood (ch. 14). The novel proceeds by means of its progressive revelations provided by these inset stories that ultimately reveal the complexities of Daddy's long life. All the inhabitants of Shelby to which we are introduced have their stories of Daddy; one might almost say that his very existence unifies the town.

My next point will doubtless have been anticipated by most readers: the majority of these inset stories, especially those of the goose-hunt and the flood, are tall tales of the kind that Mitchell presents in "The Liar Hunter." Daddy's unprecedentedly long life — he is the oldest man in Canada, indeed "older than Canada" (4) — enables Mitchell to string together a series of invented and unlikely incidents that represent popular story and are appropriately associated with an unorthodox, uninhibited, larger-than-life prairie-dweller around whom tall tales might be expected to gather. But there is another aspect of Daddy Sherry that must be emphasized at this point because it develops a characteristic that becomes habitual in Mitchell's later work. This is what Peterman calls "the unrestrained exuberance of [Daddy's] language" ("Mitchell" 13). We have heard traces of this before — in Jake the hired man, in Brian's Uncle Sean and, disguised by the mosaic of biblical phraseology, in what Laurie Ricou has described as the "prairie-sod-buster slang" of Saint Sammy (13–14) — but in *The Kite* it is offered for the first time as the dominating speech of the main protagonist. I have space for only one example, Daddy's account of his buddy Ramrod:

> "Ramrod an' me was together for . . . over twenty years. All that time I never knew him to change his socks or his underwear till they come off of their own free will. Stank like a spring bear! He stank of willah smoke an' he stank of Black Judas Chewin' Tobaccah — horse an' cow an' sheep — he stank of all the hides the Lord ever wrapped around — Ramrod ever skinned off of — a critter — an' besides all that he stank of hisself." (101–02)

Much of the effectiveness of the book derives from the exuberance of this kind of idiom, especially in its contrast with the standard "educated" cadences of most of the other characters. But, and I shall return to this point, it is a verbal effect that tends to have a centrifugal impact.

The Kite is a curiously elusive novel to comprehend or summarize. Its relations to *Who Has Seen the Wind* are numerous, and it contains profounder implications than have hitherto been acknowledged. Mitchell has changed his narrative centre from a young boy to the oldest of old men, but a link is maintained through the title-symbol, since a kite can only fly with the assistance of the invisible wind. It is a novel about Time (whose relentless reminder of mortality is symbolically challenged by Daddy at the close when he smashes his gift-clock); Keith's gift, the kite, unites past and present while the official one, the grandfather-clock, only emphasizes Time's passing. By the same token, Daddy is specifically portrayed as joining the present and the future of his country (204).

Moreover, the novel is of particular interest for the way in which it casts light on Mitchell's artistic position at this time. It is worthwhile emphasizing that David Lang, the narrator, is a figure remarkably close to Mitchell himself. He is a popular journalist and media person who becomes fascinated with Daddy's story — and the problem of how to tell it. But neither Lang nor his creator belongs to the group of "humble and self-effacing writers" who have "dissolved themselves in the one trim style so well that it seemed the material must have written itself" (6) — which is just as well, since both have to rise to the challenge of communicating Daddy's unique and boisterous personality. But the parallels go further. Lang notes that Daddy's story, as he gathers it in its "wealth of sensuous detail," was "the sort of material to stain his narrative with immediacy" but at the same time was "difficult to bring to order" (124). He also expresses a frustrated desire to break out of ephemeral journalism to the writing of more serious and more permanent literature (150–51). In articulating Lang's dilemma, Mitchell, as we shall see, addresses himself to the two issues that most affect his later work.

If Lang encounters difficulties in writing up the story of Daddy Sherry, they are as nothing to Mitchell's own problems in presenting the story of Carlyle Sinclair. A novel entitled *The Alien* was serialized (apparently in abridged form) in *Maclean's* as early as 1953–54, but Mitchell was dissatisfied with it, and it was never published separately. He eventually rewrote it drastically, and it ultimately appeared in 1973 as *The Vanishing Point*.[1] The main setting is an Indian reserve, the protagonist a middle-aged white teacher who falls in love with one of his Indian students. The background to this love-plot involves white/Indian relations, the obsolescent green world of the natural life against the asphalt jungle, and the need for "bridges" literal, moral, and psychological. The vanishing point that gives the book its title is ambivalent. Artistically, of course, it involves the technical mastery of perspective; moreover, Sinclair finds that he must change his moral and human perspective in the course of the story. But it is also, in John Moss's words, the realization that "things only seem to come together as they are diminished" (205) — an insight that becomes both sobering and sustaining.

The Vanishing Point resembles its predecessors in containing a number of compact incidents that are memorable in themselves as detachable scenes as well as forming part of a larger fictional scheme. These are mainly flashbacks to Sinclair's childhood, and include his catching his "pecker" in the magic lantern (ch. 25), his defecating in Old Kacky's desk (ch. 26), his entering the Grand Ten Thousand Dollar magazine contest and its result in his selling lingerie to Miss Rosedance and the inmates of her whorehouse (ch. 27). Once again, these are close to tall tales, as are the narrative illustrations within Heally Richards's revival sermon (ch. 21). The critical problem with such scenes is first that, amusing as they are, their preoccupation with genitals, excrement, and underwear is essentially adolescent and therefore limiting, second that they tend to deflect attention from the larger and more serious themes with which the novel is primarily concerned. The dilemma is nicely summed up in Moss's discussion. He considers the novel Mitchell's "best work" (as I do not) but then continues: "In the tradition of the comic novel, there are marvellous digressions throughout *The Vanishing Point*. Whole chapters are assigned quite arbitrarily to a retrospective of Carlyle Sinclair's early life" (205). Not only are the implications of "digressions" and "quite arbitrarily" disturbing, but they patently contradict Mitchell's own intentions, since he has insisted that "the whole answer to . . . Carlyle's human condition and to Heally Richard's [*sic*] lies back in their childhood" (Cowan 23). The critic's reading apparently refutes the author's claims. What has happened, I believe, is that a shadow has fallen between Mitchell's conception and his execution. He intended the flashbacks to relate clearly to the main theme and to culminate in Sinclair's change of heart after his initial reaction to Victoria's pregnancy. But the scenes are so vivid, so compelling as tall tales in their own right, that they indeed read like "digressions" and appear to relate "quite arbitrarily" to the rest of the book. In other words (and here, of course, I am disputing Moss's value-judgement while upholding his descriptive account), instead of contributing to the book's unity, these incidents pull it apart. The same might be said of Sinclair's endearingly vigorous idiom, which develops out of the garrulous vitality of characters like Daddy Sherry. Mitchell delights in Sinclair's slangy vernacular and in Archie Nicotine's enigmatic and ironic routines. Unfortunately, though highly creative in themselves, they further detract from the structural coherence of the novel as a whole.

Yet another weakness detracts from *The Vanishing Point*'s overall effectiveness. At the conclusion, a series of convenient happenings trivialize the serious issues with which Mitchell deals. Once Sinclair has decided to marry Victoria (interestingly enough, we never hear whether Victoria wants to marry him), he goes out for a walk in the early morning and makes two discoveries. First, he comes upon Archie Nicotine in the company of a group of his fellow Indians: Archie has at last succeeded in buying the needed parts for his truck and restoring it to working order. This has been a continuing motif throughout the novel; time and again, Archie's previous efforts have been frustrated by his weakness for alcohol and doubtful company. Suddenly he is presented as successful, though we are offered no convincing reasons for his transformation. True, his moral strength is also indicated in his defiance of the Catfaces and his rescue of Victoria, but it is surely sentimental to suppose that this gives him special power to withstand the perennial temptations of the Empress Hotel's Ladies and Escorts room. But this is not all. Earlier, we had been told that Beulah Spring, upon which the reservation depends for its water-supply, has been reduced to a trickle as a result of seismic disturbances for which an oil-drilling team had been responsible. Yet suddenly, on this magical day of transformations, the waters are freed. The whole environment, as in a comic pastoral, is made to reflect and celebrate the new promise established by Sinclair and Victoria (a promise which, given their differences — in age, education, and upbringing — seems doubtful at best, a desperate hope rather than a likely resolution). All this is cosy but forced. The symbolic dimensions of the scene are at odds with the social concern (applicable to the "real world") explored in the main plot. Here again, I suggest, Mitchell's desire for a "popular" comic ending has interfered with his ambitions to be an uncompromisingly serious novelist. His design is not in question; the artistic execution of the design seems to me flawed.[2]

Mitchell's later novels, *How I Spent My Summer Holidays* (1981), *Since Daisy Creek* (1984), and *Ladybug, Ladybug . . .* (1988), need not detain us for very long. All contain traces of the same strengths and (especially) conspicuous evidence of the weaknesses that I have identified in *The Vanishing Point. How I Spent My Summer Holidays* is clearly intended to be an adolescent *Who Has Seen the Wind*, but the thriller-plot fails to sustain a serious presentation of the change from innocence to experience. We find the same prick-and-arsehole humour — often very funny, as in the tall-tale sequence of the old man blown up while sitting in the outside privy, and legitimized to some extent by the adolescent perspective — but essentially it remains the same mixture as before. Mitchell's first full-length experiment in first-person narration, it gets into technical problems when Hughie the narrator has to be manipulated awkwardly into the right place at the right time to report on significant moments in the plot. Contrivance is more evident here than artistry. Besides, the adult world presented in the novel is a sour, restricted one — a world of mental sickness, adultery, lesbianism, even blackmail arising out of abortion — the influence, one suspects, of the sensationalist, exposé fiction of the age of permissiveness. This material seems damagingly thin when compared with the more fundamental, universal problems explored in *Who Has Seen the Wind*. King Motherwell befriends the escaped mental patient Bill the Shepherder in part because he dislikes "[s]trait-jacket restraint" (87); this seems to reflect Mitchell's own dislike of restraint that has become more evident in his later years and has exacerbated his perennial problems with artistic form. Above all, Hughie's admiration of the morally irresponsible King Motherwell is as evident in the middle-aged narrator as in his adolescent self, and this casts serious doubt on Mitchell's capacity to understand his own creations.[3]

Since Daisy Creek regains the exuberant vitality curiously muted in *How I Spent My Summer Holidays* but encounters further formal difficulties. The story of Colin Dobbs's reconciliation with his daughter is never completely integrated with the story of his mauling by the bear and the court-case over the bearskin, nor are these discrete plots easily connected with his career as a writer and teacher of writing. The memorable set-scenes — notably the death and attempted burial of the dachshund, and Dobbs's seduction by a female colleague — are amusing but even more blatantly irrelevant to the main story (or stories) than before. The dialogue, as might be expected, is convincing and the characterization vivid, but despite the serious theme of Dobbs's accident and the human intensity clearly aimed at and often achieved in the father-daughter relationship, *Since Daisy Creek* is most memorable for its isolated scenes of animated farce. Its best moments only draw attention to the almost perfunctory nature of the plot development.

In *Ladybug, Ladybug . . .* , his most recent novel, Mitchell produces a bewildering mixture of the sentimental, the psychopathic, and the metafictional. Here too connections between otherwise unrelated elements seem confined to the lower common denominator of plot: Kenneth Lyon is the centre of consciousness, but his researches into Mark Twain never connect clearly with Mitchell's recurring "little girl lost" theme or his exploration of psychological violence, and the segments of the narrative that combine the last two bear no more relation to art than the average in-flight movie (which they disturbingly resemble). Mitchell seems to have cast in his lot with the crudely popular against the subtly permanent. It seems as if we must now, regretfully, write him off as a serious novelist.

As early as the 1971 interview with Donald Cameron, Mitchell had insisted upon the need for any creative artist both to transform and to transcend the general ordinariness of everyday experience, to "go to the further things and outrageously take liberties . . . in order to make it all organically mean something" (2: 60). His subsequent career as a novelist has tended to underline the discrepancy in his own work between "outrageously tak[ing] liberties" and achieving an "organically" satisfying form and meaning. The danger signal is especially evident in a later interview, published in 1980–81, where, in discussing his own approach to the teaching of creative writing, an approach which sounds virtually identical to Dobbs's in *Since Daisy Creek*, he subordinates a mastery of "craft" to recovering all-important life-relationships from a "subconscious notebook" (O'Rourke 149–50). One can only conclude that Mitchell's recent tendency has been to venture too far in this direction. Nobody would be likely to quarrel with an emphasis on "life," but *Who Has Seen the Wind* is an eloquent example of the successful control of vital experience through "craft." Characters like Sinclair, Dobbs, and (to a lesser extent) Lyon are certainly far more immediate in impact than their equivalents in more artistically restrained fiction; in fact, their voices are so forceful that they tend to live in our memories as if the narration of their respective novels came through their mouths. We feel humanly close to them as characters, as we are close to the protagonists of Margaret Laurence's Manawaka novels, but this is not necessarily a virtue in itself. Such characters can tear a novel apart. The human immediacy of *Who Has Seen the Wind*, on the other hand, emerges because of, not in spite of, Mitchell's artistic control of the book as a whole. Ironically, that same restraint that he has combatted from *Who Has Seen the Wind* onwards — at the end of that novel "restraint" is specifically identified with Presbyterianism (298) — is the quality which the later novels have consciously avoided and most obviously lack. Vitality is desirable, but centrifugal vitality can take its artistic toll.

This rebellion against harsh restraint, at its most extreme a protest against the values of the Mrs. Abercrombies of this world, represents a popular, even "populist" stance. We end, then, where we began with Mitchell as the partial victim of an age in which it is virtually impossible to be commercially and artistically successful at the same time. *Who Has Seen the Wind* is an exception — but apparently an exception that proves the rule. The subject comes to a head in a revealing moment in the 1974 interview with *Acta Victoriana*, when he remarked: "I have been totally committed to writing for twenty-nine years. In that time there's been a compromise, but a very small compromise. It has meant a different kind of writing. Rather than corrupting what I'm writing in order to sell better, I've done documentaries and playwriting for radio and television mainly" (Cowan 16). The evidence suggests that this separation has not been as clear-cut as he hoped. That his crusade has been directed towards saving the popular from the vulgar should be acknowledged. In the same interview he made a bold statement of principle when he announced "I hate Disney," and explained the second chapter of *The Vanishing Point* as establishing a dour contrast between the green ghetto of the segregated reservation and the "Disney nightmare of fluorescent flamingos, Bambies and dwarves under toadstools" (20) that constitutes the culture of metropolitan urban sprawl. Ironically, Ricou has reported that one of his students found even *Who Has Seen the Wind* "Disneyish" (15). The student was wrong (as I hope my discussion has demonstrated): Mitchell's vision finds its appropriate artistic equivalent not in Disney but in the work of William Kurelek, who splendidly illustrated the 1976 Macmillan reprint of *Who Has Seen the Wind*. But Ricou's student would have been close to target if the adjective had been applied to *Jake and the Kid*. Mitchell, for all his distaste, teeters in this direction; the splendid achievement of *Who Has Seen the Wind* notwithstanding, it has to be admitted that this perennial temptation has left some recurrent, perhaps fatal, blemishes on his art.

CHAPTER 5

Robertson Davies

In a memorable episode half-way through *World of Wonders*, Paul Dempster, rehearsing the tightrope scene from *Scaramouche* as a double for Sir John Tresize, has difficulty with the detail of thumbing his nose at the Marquis de la Tour d'Azyr. When asked what the gesture means to him, he replies bashfully, "Kiss my arse, Sir John" (180). Sir John, only a little daunted, tries to express the effect he wants in words but eventually acts out the scene on the floor of the stage — "and there it was! Kiss my arse *with class*, and God knows how many years of actors' technique and a vivid memory of Henry Irving all backing it up" (181). This scene surely epitomizes the art of Robertson Davies himself. As ironist and satirist, Davies is continually saying "Kiss my arse" to absurdities, pretensions, and fashionable sacred cows, but he always does it "with class," elegantly, wittily, with a fine sense of timing and style. Moreover, this scene, dramatic in itself (one thinks of Eliza Doolittle's beautifully articulated "not bloody likely" in *Pygmalion*), takes the art of acting as its subject, reminding us not only of the novelist's technique, which is at least as rigorous and demanding as the actor's, but also of the dramatic dimension that is central to Davies's art of fiction.

I shall be concentrating on the dramatic element in Davies's fiction later in this chapter, but first it is necessary to discuss his particular sense of style. Paul West has observed that "Davies stands for style" ("Sluices" 63); certainly the word is continually cropping up in his novels and criticism, but the kind of style he advocates is less clear. In a review entitled "Elements of Style" (1959), for example, he refers to his "enthusiasm for a more ornate and formal style of writing than is generally recommended" (*Enthusiasms* 248). On the other hand, David Staunton in *The Manticore* is a strong champion of "the Plain Style" as practised and recommended by Dunstan Ramsay: "he insisted on essays in what he called the Plain Style; it was, he said, much harder to get away with nonsense in the Plain Style than in a looser manner. In my legal work I found this to be true and useful" (55). Everything else, we are told later, was "Baroque Style, which [Ramsay] said was not for most people, or Jargon, which was the Devil's work" (72). Staunton should not, of course, be identified with his creator, but these sentiments, especially since they originate from Ramsay, carry weight; they are upheld by various remarks Davies has made in interviews. Asked by *Acta Victoriana*, for example, how he would describe his own style, he replied: "I just try to write as clearly as I can" (Hetherington 80). Earlier, in a discussion I quoted at greater length in my introduction, he recommended "a style which compels attention and impresses by its aptness" (*Voice* 75). It is also worth pointing out that in 1964 he noted (interestingly enough, citing Ethel Wilson as an honourable exception) that "a lack of strong feeling for language is one of the principal weaknesses of Canadian prose writers" (*Well-Tempered Critic* 235). A few years later, *Fifth Business* is presented as taking its origin from a protest concerning style, Ramsay's objection to the "illiteracy of tone" (13) displayed by Lorne Packer's article in the school magazine.

Ironically, however, a recent critique of Davies by John Mills expressed strong reservations about an important aspect of his style: "Whatever else Davies is read for, it cannot be for the felicity of his prose" ("Davies" 35). Mills proceeds, unfairly, to argue his point with reference to a passage from Davies's first novel, written while he was still learning his fictional trade. He also reveals a certain bias when he uses, among other critical adjectives characterizing his prose, the word "unmetaphorical," which seems to prejudge the case by loading his dice against "the Plain Style." Certainly, one will not find any elaborate striving after complex stylistic effects in Davies (though he certainly employs more formal constructions and a larger vocabulary than many contemporary writers). Indeed, the old-fashioned "fine style" is invariably treated with suspicion, not to say hostility. Thus

78

when in *Leaven of Malice* we encounter a reference to "a world where style is rapidly becoming a thing of the past" (8), we might expect the sentiment to carry Davies's approval. In fact, it is written by a tiresome newspaper correspondent in praise of Swithin Shillito, whose style has previously been characterized as "flowery" and "drivelling" (3, 4). The point is reiterated later:

> "Writing — the light touch — the foundation of a style — you know the sort of thing I mean."
> They all knew. It meant Mr Shillito and whimsical little essays about birdseed and toothpicks. (158)

For Davies, "style" should be used in its broader sense, and clearly means something diametrically opposed to Shillito's "fine writing." It includes intellectual curiosity and vigour, a Shavian command of the dance of ideas, a wide-ranging assurance, a sharp wit, a polished (but not affected) elegance, all that Mills sums up conveniently in the term *"sprezzatura"* ("Davies" 69); it also requires a skillful control of linguistic levels (Davies is as adept as Wilson in moving from the formal to the colloquial within a phrase), and a satirical capacity for exposing contemporary excesses ranging in tone from the jocular to the pungent — in other words, "kiss my arse *with class*."

What it does not mean, if we approach his mature work with a special interest in the technical management of first-person narration, is any conspicuous differentiation between the speech rhythms of his main characters. When we turn from Ramsay's narration in *Fifth Business* to Staunton's in *The Manticore*, we are not immediately aware of a change in idiom or cadence — as we are, for example, if we move from the voice and rhythms of Laurence's Hagar Shipley to those of Rachel Cameron. Eventually, Staunton will be recognized as more caustic and impatient in tone, and rather more rhetorically flamboyant as befits a defence counsel, but the resemblances — an articulate eloquence, an ear for the witty aphorism, a sense of good narrative timing — clearly outweigh the differences. And when Eisengrim takes over the bulk of the narrative in *World of Wonders*, the radical difference in his background and education is not noticeably reflected in the way he speaks. The same is true of *The Rebel Angels*, which employs split narration, and where one would expect a strong stylistic contrast between the cadences of Maria Theotoky and Father Simon Darcourt. Minute examination uncovers some distinctions—Maria's greater impulsiveness and emotional emphasis in contrast to Darcourt's quieter, more considered pronouncements — but these are not likely to reveal themselves at a first reading. Moreover, as Mills suggests, these narrative styles all sound remarkably similar to Davies's own in his third-person novels and non-fiction writings. Ramsay's ability to "get off a good one" as a schoolboy (*Fifth Business* 29) develops into the classroom witticisms that become known as "Buggerlugs' Nifties" (*Manticore* 120). Similar effects are frequent in Davies's own prose.

It would be absurd to attribute this fact to artistic ineptitude on Davies's part. A list of characters who are not their own story-tellers but are unforgettably recorded in their distinctive speech could easily be compiled from Davies's fiction: Professor Vambrace and Humphrey Cobbler in the early Salterton novels, Ma Gall and Murtagh in *A Mixture of Frailties*, Padre Blazon and Milo Papple in *Fifth Business*, Sir John Tresize in *World of Wonders*, Parlabane in *The Rebel Angels*, Dr. J.A. in *What's Bred in the Bone*, Geraint Powell in *The Lyre of Orpheus*. It would be strange indeed if a novelist who was also a playwright could not produce such characters with ease. But when he creates narrators whose stories will extend over a whole novel, it is clear that Davies requires certain basic qualities. First, they must be supremely articulate; hence he chooses a schoolmaster, a barrister, an exceptionally gifted graduate student, a professor (Eisengrim is a slight exception here, but as a high-class magician he has had to master a clear, crisp English in order to speak in public). They must also possess an intellectual curiosity that leads them not merely to various forms of esoteric knowledge but to a sometimes idiosyncratic yet always intriguing way of looking at the world (Ramsay and his saints, Maria's saturation in Rabelais, etc.); Eisengrim once again proves an exception, this time because it is part of the point of *World of Wonders* that he offers the story while others — Ramsay, Liesl, Lind — provide interpretation. Davies clearly creates his novels so that their narrators can share his broad intellectual interests and bring an approach to them that is compatible with his own. A strong family resemblance between them is therefore scarcely surprising.

The creation of a mouthpiece is, of course, an essentially dramatic conception, involving the arts of the actor, the playwright, and even the ventriloquist. Here one begins to realize the extent to which Davies's early experience in the world of the theatre, both as playwright and as actor, had a profound effect upon the novelist that he was later to become. Clearly, he is not drawn to the special approach of the "Method" actor (an approach relevant to Laurence's art) in which the actor's personality is submerged in or even replaced by that of the subject. Davies resembles the more domineering type of actor who ingests aspects of the character he is portraying into his own personality. He has referred to this phenomenon as the art "by which an actor is both himself and another man while he is on the stage." This remark occurs not in a discussion of drama but of fiction. Davies is writing about the novels of R.S. Surtees, and observes: "When he writes about a man, he becomes that man, while retaining his watchful, chronicler's identity as well" (*Voice* 150). The effect is all the more striking when, as with Davies in so much of his work, he is not merely writing about a character but presenting the narrative through that character; in such a case, the voices of character and narrator are superimposed upon each other. The special quality that distinguishes Davies's novels derives in great part from this association. What he says of Surtees is, in fact, readily applicable to himself: "He is in the thick of the book because he knows very well that he is the best thing it has to offer, and that his knowledge and his insight are the marrow of it" (148).

It seems relevant at this point to quote a telling remark from one of Davies's early reviews, "Four Distinguished Novels," written long before he became a novelist himself: "I would far rather read a novel by a man who was the possessor of an unusual and brilliant mind, but who was an indifferent novelist, than a perfectly carpentered piece of work by a man who was a skilled artist but a person of undistinguished parts" (16, qtd. in Peterman, *Davies* 11). With this we may compare a later complaint that Somerset Maugham was "curiously without individuality of style" (*Voice* 301). Davies himself is a master of the well-made novel as well as of the well-made play; one suspects, however, that he would regard this skill, though certainly important, as little more than the basic competence assumed as a requisite for any trade. What ultimately counts is a particular quality of mind that irradiates the fiction, and the novelist's responsibility involves displaying this quality of mind. Davies is an untiring champion of the artist as performer and entertainer. But the entertainment in question should both engage the intellect and exercise the emotions; he is never more traditionalist than in his insistence on the artist's function not just to teach and to delight but to teach in the process of delighting.

Davies's ventriloquistic performances began when Samuel Marchbanks, a pseudonym originally employed for book-reviews in the *Peterborough Examiner*, gradually evolved into a curmudgeonly *alter ego* commenting on various aspects of local and intellectual life. His motive seems to have been the satirist's need for a deflecting mask, a mouthpiece for unfashionable, even unpopular opinions. As Marchbanks Davies was able to hone his satiric strategies; he managed to create a voice so blatant in its prejudices and extreme in its superseded attitudes that it need not be taken too seriously, but one through which some disturbing challenges might be insinuated. At times he could represent a *reductio ad absurdum* of certain commonly held opinions, which thereby became the object of ridicule; at others he could flaunt minority views. Many of Marchbanks's earlier contributions appeared under the byline "Cap and Bells," a reminder of Davies's *penchant* for presenting his material in the guise of theatrical clowning.

In his later books Davies has been able to employ similar effects much more subtly. His success as a novelist has been achieved against the grain of the age (a feat he was unable to bring off as a dramatist), and it is clear that he holds many views unfashionable in the mid-to-late twentieth century. Thus, like Wilson, he admires grace and poise in a literary age that sets a low premium upon such qualities; he has upheld a non-sectarian but clear moral stance (though lambasting goody-goody stuffiness) in an age of permissiveness; above all, he has championed the claims of artifice in the face of what he has called "the North American Myth of Sincerity, a myth which suggests that anything that is done skillfully, or with accomplishment, is of less value that what is botched" (*One Half* 6). He has provided, then, his own idiosyncratic but often dazzling version of a position not uncommon among Canadian novelists — a defensive statement of principles that cannot be guaranteed to arouse either the interest or the approval of their readers. We have already seen O'Hagan presenting the values of his almost superseded wilderness men through canny story-tellers like Jack Denham, and Mitchell ventriloquizing outrageously in the speeches of Saint Sammy and Daddy Sherry. More unexpectedly, we shall be encountering a similar strategy in Margaret Atwood, a writer who, like Davies, has emerged into a literary world of urban sophistication, and one who artfully creates

82

fictional situations through which to speak critically — even devastatingly — about contemporary trends.

We should now be in a better position to understand the centrality of drama in Davies's fiction. Expressed simply, he needs the novelist's equivalent of a dramatic mask. He has no pretensions to being a philosopher or a moral commentator or a preacher in the orthodox sense, yet he has something to say that many of his contemporaries would rather not hear. As a result he has become an unabashed advocate of indirection, especially that of the sugared pill. An essentially didactic entertainer, he has learned the virtues and advantages of adopting personae. Marchbanks is clearly a satiric device like Swift's Gulliver, but one that can be manipulated in an almost Borgesian spirit of play, as attested by the recent reissue, *The Papers of Samuel Marchbanks*, with Davies assuming the role of decorous and deferential editor to his own creation. But Davies has learned to don more complex masks. The masked fancy-dress party in *A Mixture of Frailties* reveals itself at this point as one of his expansive fictional metaphors, not merely a plot device. Above all, he has been able to exploit the manifold possibilities of drama for his more exploratory and more profound fictions.

Before I embark on a discussion of the dramatic element in Davies's fiction, however, one point must be made clear. Davies once observed that, when he published his first novel after becoming known as a dramatist, "all the critics of novels said that I wrote like a playwright" (*One Half* 15). The context is facetious, but one suspects a genuine irritation behind the remark. I wish therefore to dissociate myself from any imputation of slurring Davies's achievement in this regard. I am not arguing that his novels are somehow potential plays written in the guise of prose fiction; rather, I am saying that his fascination with drama and the theatrical in all its manifestations is as evident in his novels as in his plays. Elspeth Buitenhuis, writing of *Tempest-Tost*, maintains that it is "best when it is dramatic" (39), and this seems to me a perfectly acceptable position — especially since we now know that Davies originally conceived it as a play (Peterman *Davies* 81). His previous (or in the case of the earlier fiction contemporaneous) experience in drama was an undeniable asset to his qualifications as a novelist and in no sense a liability. That point being established, I can now proceed to an analysis of the various dramatic characteristics present within his fiction.

In *Tempest-Tost* and *World of Wonders*, of course, theatrical activity is at the centre of the plot. Elsewhere, the use of dramatic imagery and allusion continually catches the attention. Crucial references to "the theatre of their minds" (*Mixture* 65) and "the theatre of life" (*Fifth Business* 22) are hardly remarkable, but they may remind us of Jaques's famous "All the world's a stage" speech in *As You Like It*, which is alluded to in a comic sequence in *Tempest-Tost* and quoted at length by Murtagh in *A Mixture of Frailties*. It is a powerful image that Davies develops profoundly, as we shall see in a moment. Other aspects, especially in the earlier novels, remind us of dramatic structure. *Leaven of Malice*, for instance, though containing hardly any specific reference to drama at the plot level, has an inescapable theatrical quality, particularly notable in the type characters, the carefully constructed scenes (culminating in the climactic revelations in the lawyer's office), all the polished artifice of the well-made play. (Not surprisingly, perhaps, Davies later adapted this novel for the stage.)

Again, Davies's dialogue becomes increasingly dramatic as his career as a novelist develops. The opening scene in *Tempest-Tost* introduces the subject of drama and represents dialogue imaginable in a play, though written out according to the conventions of prose fiction. This process has developed by the time he writes *A Mixture of Frailties* so that, in the scene where Domdaniel first interviews Monica in London, the fictional "he said . . . she said" falls away and for over a page we are offered dramatic dialogue pure and simple (104–06). In *The Manticore*, many of the meetings between Staunton and Dr. von Haller are presented as dramatic dialogue with the characters identified before each speech. It is not uncommon in the later novels for readers to be confronted with snatches of unalloyed dialogue, the identities of the speakers only becoming evident as the conversation proceeds. In *What's Bred in the Bone*, the celestial dialogue between Francis's Daimon and the Biographical Angel provides a theatrical framework for a cosmic perspective.

But Davies's dramatic foundation for his novels is more than a matter of formal techniques. The seeds of his later mature style are evident as early as *Tempest-Tost*. This novel depends upon a realization that the main characters are as much a part of a play when off-stage as when they are rehearsing and performing *The Tempest*.

The plot insists on the theatrical image, and this becomes only slightly more complex when, for instance, Griselda is described as "an amused observer of the human comedy" (162). Davies takes a great step forward, however, when he pictures Hector Mackilwraith becoming aware of his role-playing off-stage as well as on: "In his little mental drama he was the principal figure, and Griselda was a supporting player. But as time wore on the emphasis shifted, and Griselda became the chief person of the drama, and he was a minor character, a mere bit player, aching for a scene with her" (153). In other words, though the point could not have been made in this way when the novel was first published, Mackilwraith finds himself assuming the role of Fifth Business in Griselda's personal drama.

This fruitful idea of human beings gradually playing out roles in a drama larger than they comprehend may be seen developing with remarkable consistency in Davies's work. In *Leaven of Malice* we are told how Martin Snelgrove, half consciously, half deliberately, took on not only the profession of a lawyer but also the image of the archetypal lawyer as presented in hosts of novels and plays until "it was often impossible to tell whether he was really a lawyer or an indifferent character actor playing the part of a lawyer" (73). *A Mixture of Frailties* is full of role-players. Ma Gall is shown debarred from "playing her role as the Earth-Goddess, the Many-Breasted Mother" (81); John Ripon, the American in England, finds that "over here I have to play a part, or disappear" (195); Monica is determined that "Patient Griselda was only one of the parts she meant to play in the life of Giles Revelstoke" (225); Domdaniel admits to role-playing while assuring Monica that he is "too old to get any pleasure out of playing the sage" (242) — a role he plays impressively throughout the book.

Fifth Business is, of course, central to this development in that the idea becomes explicit here, and is exploited to carry the burden of the whole novel. The book could in fact be described, as Davies himself describes Joyce Cary's trilogy, as "a triumphant exposition of the truth that we are all, unwittingly, playing supporting roles in each other's personal dramas" (*Voice* 247). Dramatic imagery is never far from the surface of the prose. As early as the first chapter, Ramsay observes that, in reporting the snowball incident to his parents, he stressed his "own role as the Good Samaritan" (11). Later, when he is awarded the Victoria Cross, we find him meditating on our treatment of heroes and prominent people: "we cast them in roles, and it is only right to consider them as players, without trying to discredit them with knowledge of their off-stage lives — unless they drag it into the middle of the stage themselves" (87). All the world's a stage, indeed. We begin to realize that Mills is inaccurate when he describes Davies's style as "unmetaphorical." On the contrary, it could be argued that Davies is highly metaphorical, not in the use of small verbal effects within individual sentences, but in the larger concepts that dominate his novels — psychological archetypes in *The Manticore*, the theatrical imagery of *World of Wonders*, the excremental vision that dominates and to some extent organizes *The Rebel Angels*.

In *The Manticore* the theatrical principle is carried still further in that the whole subject is given a broader, psychological dimension. Not only does Dr. von Haller identify recurrent types and roles in Staunton's dreams and autobiographical accounts but also openly admits that her own function contains a dramatic element: "It is part of my professional duty to assume these roles; . . . now we have reached the Anima, and I am she; I am as satisfactory casting for that role as I was for the Shadow or the Friend" (182). Later, she calls these figures "the Comedy Company of the Psyche" (229), a phrase that elevates the dramatic image to a central place not only in fiction but in the way our experience (the universe that we inherit) works. This world-view is developed toward the end of the novel by means of the non-dramatic but highly resonant image of a multi-dimensional chess-game played out on several levels at once.

One finds similar elements in later novels, though these represent a consolidation rather than a development of the effect already established. In *World of Wonders*, of course, drama is once more at the centre, though the juxtaposition of dramatic content with the film in which Eisengrim is acting, the discussion of the "sub-text," and the initially theatrical but later psychological presentation of the double all add complexity to the subject. As Liesl points out, a story will change depending upon which participant is telling it. "Somebody," she observes, "has to play Judas" in someone else's Passion, "and it is generally acknowledged to be a fine, meaty role. There's a pride in being cast for it" (137). In *The Rebel Angels*, among other dramatic allusions, Simon Darcourt comes to realize that "the Imitation of Christ might not be a road-company performance of Christ's Passion, with me as a pitifully badly cast actor in the principal role" (56).

In addition, Ozy Froats's physiological types complement von Haller's psychological ones, and indicate the centrality of the type as a concept within Davies's imagination. *What's Bred in the Bone* transfers the image to a cosmic level, where we observe two supernatural beings stage-managing Francis's life and nudging him into the roles he plays. Finally, at least at the time of writing, *The Lyre of Orpheus* returns to the pattern of *Tempest-Tost* and rings elaborate changes between the tangled emotions presented in a restored opera and those of the people involved in its production.

But the significance of the dramatic image has another vital dimension arising out of von Haller's phrase, "the Comedy Company of the Psyche." A year after *The Manticore* was published, Davies made a similar remark when, in a speech to a group of psychologists, he referred to "the Jungian Theatre Company of the Archetypes" (*One Half* 150). This is no mere literary artist's rhetorical flourish. Davies's dramatic and Jungian interests converge as soon as we realize that the characters in his novels, like ourselves in "real life," are not just assuming roles but are simultaneously acting out mythic patterns. At his father's funeral, for example, Staunton found himself forced "almost without thinking" into the role of "the Only Son" while Caroline played "the Only Daughter" and Denyse "the Widow" (*Manticore* 36–37). Dr. von Haller, as we have seen, professionally and so deliberately takes on various archetypal roles as Staunton's inner exploration proceeds. But Staunton was not Ramsay's pupil at Colbourne College for nothing, and he has learned how myths "contained some truth that was applicable to widely divergent historical situations" (118), or, to put it another way, that historical figures also tend to act out the basic patterns prefigured in primordial myth. Ramsay, we remember, has gone through a symbolic death and rebirth in the First World War. Eisengrim makes a similar point flamboyantly but specifically in *World of Wonders* when he refers to "the day I descended into hell and did not rise again for seven years" (17), and the pattern recurs in Parlabane's life as recounted in *The Rebel Angels* (64). Staunton's own mythic journey is more complex. He performs it psychologically during the processes of analysis and self-analysis presented in the main section of the book, but he must also make a literal journey to the depths that is at once a journey in time, a journey to the centre of the earth and the heart of darkness, and a journey that reveals his inner self.

The Manticore is obviously the central text here, but Davies makes related points elsewhere, notably in *What's Bred in the Bone*, a novel told, unusually for the later Davies, in third-person narration. Here too the protagonist, Francis Cornish, acts out mythic patterns; he is constantly seen as a Grail Knight of Art passing various tests, and even suffering with Eisengrim his own "descent into Hell" (77). But this novel seems to take its form from a casual comment by Liesl in *World of Wonders*, where she observes how the medieval *Weltanschauung* was ready "to see the hand of a guardian angel in what we are apt to shrug off ungratefully as a stroke of luck" (287). In the later novel Davies substitutes a Daimon for a guardian angel (Darcourt explains the distinction [17–18]), but the basic principle remains. Darcourt and Maria, who is said to "think medievally" (15), soon give way to the Lesser Zadkiel, Angel of Biography, and the Daimon Maimas who rehearse the circumstances of Cornish's life. Some reviewers regarded this as a facetious and tiresome contrivance; in fact, it is integral to the main point upon which Davies is insisting. The device demonstrates how Cornish is propelled by outer forces towards his destiny. These forces have determined, to a considerable extent, the roles he must play. The novel is thus based upon a premise of "special celestial guardianship" (308), curiously reminiscent of Ethel Wilson's structure in "Tuesday and Wednesday," that makes omniscience essential; no human agency (except, of course, the magician-creator, Davies himself!) could explain the circumstances that mould this particular life. The celestial structure of *What's Bred in the Bone* may therefore be seen as a culmination of Davies's interest in dramatic and psychological patterning.[1]

What's Bred in the Bone is important, however, for another reason. It is a novel about art and art criticism, about the genuine and the fake and the fine line that separates the two, about the evolution of an artistic sensibility, and (as a result of all these) about the complex organization of any individual work of art. One reviewer, Wilfred Cude, pointed out shrewdly that it was Davies's explanation "of how his own art is to be read" (46). Taking up this hint, we can see more clearly that, throughout his career, Davies has been concerned with artistic organization and with the fact of artifice. Nearly all his novels contain a figure who, though not always a creative artist in the strictest sense, is in some way or other involved in the production of a work of art. Such figures include Valentine Rich, the theatrical director in *Tempest-Tost*; Domdaniel, the orchestral conductor in *A Mixture of Frailties*; Ramsay, both academic historian and fictional autobiographer in *Fifth Business*; Lind, the film director in *World of Wonders*; and Darcourt, the "new Aubrey" in *The Rebel Angels* struggling, like Davies while writing the novel, to catch on paper the elusive and volatile human essence of a university. Less obviously, Gloster Ridley, the newspaper editor in *Leaven of Malice*, is one who collects, organizes, and presents information, while von Haller's function in *The Manticore* is to reveal an order and meaning within Staunton's troubled psyche. It is not an exaggeration to say that all these characters in their different ways are actively concerned with the large questions of artistic form.

The central position of art in human life is a subject that has preoccupied Davies throughout his career. In his early work, indeed, the attitudes of his characters towards art are a clear index to their qualities as human beings. Thus in *Tempest-Tost* the uncultured Forresters are symbolized by their library "accommodated in a single case" (27) whereas Mr. Webster "liked books and had a great many of them" (31); we realize that Mackilwraith has much to learn as soon as we find that for him literature consists of "ambiguous and unsupported assertions by men of lax mind" (50). Here, and in the Salterton trilogy in general, a model is provided by the unconventional but totally committed Humphrey Cobbler, who sums up his own *credo* (and, one suspects, Davies's) as follows: "we're too solemn about the arts nowadays. Too solemn, and not half serious enough" (171). Later, the "wonder" that becomes increasingly important in the Deptford trilogy is frequently communicated through art, whether it be the high art of Ramsay's madonna-statue or the various popular theatrical forms, from Tresize's romance melodrama to Eisengrim's magic illusions. Furthermore, in the course of his writings, both fiction and non-fiction, Davies gives expression to a number of his artistic convictions that are likely to prove controversial because they challenge either entrenched Canadian prejudices or the pervasive myths held by influential contemporary practitioners. In the first category belongs his insinuation, expressed through Domdaniel in *A Mixture of Frailties*, that Canada suffered from "cultural malnutrition" (54) — exemplified by Monica's study of one or two

Shakespeare plays at school without ever having "associated them with any idea of entertainment" (117) — and the sentimental notion that "nobody who was serious about art ever had a bean" (140). To the second category may be attributed Davies's firm insistence on "the artist's obligation to find form and meaning" (*Voice* 111), unwelcome to the advocates of free expression and supposed artistic sincerity; his serious (but, like Cobbler's, not solemn) emphasis on the moral element in art; his unabashed didacticism (so long, once again, as it is also entertaining); and, above all, his unfashionable but reiterated refusal to recognize any connection between art and the nostrums of democracy (his insistence, for example, that art is aristocratic, not democratic, by which he means that it is produced, not "by high-born people for high-born people," but "by special people for people who can understand" [Twigg 39]).

This courageous, if sometimes deliberately provocative, expression of unpopular opinions helps to explain why, despite his eminence and relative popularity, there has always been an undertow of hostility to Davies, a resistance that occasionally becomes extreme in its contemptuous dismissal. Part of this may be simply attributed to envy, or explained as irritated reaction to his poise and apparent assurance. In some instances, one suspects an element of misinterpretation, a tendency to read into Davies some of the more outrageous opinions of Samuel Marchbanks (the kind of risk a satirist always runs). The more persistent charges which need to be considered in more detail are as follows: that his attitudes are old-fashioned and outdated, that he is an elitist, and that he shows signs of Anglophilia.

Even if the last charge were true, there would be something ludicrous about it: would Francophilia be equally objectionable? Would Anglophobia be acceptable? But it is not true. Such positive examples of English culture as Cobbler and Domdaniel are in fact outnumbered by doubtful figures like Swithin Shillito and Bevill Higgin in *Leaven of Malice*, Roland Ingestree in *World of Wonders*, the dishonest and manipulating Ismay in *What's Bred in the Bone*. Davies's own succinct comment on the matter was recorded in 1972: "The English influence in Canada has not, I think, in general been a happy one. . . . My background is not English, it is Welsh and Dutch, and I look at the English with a fairly cold eye" (*Enthusiasms* 313). I see no reason to question this self-assessment; Davies's tone and style may well blend more comfortably with the English literary tradition than with the American, but this fact is essentially separate from social and moral judgements. Ironically, one of the chief butts of Davies's satire is the very attitude that careless readers attribute to him. It is Mrs. Bridgetower, after all, who talks about learning all we can "from Older Civilizations" (*Leaven* 162) — a by no means unreasonable aim in itself, though predictably she is not prepared to learn anything from Cobbler. Especially in his early books, Davies casts an equally cold eye on Canadians who profess an essentially phony Englishness. His position depends upon intricate distinctions that some of his lesser critics seem unprepared to make.

The "old-fashioned" and "elitist" charges are really variants on the same basic complaint. That Davies *is* elitist may be granted; it is a part, surely, of his realistic clearsightedness. Ironically, the charge comes as often as not from members of universities which, as centres dedicated to excellence, would have no *raison d'être* if they were not elitist themselves. Since we all necessarily express discriminating value-judgements every day of our lives — whether on novels, student essays, literary theories, political parties, brands of merchandise, or sports teams — gradations are inevitable. All this constitutes elitism; I see no objection to the label and suspect that Davies's response would be similar.[2] As for "old-fashioned," this charge is verbally slanted since it amounts to little more than a synonym for "traditionalist" employed by someone less skeptical about "progress" than Davies himself. All these terms — old-fashioned, elitist, Anglophile — are in fact critically neutral; a writer can display these qualities on a spectrum ranging from the justifiable to the culpable. Blanket condemnation of this kind serves little purpose without specific instances, each of which needs to be judged on its own merits.

Other criticisms are, however, more cogent. Among articles that express reservations about Davies's work, the most thoughtful and stimulating that I know is Sam Solecki's "The Other Half of Robertson Davies." His main argument is that *Fifth Business* " 'dances' " while the later novels " 'walk' and even stumble" because they "become increasingly static, cluttered with the flotsam of Davies' store of learning" (31).[3] Solecki, it should be noted, is not averse to novels of ideas; what troubles him is Davies's undisguised didacticism, and especially what he calls "the author's guiding hand on our shoulder" (30). The case is made intelligently and responsibly. Even here, though, one suspects a radical and unbridgeable gap between critic and author in their artistic preferences — with the critic, ironically enough, embracing the more conventional stance. Solecki appears to favour the traditional, socially committed novel to the more original intellectual romance that Davies has developed. Solecki complains: "these novels are accessible, even comfortable, in a way that the major works of modernism and post-modernism are not" (31). Perhaps so, though one can question whether there is any particular virtue in literary inaccessibility and discomfort. I find himself wondering, indeed, if Davies's ideas have troubled Solecki by challenging the literary *status quo*. His effects are so often double-edged. When, for instance, Davies makes one character refer to "the fashionable modern twaddle about the anti-hero and the mini-soul" (*Manticore* 295) or another observe that the "notion that everybody wants the latest is a delusion of intellectuals" (*World* 225), readers who sympathize with such sentiments may well feel comfortable while others (possibly including Solecki) may feel the reverse.

A little later, Solecki goes on to make the revealing comment that a comic mode "may not be a suitable medium for a certain kind of subject" (47). The wording is somewhat vague, but it may well refer to a quality which can just as readily be regarded as one of Davies's greatest strengths: his capacity through humour to prick the bubble of contemporary earnestness. In the opening pages of *The Rebel Angels* (which Solecki is reviewing), his light and witty but maturely serious treatment of the "sexual harassment" issue, generally debated so solemnly and priggishly, is a case in point. Here and elsewhere Davies offers the responsible argument that seriousness can paradoxically cease to be worthy of genuinely serious consideration if it neglects its context within the human situation which, whatever the humourless may say, can legitimately be regarded as "the human comedy." What all his detractors suggest (and let me reiterate that Solecki is the most informed and cogent of them) is that they are acutely disturbed by Davies's satire, that his writings have challenged a number of contemporary sacred cows, that an attempted refutation of the satirist may be more effective than closely focused arguments about the issues involved. If it is indeed "the artist's obligation to find form and meaning," then many highly praised contemporaries, connoisseurs of chaos and meaninglessness, may ultimately be found wanting; if there is an intimate connection between art and morality, then numerous modern-day writers are on the wrong track; if

Davies's traditionalism still retains an appeal, then the challenge of a revolutionary avant-garde may prove to be ephemeral.

This, of course, is itself a "conservative" argument, but there are strong grounds for giving it due weight. In 1970, when *Fifth Business* first appeared, it seemed far more "old-fashioned" than it does today. In tracing the far-reaching implications of a child's action in throwing a snowball, it took its origin from a supposedly outmoded "well-made" plot; it did not eschew coincidences (though these are updated into Jungian "synchronicities" [126]); it concerned itself with a lot of exploded esoteric subjects like magic and hagiography; it portrayed the comparatively well-to-do and articulate rather than the "non-verbal" down-and-out; it exhibited stylistic polish when it should have been drably stark; in a world of kitchen-sink realism it offered intimations of "wonder." *Fifth Business* became a success, in part at least, because its old-fashioned virtues suddenly manifested themselves as fresh, original. Its great contribution was not so much that it transcended the confining boundaries of realism but rather that it extended these same boundaries to include areas previously considered alien to realistic presentation. Ramsay discovers that "the marvellous is indeed an aspect of the real" (199). In so far as it shows close connections with the more imaginative, exploratory Canadian fiction that followed it in the 1970s and 1980s than it does to the work of the previous two decades, the inadequacy of the "old-fashioned" charge is especially evident.

These criticisms have had the curious effect, however, of deflecting attention from the area where, in literary-critical terms, Davies is most vulnerable. If there is one predominant "message" that rings loud and clear through his writing, it is the importance of the emotional life and its tendency to be ill-developed or stifled in twentieth-century Canada. With the gift of hindsight, we can recognize in the misadventures of Mackilwraith in *Tempest-Tost* Davies's earliest treatment of a theme he will return to again and again. Monica in *A Mixture of Frailties* is another example of the Canadian possessing intelligence but (at least initially) lacking in feeling; as Domdaniel points out, "feeling really *does* have to be learned" (214), and the novel concerns itself as much with her emotional as with her artistic education. Ramsay's personal odyssey in *Fifth Business* represents a continuing urge to shake off mental and sexual inhibitions. The prime example in Davies's writings of a character who needs to be educated in the feelings is, of course, David Staunton in *The Manticore*, but the subject continues to be explored through Clem Hollier in *The Rebel Angels* and Francis Cornish in *What's Bred in the Bone*.

But Davies's difficulties with this subject become evident when we realize that his books tend to be *intellectual* arguments in favour of emotion. Speaking generally, he has observed: "there may be something wrong with us; we hate to have our feelings touched" (*One Half* 219). The first-person plural, of course, includes Davies himself in the dilemma. Although he classifies himself in an interview as "a feeling person with strong intuition" (D. Cameron 1:42), it is his intellectual qualities (albeit a playful and imaginative intellectualism) that display themselves most prominently in his writings. Moreover, while he finds himself advocating the importance of feeling in life, at the same time he is constantly insisting on the supremacy of intelligence in art. Domdaniel may emphasize Monica's need to educate herself in the emotions, but he also claims that her intelligence gives her an advantage over "one of those little southern passion-pots. . . . *She's* got feeling; *you*'ve got intelligence. She's a sprinter; you're a miler" (136). The potential contradiction involved here is nicely illustrated in *A Voice from the Attic* where on one page he argues that "good fiction asks the reader to feel" (11) and two pages later wonders whether readers "*know* what they themselves are" (13; my emphasis). Significantly (since Davies is essentially a comic writer) he observes later in the same book that humour "is a thing of intellect rather than emotion" (217).

It is important to acknowledge, of course, that Davies is not advocating feeling *over* thought but is seeking for a balance. Yet the moments of genuine human emotion in his work are comparatively few, as a momentary comparison of his fiction with that of Margaret Laurence will demonstrate. The passion he can project most convincingly is "intellectual passion," though it is significant that, when Clem Hollier uses the phrase of himself in *The Rebel Angels*, Mamusia, the wise if grotesque gipsy woman, replies: " 'Pride, Hollier, give it its real name' " (269). In such dramatic exchanges, Davies reveals, of course, that he is himself fully conscious the problem. While it would be folly to downgrade the intellectual dexterity and flexibility that is so refreshing a part of his humorous and satiric wisdom, we should acknowledge a limitation here. Davies does not seem able to achieve that ultimate impersonality that would allow him to transcend the anomalies and contradictions that he can recognize and display so adroitly.

A balanced estimate of any writer's literary achievement is always a delicate operation, and in Davies's case, because he occupies so individual (almost idiosyncratic) a place within Canadian fiction, it proves especially difficult. In his own area of achievement he is inimitable, and it is a matter of classification rather than evaluation to acknowledge that there are areas in which he is less at ease. That intensely sympathetic expression of human fallibility which writers like Mitchell and Laurence (at their best) manage so well is beyond him. Nor can he catch the intricate texture of relationships within a closely knit community like Munro, and his sense of human beings in the grip of historical movements, though a subject that interests him, is superficial when compared with Mavis Gallant's. But he is second to none in his ability to indicate the complex of influences impinging upon an individual life, and in his awareness of the way in which we all live in a "muddle of eras" (*Rebel Angels* 124). Hence his characteristic long passages of narrative in which a person's intricate background — a mixture of inherited traits, psychological urgings, abstruse intellectual interests, and the impact of the spirit of the age — is sketched in with sagacity and grace. He has a strong and unabashed capacity for artifice, and never tries to palm off artistic patterning as run-of-the-mill realism. Above all, his humour, like Rabelais' as celebrated in *The Rebel Angels*, is "the big salutary humour that saves" (118). This is a strong if unusual brew of fictional qualities, and he will remain important to all readers who believe with Darcourt in the same novel "that learning could be amusing, and that heavy people needed stirring up" (38).

CHAPTER 6

Mavis Gallant

There are doubtless many reasons for the comparative neglect of Mavis Gallant by Canadian critics and teachers until the late 1970s. The most obvious are her foreign domicile, her reluctance to discuss the details of her private life (both liabilities in a country where public appearances are so intrinsic a part of the artistic scene), her refusal to limit herself to supposedly Canadian themes (she gained a long overdue Governor General's award only when *Home Truths: Selected Canadian Stories* appeared), and her related insistence on seeing herself as a writer in the English language first and as a Canadian writer second. But these reasons are not in themselves sufficient to account for the lack of proper recognition. When Robertson Davies, of all people, can admit that the language of literary criticism failed him when he attempted to characterize her writing (*Well-Tempered Critic* 280), one detects a more intricate problem. Davies himself doubtless took the first step towards explaining the anomaly when he observed that her stories "yield up their secrets slowly" (284). On a superficial level she is deceptively straightforward. The apparent effortlessness with which she achieves her effects tends to discourage awareness of her subtlety. Each story is so perfectly fashioned that we are content to appreciate its individual merits instead of regarding it as part of a larger and extraordinarily impressive *oeuvre*. As a result, we are still in the initial process of coming to terms with her importance as a writer and with the unique qualities of her art.

A forceful attempt to remedy the situation has recently been made by Janice Kulyk Keefer in two pioneering and closely interrelated articles, one in the *Dalhousie Review*, the other in the *University of Toronto Quarterly*. In the former, reacting against what she sees as a limiting tendency to praise Gallant's work for the excellence of her presentation rather than for the importance of her content, Keefer has defined her prime achievement as "an acute social, political and historical sense which finds expression in her detailed exploration of two areas central to human experience in our century: the world of women and the collective memory of shattering events we own as history" ("Criticism" 722). The latter article concentrates on Gallant's politically oriented attitude to history and on her unceasing preoccupation with "history-as-everyday-living" ("Gallant" 288). Keefer gets to the heart of Gallant's self-imposed artistic challenge in a passage which I consider the most profound analysis of her significance that has yet been offered:

> Gallant, as a writer, faces the dilemma of wanting to incorporate catastrophic historical events and terms in her fiction without exploiting them as kitsch; she uses, and shows her characters using, events such as the deportation of European Jews to death camps, not to drop a penny in the slot of instant poignancy and horror but to differentiate history from, and relate it to, the process of everyday living. It is both a sacrilege and a human necessity that an event which no language can describe or explain and no person, save its victims, can know, should become a kind of shorthand for general human catastrophe: the Holocaust. And yet without a tremendous effort of Imagination to fathom that event in the terms of one's own possible experience, it becomes irrelevant, annulled. (288)

I cannot think of any other Canadian novelist who demands this kind of subtle intellectual discrimination — which may explain in part why Canadian criticism has not yet evolved a way of providing it.

At the same time, brilliant as Keefer's discussion undoubtedly is, it should not be accepted without question, and certainly not to the extent of displacing alternative fruitful approaches. While I applaud her concentration on Gallant's profound meditation on the processes and effects of history, I suspect that her emphasis on "the world of women" may be an understandable exaggeration resulting from the feminist sensitivity characteristic of our times. That this is part of Gallant's concern is unquestionable — one would be surprised if it were not — but a remarkable and rare feature of her writing is surely her capacity to enter into the minds and emotions of representatives of either sex with total conviction. I am never conscious while reading Gallant — as I am sometimes with Alice Munro or even occasionally with Margaret Laurence, not to mention lesser writers like Marian Engel and Audrey Thomas — that her female protagonists are primarily representing women rather than all human beings in their time and place. Here Davies is useful in providing a provocative but shrewd counter-statement: "Mavis Gallant's stories of miserable women stand apart from most writing of the kind because there is no current of anti-masculine grievance in them — no sound of an axe being remorselessly ground without ever achieving an edge" (*Well-Tempered Critic* 280). The truth doubtless lies somewhere between the two extremes (it is a token of Gallant's quality that discussion of her work tends to involve the continual refinement of generalized distinctions). To be sure, her presentation of war and its effects depends upon the unstated but everpresent awareness that political decision-making is primarily a male preserve but that women suffer equally from the results. Similarly, the Linnet Muir stories in *Home Truths* are properly bitter about inequities of pay ("As soon as I realized that I was paid about half the salary men were earning, I decided to do half the work" [322]). Nonetheless, her sharpness of judgement and breadth of observation extend far beyond the limitation of gender boundaries. Her women are always human beings first, women second.

I also believe that, in the doubtless justified (and certainly understandable) interests of enforcing a neglected truth, Keefer approaches another extreme in her strictures against the emphasis of certain literary-critical predecessors, notably Davies and George Woodcock, whom she accuses of having "presented Gallant as a white-gloved Queen of Fiction unacquainted with those sub-aesthetic thugs, politics and history" ("Gallant" 283). The uncharacteristic shrillness here signals a false note. While it is true that both commentators, especially Davies, emphasize her artistry and fail to do full justice to her content,

I suspect that this happens not because her preoccupations are unrecognized but because they are regarded as self-evident. Be that as it may, this seems a rare instance — possibly unique in the present climate of Canadian criticism — of a thematic concern downplayed at the expense of predominantly artistic emphasis. Therefore, since my own approach within this book is specifically concerned with the art of fiction, I wish to make two preliminary points: first, that such an emphasis in no way detracts from the significance of Gallant's preoccupations; second, that (while I applaud Keefer's cogent and forceful discussions as a major breakthrough in Gallant studies) I acknowledge in both Davies and Woodcock insights that should not be forgotten in any study of Gallant's literary achievement.

Davies's article is curiously defensive in tone, and was clearly offered as one writer's appreciation of the excellent but very different work of a contemporary. It has no pretensions towards literary-critical depth, yet it makes an important point by insisting that Gallant "deploys, displays, exhibits, and leaves the judgements up to us" (*Well-Tempered Critic* 281). This indirectness may well explain Keefer's complaint that her continuing preoccupation with the nightmare of history has received insufficient notice; Gallant never draws *explicit* attention to her themes, which can be scanted in consequence. (I would also argue that, though she gives readers freedom to manoeuvre, her deepest moral judgements are never in doubt.) Woodcock's article, on the other hand, is longer and more ambitious. It makes, I believe, a permanent contribution to our understanding of Gallant's art. While his statement about "the autonomous worlds of all Mavis Gallant's short fictions" is challengeable, he is excellent on her special kind of realistic fidelity: ". . . absolute plausibility demands absolute artifice, not faith to actuality, which is why Flaubert outshines Zola and Chekhov outlives Guy de Maupassant. It is also why Mavis Gallant . . . outwrites most other Canadians" (*World* 93). Or, again: "[Her fiction] is not a naturalistic fiction, but it is a fiction of enhanced reality, in which life is reshaped by artifice, but not distorted" (96). Woodcock is here arguing (in my view, justly) that Gallant has achieved fully what Laurence, as I indicate in the next chapter, achieved only in part: a fusion between characterization appropriate to "enhanced reality" and an equivalent credibility in terms of plot. Artistically speaking, this is a crucial distinction, and it is to Woodcock's credit that he makes it so clearly and shrewdly.

The discussions of Davies, Woodcock, and Keefer, together with the carefully argued scholarly articles by Ronald Hatch that have been appearing in recent years,[1] have now set literary-critical approaches to Gallant on a seemingly contradictory but in fact solid footing. Keefer is undoubtedly right to emphasize Gallant's "strong public sense of reality" and to insist that her fiction "presents a vision of history *as* lived experience" ("Gallant" 299, 300). But a vision can only be communicated through art, and a concentration on the literary techniques that facilitate this communication in no way detracts from a serious appreciation of the vision itself. In the following sections I intend to explore Gallant's fascination with language and the way in which it both transmits and embodies her central concerns, and then, through an emphasis on the Linnet Muir stories, to tackle the larger question of how she uses art both to convey and to illustrate her artistic procedures.

According to her own account, three weeks after her fourth birthday Gallant was taken to her first school, a French Catholic school in Québec: "My mother said, 'Just wait, I'll come back.' But she didn't come back." Gallant, who bitterly describes her mother as someone "who should not have had children," remarks of this action: ". . . it was more than a betrayal. It was insane" (Gabriel 26). The experience obviously had a deeply traumatic effect upon the future writer, and we can trace direct echoes of it in at least three memorable scenes in her published fiction. *Green Water, Green Sky* begins as follows: "They went off for the day and left him, in the slyest, sneakiest way you could imagine. Nothing of the betrayal to come showed on their faces that morning. . . . Oh, they had managed it beautifully. First they were out on the hot terrace, offering him gondoliers, then he was abandoned . . . " (1, 3). In "An Autobiography," some Swiss parents are shown behaving in a similar way: "They tricked the baby cruelly, taking her out to feed melon rinds to Coco, the donkey, in his enclosure at the bottom of the garden. When she came back, clutching the empty bucket, her family had disappeared" (*Pegnitz* 107–08). And in "Piotr" Laurie Bennett talks of "an Anglican boarding school where she had been 'left' and 'abandoned' and which she likened to a concentration camp" (*Fifteenth District* 170). (This last is a consummate instance of Gallant's ability to combine two predominant thematic images into a new and original synthesis.)

I present what may seem a rather quaint exercise in an officially outmoded form of biographical criticism to make a basic but extremely important point. In her major work Gallant begins almost invariably with personal experience of some kind. In these cases the events ultimately derive from an experience of her own, but — and this is crucial — the autobiographical details are immediately subsumed into detached artistic creation. We would not be likely to suspect an autobiographical urgency behind the writing if the clue from the interview were not available. A careful reading of her work, however, backed up by this biographical knowledge, will reveal how frequently her plots depend upon the concept of abandonment or betrayal. In *A Fairly Good Time*, for example, Shirley's second husband deserts her at the opening of the narrative, and the word "abandoned" echoes continually within the text. Most poignant, perhaps, is the narrator's summary of Shirley's religious attitudes: "*We have been abandoned* was all she knew about the universe" (49). Yet Gallant never elaborates on the *theme* of abandonment; she does something much more significant — she shows us human beings who have been abandoned, and the desolating effect upon them. She allows us as readers, if we wish, to extend the specific fictional instance so that it becomes universally applicable, a representative event in our understanding of the "real" non-fiction world that we inhabit; but she doesn't insist on such a reading. As Davies says, "she leaves the judgements up to us," though it is important to note that (unlike Munro, as we shall see) she maintains strict control over the limits of legitimate interpretation.

There are, of course, numerous ways of being abandoned or displaced. Most obviously, as Keefer demonstrates, war and its immediate effects are a prime cause, and here Felix in "The Other Paris" provides almost a casebook example. His relatives "had all been killed at the end of the war, in the final bombings," and he is "in Paris illegally, without a proper passport or working papers" (*Other Paris* 10). *The Pegnitz Junction* is full of clear-headed but sympathetic accounts of the social and psychological damage caused by related or similar experiences. Long-term effects of political decisions within history may also be involved. Thus a French-Canadian in "The

Burgundy Weekend" observes: "We suffer from the Oedipus feeling of having been abandoned. . . . Abandoned by the mother, by France, by *you*" (27). Not infrequently (as with Shirley) the breakdown of a marriage precipitates an overpowering sense of desolation and loneliness. Whatever the reason, established patterns are uprooted, traditions expunged. Adaptation to new conditions of living is difficult. (Some are not so much displaced as "distimed," like her English expatriates retreating to the Riviera.) Above all, and this was an additional shock for the young Mavis Gallant at the Québec school, the cruellest displacement involves language.

Characteristically, Gallant displays her most subtle qualities as a writer through her sensitive presentation of the supreme importance of language in the difficult art of living. The fact of language naturally affects us all, but she concentrates on types or groups who are especially vulnerable. These include children bombarded and frustrated by words whose meanings are never explained, or disoriented by the discovery that the same words have varying meanings or nuances in different places; articulate adults rendered literally wordless by finding themselves in a community whose language is incomprehensible; whole peoples (French-Canadians are Gallant's favourite examples for obvious reasons) fated to witness their own language altered, defamiliarized, and possibly undermined by a stronger linguistic influence, and forced to master a foreign tongue in order to survive. It is also worth noting that Gallant frequently presents disorientation caused by language as a powerful image for a more general breakdown in communication. A whole book could be written about her treatment of the human effects of language. Here I must confine myself to two important instances, "Orphans' Progress" and "Careless Talk," before moving on to a more detailed examination of the centrality of language in *A Fairly Good Time*.

"Orphans' Progress" is a story which repays attention because it combines so many of Gallant's preoccupations. It begins significantly: "When the Collier girls were six and ten they were taken away from their mother, whom they loved without knowing what the word implied" (*Home Truths* 56). The story chronicles how they are relentlessly separated from their origins and ultimately from each other. Initially transferred from Québec to a grandmother in Ontario, they encounter subtle but disturbing changes in the way words are used: "When their new friends liked something they said it was smart.

A basketball game was smart, so was a movie: it did not mean elegant, it just meant all right" (56). Brought up by their French-Canadian mother to speak both French and English, they are now told that "French was an inferior form of speech" (57), and are puzzled by contradictions communicated through words — when, for example, a maid describes their grandmother first as "a Christian" (58) and then as "a damned old sow" (59). They are further confused when, after their grandmother's death, they are shifted back to other relatives in Québec, and the linguistic tables are turned: "Language was black, until they forgot their English. Until they spoke French, nothing but French, the family pretended not to understand them. . . . They very soon forgot their English" (60). They are subsequently sent to a convent school, and the younger is adopted (and her name changed) by yet another relative. They become so disoriented — one is tempted to say "brainwashed" — that their earlier life and relationship is blotted out. They no longer share the same surname and have nothing to say to each other when they meet. The climax comes when the younger does not even recognize her old home when it is pointed out to her. Gallant's clipped, detached, emotionally deadened style here contributes in large measure to the terrifying pathos of the story; in a very real sense we can say that the sisters are orphaned not merely by physical separation from their parents but by language and the ways that language can be manipulated.

Perhaps the most moving account of the relation between language and despair occurs in "Careless Talk," first published in 1963 and only recently collected in *In Transit*. Iris, the central character, is an Englishwoman married to a French farmer. The shock of moving to a rural and so comparatively isolated area proves disorienting, all the more so because she is also moving into the linguistically alien: "No homely object was like anything she had seen; a chair was not a chair now because it was *une chaise*" (124). She finds that "safety came down to language now French was quicksand and English the rock" (124). When she is forced by circumstances to speak French to her own children, she not only feels the wrench from her own culture ("They'll never know my rhymes" [129]) but even comes to doubt "what being Iris meant" (127). She forms a friendship with a woman who was born in France of Irish parentage but is considered "*très americaine*" by Iris's French husband and "*très anglaise*" by the village (125). Language becomes overpowering: "The stones of the house understood nothing but French. . . . The mud in the courtyard was French, soaked in French" (129–30). "Careless Talk," so ironically titled, may well contain the most probing examination within her short fiction of the way that language isolates.

Gallant's emphasis on language receives its most varied, and certainly its wittiest treatment in her longest work of fiction to date, *A Fairly Good Time*. This is one of the most brilliant and original of her writings, and its shocking neglect stems from the fact that Gallant criticism has not yet recognized the centrality of the linguistic concerns that I am emphasizing here. When that happens, *A Fairly Good Time* will establish itself as a seminal text. It is crucially important to my argument because the combined themes of abandonment and language are perfectly integrated within the art of the novel. Since it is decidedly less familiar than other major works discussed here, a summary of the narrative may be in order. The plot centres upon Shirley, a Canadian girl in her twenties whose first husband had been killed in an accident while they were on their honeymoon in Italy. Sequentially (though we do not hear the circumstances until later in the novel), this is the first of a series of disorientations in Shirley's young and untidy life. Instead of returning to North America, she remains in Europe, moves to Paris, and gets married again. Her second husband, Philippe Perrigny, is a mediocre journalist with pretensions, who writes articles on widely differing topics — the Berlin wall, the Canadian situation, contemporary drama — that invariably contain within their titles the paradoxical phrase "The Silent Cry." At the beginning of the book, Philippe has deserted her, and the novel concerns itself with the effects of this abandonment upon Shirley's consciousness. And it is exclusively from Shirley's consciousness, mediated through third-person narration, that the story is told.

If one recounts the basic plot in this way, it sounds like a traditional modernist novel written under the influence of Henry James, and this suspicion is strengthened by the title which, as an epigraph indicates, is derived from a short story by Edith Wharton. Here, surely, is an intellectual comedy of manners displaying a sophisticated narrative technique, in which North American innocence comes into contact with European experience, one more polished analysis of the

Jamesian complex fate. Thus Brendan Gill, reviewing the novel in *Time*, described Shirley as "kin to a long line of unworldly New World girls, starting with Daisy Miller, who have pitted their innocence against Old World ambiguities of Europe and pluckily gone under" (62). But this is, at best, a half-truth: the effect of the book is ultimately very different. We are confronted by drastic and initially puzzling shifts of tone, and the narrative moves bewilderingly between Shirley's outer and inner worlds, between her everyday experiences and her dream fantasies. She is herself bewildered, as the following passage makes clear:

> [She] felt as if she had been invited to act in a play without having been told the name of it. No one had ever mentioned who the author was or if the action was supposed to be sad or hilarious. She came on stage wondering whether the plot was gently falling apart or rushing onward toward a solution. Cues went unheeded and unrecognized, and she annoyed the other players by bringing in lines from any other piece she happened to recall. (179–80)

Readers, I suggest, find themselves in a similar situation. We are reminded at different times of writers as varied as Jane Austen, Lewis Carroll, Stella Gibbons, and Nancy Mitford — and these are not accidental or personal associations on my part, since all these writers (or works by them) are alluded to in the course of the novel.

But let us begin at the beginning. The first chapter consists of the text of a letter written to Shirley by her mother, Mrs. Norrington. It concentrates on the identification of a wild flower, a bluebell, that Shirley has sent her, but moves off in rather scatter-brained fashion to anecdotes and assertions that bear no obvious relation to the subject at hand. One extract in particular is both illustrative and revealing:

> I am assuming this is what your nine-page letter was about. I could not decipher what seemed to me to be an early Teutonic alphabet. Neither of your marriages ever improved your writing. You may retort that legibility is not the purpose of marriage. I am not sure it has any purpose at all. (4)

This seems witty, a little zany, and somewhat unsettling. Thirty pages later, we learn something of the background. Shirley reports to a friend:

"I've had this *long letter*. . . . It's about bluebells, all the history of bluebells. I don't know why. She says she can't make out my handwriting. . . . I told her I thought I was messing up my marriage, doing all the wrong things. I can read *her* writing, but I don't always know what she's driving at." (34)

Shirley sums up the situation with admirable succinctness a few pages later: "Everything between two people is equivocal" (39). In this instance, one correspondent writes seriously but illegibly, the other legibly but incomprehensibly. As the narrator notes, "[t]he correspondence between mother and daughter, Montreal and Paris, was an uninterrupted dialogue of the deaf" (45).

All this suggests that at least one of the novel's primary concerns is (if the banality can be forgiven) the problem of communication. Indeed, many of its more disorienting sentences — sentences that produce in readers what I can best describe as an intellectual double-take — involve troubling matters of language, in part (but only in part) arising from Shirley's imperfect command of French. She explains at one point:

"When Philippe and I talk English he's at a disadvantage, and when it's French I'm never sure. I understand every word, but do I understand what French means? I might know every word in a sentence, and still not add up the meaning." (154)

"Again," we have just been told, she was "deceived by language" (148). Let me quote a few examples of these disorienting sentences (which occur throughout the novel), both to illustrate what I mean and to establish the curious stylistic tone which is so prominent a feature of the book:

Each time the story she was composing for Philippe touched on the truth, it became improbable. (50)

. . . by the time she remembered the French word for "toast," which was "toast," [the waiter] had vanished. (67)

On the rim of a traffic circle, *contradictory signs* directed them back to Paris. (81; my emphases)

106

With women, "trouble" means "I am in love" or "I am not in love" or "I am pregnant." (201)

There are numerous other examples where the paradoxes, ambiguities, and seductions of language are built into the narrative situation ("Language is Situation," Shirley realizes at one point [22]). Thus Philippe is obsessed with finding esoteric meanings — political, historical, and even prophetic — in the nursery-rhyme "Goosey Gander." "How to decipher this?" he asks (307), and so attempts to impose a meaning that isn't there. Once he took Shirley to a meeting "at which the language probably spoken by the aristocracy on lost Atlantis had been discussed, and during which someone tried to prove a link between the name Mao and the noise made by a cat" (17). The linguistically futile is followed by the linguistically irresponsible, though in the latter instance it may be worth noting that the sound of a word (Mao) is desperately linked with a "cry." On another occasion, James (a Greek neighbour and sometime lover of Shirley) appropriates one of her party-piece stories, but in so doing "missed telling what the story was about" (114). Towards the end of the book, Shirley sees a sequence of meaningless letters scrawled on a wall by a child, but decides that they "meant, in code, that Philippe had come back to her" (275). The meaningless, in this novel, has a habit of being found by the characters to be more meaningful than meaning itself.

Characters talk at cross-purposes throughout the book. Here is a classic example where Shirley is talking with the somewhat sinister Madame Roux:

" 'A woman of seven-and-twenty can never hope to feel or inspire affection again,' " Shirley had quoted . . .
. . . "True," said Madame Roux, "but, at the same time, nonsense. . . . Who were you quoting? . . . Balzac?"
Jane Austen had said it.
Who was Jane Austen? The author of *Wuthering Heights*?
No — Jane Eyre was the author of *Wuthering Heights*.
Had Laurence Olivier played in that?
Yes, Shirley thought he had. It was an old movie — almost as old as the book. In that case Madame Roux knew about it, though she could not remember when Laurence Olivier had made that remark. (94)

107

This sounds like an intellectual comedy-routine, a hyperliterate *Goon Show*. Yet it occurs, as a flashback, at a time of marital disaster, the moment when Shirley is forced to recognize the finality of Philippe's abandonment. Clearly, we have come a long way from a novel in the style of James. This sounds much more like a contemporary meta-fiction, an exposé of the absurd intent on preventing any signifier from making contact with a signified.

What are we to make of a novel in which the "sad" and the "hilarious" are so oddly intertwined, in which subjects such as abortion, incest, and attempted suicide are conspicuous at the edges, or just beneath the surface, of what appears to be a witty social comedy? The thematic approach will obviously not help us here. Is it enough to find a unifying concern in "the problem of communication," to argue that we are led with Shirley through a disorienting experience so that we ourselves become disoriented? Surely not. Should we place our emphasis, in the contemporary fashion, on the extent to which Shirley "invents" her own story? Not altogether; that is at best a minor strand in a book with far more complicated concerns. Let us return to the first chapter where Mrs. Norrington identifies the bluebell when Shirley (as we learn later) has written in desperation about making a mess of her marriage. Ronald Hatch has provided a clue when he describes Shirley's letter as "a cri de coeur" ("Creation of Consciousness" 59). A letter containing a cri de coeur is necessarily a silent cry. Philippe's phrase, which part of the novel parodies as meaningless, is suddenly seen to contain a potentially profound meaning. Ironically, in a passage I have already quoted, Mrs. Norrington does allude to marriage and the purpose (or, rather, purposelessness) of marriage in her letter about bluebells, so it seems that something has been communicated after all. Shirley's distress seems to have got through, in obscure fashion, to her mother, though Shirley has not picked up the relevance of her reply. Moreover, we eventually realize that Shirley's whole story, as we have it in the novel, is an extended cry, silent not in the literal sense (she seems to be talking continually to someone) but because she is never able to translate her full meaning into terms that any other individual can understand.

I use the word "translate" deliberately, because this intricate linguistic situation is central to Gallant's concerns both in this novel and elsewhere. Many of the conversations in the book, though they are in reality (that is to say, the sense of reality proposed by the fiction) conducted in French, are presented to us in English; at other times, the problems of translation are specifically alluded to (albeit sometimes at a comic remove, as in the line about Shirley's forgetting the French for "toast" — which was "toast"). Moreover, even in conversations where the participants share the same language, ideas have to be converted into words, transmitted, and then recoded in that subliminal act of simultaneous translation that we engage in at all times. Thus the difficulties of language and meaning are close to the surface in the section (towards the end of the novel) where we hear of the early meetings between Philippe and Shirley. "Whenever I did not know why something had been said," Shirley recalls, "I thought it was because I did not understand French well enough or else that I was stupid. I translated us both from the beginning into characters out of books, but they were children's books [Philippe] had never heard of" (267). (He was presumably too busy reading impossible meanings into "Goosey Gander.") And at a crucial point, when Philippe's inquiries are clearly indicative of a deeper — even "romantic" — meaning behind the conversation, we find Shirley saying something different from what she intends and then discovering that what she had said is in any case ambiguous. Philippe has asked: "Who is responsible for you? . . . Is anyone?"

> The answer that came to mind was, "At my age?" but "No one who can stop me giving everything away" was what I said. This had a double sense in English. It meant also, giving away the end of a story, revealing the point too soon.
>   This conversation and *the knowledge of what it was really about* had cut my appetite. (272–73; my emphases)

"This had a double sense in English," but they are evidently speaking French, a language which may well contain meanings of which Shirley is unaware. The "translation" experienced by an English-speaking Canadian living in France thus becomes an emblem of the more radical act of translation when, in whatever language (including our own), we try to interpret the nuances that lie just beneath the surface of apparently clear (or "innocent") words and gestures.

If *A Fairly Good Time* is Gallant's most detailed examination of the perilous relationships between language and the everyday routines and processes of living, the Linnet Muir stories link this theme with her other literary concerns. These are stories about time and meaning, about change, about the past and the ways it can be recreated (or even created). The question of language is obviously central, but these stories extend the subject to take in the art that language makes possible. Mavis Gallant, Linnet Muir: the pun on singing birds (mavis [= thrush] and linnet) alerts us to an intriguing relation between creator and creation. Furthermore, the stories appear as a culmination to the volume entitled *Home Truths,* and so invite us to wonder whose home and what truths are involved.

The circumstances which led to their writing are of particular interest. While engaged in research on her projected book about the Dreyfus case, Gallant felt the need to saturate herself in the physical immediacy of Dreyfus's Paris, then some eighty years or so back in the past. She knew already, of course, that since his time Paris had changed out of all recognition (see not only ''The Other Paris'' but, more particularly, the stories gathered in *Overhead in a Balloon*). This led her to think of the similar fate of Montreal since she had first known it as a small child in the late 1920s and as a young woman during the war years. The two processes of recreation — one historical, one autobiographical — seemed to fuse: ''there began to be restored in some underground river of the mind a lost Montreal'' (xxii). But Gallant is too experienced and too intelligent a writer to ignore the pitfalls and betrayals of memory. To what extent *can* the past be restored? Here Gallant boldly explores the question of possible fictionalizing through the medium of fiction itself. She invents Linnet Muir who, as she insists, ''isn't *myself* but a kind of summary of some of the things I once was'' (Hancock 88), and then takes her through the same Proustian journey *à la recherche du temps perdu* upon which she herself is engaged. (The Mavis/ Linnet connection is surely related to that of Proust/Marcel.) Linnet confesses: ''Anything I could not decipher I turned into fiction, which was my way of untangling knots'' (261); Gallant is engaged in an identical process even as she makes Linnet pen those words. The resultant stories read like memoirs, but memoirs separated by at least two removes from personal recollection. They constitute a splendid meditation on the very intricacies of thought and invention that makes such fiction possible.

The first story, ''In Youth Is Pleasure,'' begins with the bald statement, ''My father died'' (218). The event occurred during

110

Linnet's childhood and, like so much else, the precise circumstances "had been kept from [her]" (228). Like Gallant trying to clarify the mystery of Dreyfus, Linnet is eager to penetrate the tangle of rumour and fable surrounding her father's death. Because these stories make up a developing portrait of the artist as a young woman, Linnet is presented (i.e., Gallant presents her) as a writer of politically oriented poems and as a compulsive diarist and notebook-filler, one who "made symbols out of everything" (221); but the older Linnet — not to mention Gallant — is continually looking over her shoulder, drawing attention to the things she did not know. She considers herself "an artist" at getting adults to reveal "the truth" (228), which she still thinks of, in the terms of a later story, as "Truth with a Capital T" (318), but all she can extract is conflicting hearsay — an illness, a botched operation, a possible suicide, a possible death at sea.

At this point Gallant embarks on an audacious technical manoeuvre by inserting an apparently digressive anecdote:

> I know a woman whose father died, she thinks, in a concentration camp. Or was he shot in a schoolyard? Or hanged and thrown in a ditch? Were the ashes that arrived from some eastern plain his or another prisoner's? She invents different deaths. (234)

This woman emerges ultimately as an emblem of the bad artist in contrast to Linnet/Gallant. In an important distinction between "invention" and "creation," soon to be exploited by Jack Hodgins, Gallant shows Linnet to be a true artist by acting firmly and consistently in "making" the truth about her father and sticking to it: "I had settled his fate in my mind and I never varied: I thought he had died of homesickness; sickness for England was the consumption, the gun, the everything" (235). In other words, she has created a "home truth," which may not be literally true but is symbolically right. The act has important repercussions for Gallant's fiction. Historical reconstruction (and she is adamant on the importance of accurate detail and authentic atmosphere) can only go so far; there are always gaps, and these must be filled by the responsible imagination. It is not by chance that Gallant quotes Jean Cocteau's "*Je suis un mensonge qui dit la vérité*" in her introduction, not as "the last word about the writing of fiction" (xxii) but as close to the last word as can reasonably be expected.

This paradox is extended as the Linnet Muir series develops. Her father's death had been a historical problem like the Dreyfus case, but subsequent stories seek to reproduce her own past. To what extent is memory itself *"un mensonge qui dit la vérité"*? In "Between Zero and One," which recounts her experience as a reluctantly employed woman in a hitherto male wartime office and her brush with a bullying woman-professional, Linnet ends with an image of herself standing with Mrs. Ireland at the office-window under circumstances that seem, in sober and unimaginative truth, impossible:

> We could never possibly have stood close, talking in low voices. And yet there she is; there I am . . .
> Mostly when people say "I know exactly how I felt" it can't be true, but here I am sure — sure of Mrs. Ireland and the window and of what she said. The recollection has something to do with the blackest kind of terror, as stunning as the bits of happiness that strike for no reason. (259, 260)

We may remember Jean Price, the narrator of "Its Image on the Mirror" in *My Heart Is Broken*, a story that also attempts to recreate the "lost Montreal" presented here. Jean reminisces about the past while at the same time admitting that other participants deny her version. But here, as with the matter of her father's death, Linnet *makes* it the truth by presenting it convincingly in words. Similarly, in "Varieties of Exile," she creates a background for the remittance-man (if that is indeed what he is — how can we know?) and composes a story within the story entitled "The Socialist RM." Much later, when she is in the process of destroying this story, we are abruptly told that she "found a brief novel I had no memory of having written" (281). It is based not on Frank Cairns the remittance-man himself, but on a friend of his whom Linnet had invented to fill a biographical gap. So fiction extends itself, and becomes (in terms of our world) false; yet the story in which this truth is learned is itself fiction.

Two later stories, the evocatively titled "Voices Lost in Snow" and "The Doctor," develop Gallant's interlocking subjects of interest still further. So far the narratives have been set in the early years of the Second World War when Linnet (as well as her creator) was in her late teens and early twenties. The continued references to "journals" kept at the time (albeit imagined journals within a fiction) suggest the possibility of checking present memory against past document. But what of our earliest memories, things seen and felt but inadequately understood by young children before diaries are a possibility? How far can such memories be trusted, and of what do they consist? Characteristically, what Linnet remembers, like children in Gallant's earlier stories, are the bewildering traps of language — getting into trouble for calling a neighbour "old cock" (283) or the puzzlement at her father's saying "Fix your hair" after having told her "not to use 'fix' in that sense" (290). The older Linnet realizes that, as in fiction, memory tends to coalesce into a retainable composite image: "These Saturdays have turned into one whitish afternoon, a windless snow-fall, a steep street" (283). Memory has here remade the past but in a vivid and artistically authentic form. The dangers of distortion in such a process are, however, embedded within the story in the account of Linnet's mother who "often rewrote other people's lives, providing them with suitable and harmonious endings" (287) — another (false) way of attempting to make truth. Linnet eschews this, and the story ends on an inconsequential note that is credible but subtly *in*harmonious. In "The Doctor," the greatest surprise occurs at the end in the revelation that "Uncle Raoul" was not merely family friend and pediatrician but a writer, that this man had a whole imaginative dimension which was closed to her. At the same time, the realization demonstrates how her own portrait of him, though artistically self-sufficient and apparently authentic, was radically incomplete, thus proving that all recreations are necessarily partial.

"With a Capital T" is a story illustrating the unattainability of its title. Here we return to the Montreal of the 1940s where Linnet, now working as a reporter, interviews her godmother whom we have already met under equivocal circumstances in "Voices Lost in Snow." The story opens with a long and amusing discussion, the celebrated "boy eats bun while bear looks on" sequence, that points up the impossibility of providing a clear and watertight account of even the most straightforward incident without risking ambiguity or misinterpretation. This serves as an oblique introduction to the awkward interview in which so much has to be left unsaid. Linnet goes on to write what she calls a "true account" (329) of the godmother's committee-work and so effectively alienates her forever. She knows, of course, that this article is not the whole truth, still less Truth with a capital T. Ironically, the story that contains her account, though itself a fiction, comes closer to authentic representation if not to

"Truth" by catching an atmosphere of uneasy suspicion through the deft handling of nuance and suggestion.

Yet despite her droll portrayal of the communication problem in *A Fairly Good Time*, and despite the acknowledgement here that Truth with a capital T is a chimera, Gallant is confident that an imaginative artist skilled in the full range of verbal resources can achieve an acceptable and satisfying approximation. It would be a serious mistake to assume, here or elsewhere, that she is approaching a post-modernist statement about the inadequacy of language. Nothing could be further from her artistic principles. In the interview with Geoff Hancock, she makes one of her extremely rare allusions to her more avant-garde contemporaries when she observes, in a comment clearly intended to inhibit further discussion, "I find Robbe-Grillet very boring, don't you?" (102). And on the same occasion she spoke with unqualified enthusiasm for the potentiality of English as a literary medium: "it's an absolutely fabulous language. It's so misused, so underused" (86). Even more significant, perhaps, is the introduction to *Home Truths*, a statement as close to an artistic *credo* as anything we have yet had from her. "Memory," she insists, "is inseparable from language" (xv), and the subject of "language and meaning" is "vital" (xvi). She pins her faith on "a strong, complete language, fully understood, to anchor one's understanding" (xvii) and adds, in a remark especially interesting given her domicile and the linguistic background to so much of her work: "I cannot imagine any of my fiction in French, for it seems to me inextricably bound to English syntax" (xviii).

This sensitivity to English syntax — I am bound to say, with regret, that I can think of very few other Canadian writers (Hugh Hood? Clark Blaise? John Metcalf?) who would be likely to make such a remark — is what distinguishes Gallant as a writer of fiction. It is a quality that manifests itself in her command of the niceties that constitute "style." Gallant has, of course, written on this subject in her article "What Is Style?" in *Paris Notebooks*: "Style is inseparable from structure, part of the conformation of whatever the author has to say" (177). What Gallant "has to say" may involve the frustrations of communication and our all-too-frequent failures to make ourselves understood, but in facing up to the problem she has taken the first step towards countering it. The artist, as T.S. Eliot says in "East Coker," inevitably encounters "the intolerable wrestle / With words and meanings" (125), is forced to conduct "a raid on the inarticulate / With shabby equipment always deteriorating" (128). At the same time, the conscientious and skilled writer can keep the misunderstandings and ambiguities to a minimum, can even use them (as James Joyce did supremely) to artistic advantage.

Gallant's capacity to find the right word and the appropriate cadence may well surpass that of any contemporary Canadian writer. An excellent example comes from the opening page of the first Linnet Muir story, "In Youth Is Pleasure." Linnet first describes her mother's attitude towards her: "She had found me civil and amusing until I was ten, at which time I was said to have become pert and obstinate." A few lines later, she describes her own lack of interest in her mother: "It was not rejection or anything so violent as dislike but a simple indifference" (218). The gradations that separate "civil and amusing" from "pert and obstinate," the fine distinction that chooses "indifference" over "rejection" and "dislike," are masterly. This seemingly effortless, smoothly flowing prose employs verbal discriminations of extraordinary subtlety. Reading these lines, I am always reminded of Eliot's more positive expression of his verbal dilemma in "Little Gidding," when he describes a never-ending quest for

> The word neither diffident nor ostentatious,
> An easy commerce of the old and the new,
> The common word exact without vulgarity,
> The formal word precise but not pedantic. (144)

A similar, exquisite discipline is involved here.

If the whole of *A Fairly Good Time* is Shirley's "silent cry," it is a silent cry that *does* ultimately communicate. To recreate the past with total accuracy and authenticity may be impossible, but in the Linnet Muir stories we receive the paradoxical impression that the "lost Montreal" she invokes may be *"un mensonge"* yet it still speaks *"la vérité."* Unlike some of her more conspicuous but perhaps less talented contemporaries, Gallant has never lost faith in the adequacy, the power, and even the glory of language. Art may well be defined as a cry that communicates in silence; it may succeed occasionally in presenting voices lost in snow; and Gallant is supreme because she has shown us, again and again, how it happens.

CHAPTER 7

Margaret Laurence

At the close of the short story "To Set Our House in Order," in *A Bird in the House*, Vanessa MacLeod rides out on to the prairie and tries to come to terms with the complex events and tangled emotions that she has noticed in her family during the critical period culminating in the birth of her brother. She has just spent several unhappy weeks under the irksomely ordered rule of her grandmother, who has told her: "God loves order — he wants each one of us to set our house in order" (46). Vanessa has also learned much about the hopes and fears and secrets and unhappiness of her relatives. The last two paragraphs read as follows:

> I thought of the accidents that might easily happen to a person — or, of course, might not happen, might happen to somebody else. I thought of the dead baby, my sister, who might as easily have been I. Would she, then, have been lying here in my place, the sharp grass making its small toothmarks on her brown arms, the sun warming her to the heart? I thought of the leather-bound volumes of Greek, and the six different kinds of iced cakes that used to be offered always in the MacLeod house, and the pictures of leopards and green seas. I thought of my brother, who had been born alive after all, and now had been given his life's name.
>
> I could not really comprehend these things, but I sensed their

strangeness, their disarray. I felt that whatever God might love in this world, it was certainly not order. (59)

This is a seemingly apt conclusion, but, as Michael Darling has remarked in an excellent analysis of the story, the mature Vanessa, as narrator, "is trying to order her past, with the understanding that art can improve upon life in the imposition of order upon chaos" (199). For this reason, "the text itself disproves Vanessa's conclusion.... In telling the story, Vanessa has finally put her house in order" (202). Or, as I would rather put it, Laurence, in making Vanessa tell her story in this particular way, has enabled her to set her house in order.

Laurence has employed a number of artistic effects here in the process of drawing attention to the order/disorder paradox. She has, first, given Vanessa at this point an unusually and conspicuously formal rhetorical prose ("I thought of . . . I thought of . . . "). She has used the grandmother's phrase for the title of the story as a way of balancing Vanessa's final phrase. And in these final paragraphs she has made Vanessa think back to certain earlier experiences — awareness of "the baby who would have been my sister if only she had managed to come to life" (42), her grandfather's Greek books, her grandmother's luxurious tea-parties, and so on — that take on a fictional order by becoming part of her total consciousness. Above all, she has "ordered" Vanessa's words so that the story that carries intimations of chaos ends with the word "order." If we respond to Laurence's art, we appreciate the neatness of the ending but are uncomfortably aware that the story itself suggests that life is anything but neat.

The paradox involved here is, of course, one that continually arises in the study of literature, and especially perhaps in the discussion of fiction. One thinks of Henry James's famous remark about "[l]ife being all inclusion and confusion, and art being all discrimination and selection" (120). It is, moreover, a paradox that seems to lie at the heart of Laurence's work — partly, one suspects, as a result of her particular temperament. For example, in the matter of order versus disorder Laurence shared the sentiments of Vanessa. In an article written early in 1967, three years after "To Set Our House in Order" was first published, she insists that "living disorder is better than dead order" (*Heart* 95), and in an essay that appeared in 1972 and discusses *A Bird in the House* she speaks of "the fluctuating and accidental quality of life" and remarks parenthetically: "God really doesn't love Order" ("Time" 158).

To Laurence, then, art offered through form and structure the vision of an order that God had failed to deliver. Beyond this, however, there is no evidence that she had thought deeply about the aesthetic aspects of fiction before she began writing novels and short stories. Apart from a few competent but hardly exceptional stories published in a student magazine while she was an undergraduate, she showed no signs of being impelled into the writing of fiction until the time of her African experience, whereupon she wished to employ a medium that would communicate what she wanted to say as efficiently and as effectively as possible. The qualities of traditional fiction — an absorbing plot, convincing characterization, vivid background — were all necessary and desirable. Laurence seems to have accepted, without notable questioning, a conventional realism that, while not going so far as to imitate "the fluctuating and accidental quality of life" obeyed certain requirements in keeping with the limits of the credible and the possible.

Her own mature brand of realism was, of course, psychological rather than social, and she has distinguished between these two in an important passage in her interview with Donald Cameron:

> For me and for most of my generation, in Canada anyway, that kind of social realism which took in an analysis of the whole social pattern was not necessary because it had been done by people like Hugh MacLennan, like Ernest Buckler, like Sinclair Ross, and various other people — Morley Callaghan — so when I began to write I realized quite quickly that . . . what I really would like to do the most in a novel, was to, as far as possible, present the living individual on the printed page, in all his paradox and all his craziness. (1: 103)

A little earlier, she had compared this process with "Method" acting, which implies an emphasis on immediacy, on the closest possible empathy between writer and character. Such fiction stands or falls by the ability of the reader to accept the character — Hagar Shipley, Rachel or Stacey Cameron, Vanessa MacLeod, Morag Gunn — as totally credible. Although she knows, and goes on to insist immediately, that "Art is never life" (1: 104), her characters must be accepted as capable of living in "the real world." And for this reason the authenticity of their voices and personal idioms is crucial.

The successful blending of personal story with individual idiom is what constitutes Laurence's distinctive "style," a term that invites use despite her own dislike of it. At the same time, it is important to realize that her first works of fiction, the novel *This Side Jordan* and the collection of short stories entitled *The Tomorrow-Tamer*, belong rather to her category of "social realism" — inevitably, since they are set in the Gold Coast, now Ghana, and deal with issues that are as much political, social, and historical as personal, individual, and psychological. Only when she began to explore her own tribal and ancestral past could she move on to her preferred fictional approach. It is a commonplace of Laurence criticism to say that she learned, while in Africa, the complex fate of being a Canadian, and that her presentation of her Manawaka world required the radical distancing of perspective that her stay in Africa provided. I would like to go further, however, and suggest that her African fiction rooted her in a tradition of novel-writing that, despite her predilection for a newer mode, she never wholly outgrew. Her fiction occupies a position, I believe, between the old fiction and the new. *This Side Jordan*, for all its merits, now looks somewhat dated and technically old-fashioned, and occasional novelistic contrivances jar even within the Manawaka series. My own view is that, when she made her personal break-through on first hearing the authentic cadences of Hagar Shipley speak through her, she never quite realized that this new fictional method was not readily compatible with the formal and generic conventions of the traditional novel, that the more fluid and intimate speech-rhythms could be cramped within the stricter form of a well-made plot. Laurence's characteristic tone, her "style" in the larger sense of that term, is the often magnificent but sometimes imperfect result of this blend. In order to see this development in process, we must examine the African fiction before going on to consider her more representative Manawaka novels.

Laurence tells us in "Gadgetry or Growing" that she wrote "the last few pages [of *This Side Jordan*] first," and insists that, in structuring the novel, she "did not want to superimpose a false order and shape on it" (81). Nonetheless, that she did impose an order or shape of some sort, false or not, can hardly be disputed. The novel follows the fortunes of the white Johnnie Kestoe and the black Nathaniel Amigbe alternately throughout the action; their lives continually interconnect, often uncomfortably, and at the conclusion they are brought together (at least in terms of fictional structure) when their wives give birth at the same time and in the same hospital. The whole of the novel, indeed, depends formally on a principle of juxtaposed balance. This is evident on the first page where, after a brief description of Johnnie dancing with an African girl, we find this all-important paragraph, which I quote in full:

> At one of the tables around the outdoor dance floor, a young European woman [Johnnie's wife] watched thoughtfully. At another table an African man [Victor Edusai, the girl's lover] watched, then turned away and spat. Both were angry, and with the same person. (1)

This tableau is as dramatically powerful as it is blatantly artificial, the artifice manifesting itself in the conspicuously balanced syntax of the sentences. Such deliberate balancing of character with character, and emotion with emotion, is often technically effective; in the third chapter, for example, an opening conversation between whites (Johnnie and James Thayer) is followed by two mixed confrontations (first Johnny and Victor, then Nathaniel and the Kestoes), and the chapter closes with a conversation between blacks (Nathaniel, his wife, and Victor). The basically realistic presentation of before-Independence Ghana is not distorted by this conscious patterning, and the artistic control evident in the organization is aesthetically satisfying.

This principle of balance can decline all too easily, however, into a distracting contrivance. The flashback to Johnnie's traumatic experience at the time of his mother's death too obviously echoes Nathaniel's response to his father's death, also presented as a flashback. In this instance the obvious artificial patterning works against fictional credibility; we suspect the parallelism as being too neat to be true. Later, both Johnnie and Nathaniel betray their best selves in the interests of an essentially selfish expediency. It would be difficult to find fault with this linkage, but a little later still Laurence desperately contrives that the two men should both go in unlikely circumstances to the same high-life night-club on the same evening and become involved in a thematically convenient confrontation. An even more self-conscious patterning is visible, this time in a scene comparing

Johnnie and Victor, when each responds to an allusion to the other person, according to Cameron Shepherd, with the same reaction and in the same words (279). At the end, the juxtaposition of the two wives and their simultaneous child-bearing might be acceptable in itself, but when Johnnie and Nathaniel both receive encouragement in their jobs at the same time (promotion for Johnnie, a position of trust for Nathaniel), the artifice undercuts any sense of realistic portrayal. The convention of novelistic closure is at odds with the requirements of socio-political commentary. The ending suffers in comparison with E.M. Forster's balanced *lack* of resolution in the final chapter of *A Passage to India*. One might well argue that the "order and shape" are indeed "false" since in drawing attention to themselves they weaken any moral or didactic connection with the world of public events.

I do not want to give the impression that *This Side Jordan* is a bad novel; on the contrary, it contains scenes of great power and has been properly praised for its compassionate and independent insights into the realities of the colonial situation that it portrays. The speech patterns of a wide range of characters are skillfully reproduced; the descriptions of African life are admirably detached (even if Laurence's similes often betray an outsider's — almost a tourist's — sense of exoticism); and a workmanlike competence is evident on every page. It is fair to suggest, however, that the book is more a product of Laurence's moral and political conscience than of her artistic imagination. Indeed, with the gift of hindsight we can recognize the most characteristic Laurence effects not in the male world of political and professional strategies but in the scenes presenting Helen Cunningham and Cora Thayer, especially the magnificent seventh chapter where we are suddenly confronted with Helen's confession of the hopelessness of her situation and Cora's pathetic defence-reaction of decorating a totally un-African bungalow in which she lovingly fingers her useless fragments of brocade. In these neurotic, suffering, lonely women, presented with a combination of firmness and genuine sympathy, we see the beginnings of the mature novelist that Laurence was to become.

A comparable demonstration of balance is manifest in the stories that constitute *The Tomorrow-Tamer*. In some cases, this balance is achieved by the simple confrontation of black and white characters — the white narrator and Kwabena his black "brother" (in the sense that they were both suckled by the same woman, Kwabena's mother) in the opening "Drummer of All the World," and Mammii Ama and the white woman in the closing "Gourdful of Glory." (The patterning of the volume, as well as of the stories within the volume, is evident here.) More subtly, in "The Perfume Sea," the white hairdressers Mr. Archipelago and Doree, neither of whom can admit to a past, are assured of a future through the African Mercy Tachie, who wishes to look like a city girl and so to deny her own past (as James Harrison has noted, they switch "from curling European hair to uncurling African hair" [245]). In "The Tomorrow-Tamer" we see the basic facts of a tragic event in the village of Owurasu interpreted in totally different ways by the white technicians and the black natives; in "The Rain Child" the tension in the story develops from the series of comparisons and contrasts set up between Violet Nedden, the elderly white teacher who will soon be forced to retire back to an England in which she is a stranger, and Ruth Quansah, the young African girl born in England who finds it almost impossible to adapt to the ways of life of her own country; in "Godman's Master" the relation of master and servant-slave shifts and varies as Moses Adu finds himself more and more involved in and responsible for the future of the ironically named dwarf Godman. The list could be extended. In religious terms, white Christianity and black Fetish are contrasted and juxtaposed throughout the book; in political terms, the collection as a whole is subtly poised between a sympathetic presentation of the Africans' hopes of "Free-Dom" on the one hand and the poignant realization that many of these hopes cannot possibly be fulfilled by the fact of Independence on the other. And almost invariably, this balancing of character with character or concept with concept enhances the stories and in no way detracts from their effectiveness. The artifice contributes to the complexities of these stories but never dominates or falsifies.

The publication of *The Stone Angel* in 1964 represented a dramatic breakthrough in Laurence's career as a novelist. While it would not be true to say that she found her voice in this novel, she certainly discovered and exploited the potentiality of voice and personal language. "[O]nce I began *The Stone Angel*," she recalls, "it wrote itself more easily than anything I have ever done. I experienced the enormous pleasure of coming home in terms of idiom" ("Ten Years" 31).

Time and again, she has commented on her confidence about the authenticity of Hagar's voice: "I kept feeling that I *knew* I was getting the speech *exactly right*! It was *mine* . . . phrases, bits of idiom, would come back to me that I had forgotten, that I didn't know I even remembered, from my grandparents' speech" (Sullivan 68). As B.W. Powe has noted (in one of the few studies to date that offer a discriminating rather than exaggeratedly eulogistic account of her work) Laurence is important as "an 'ear-witness' " because at her best "her sense of voice never goes wrong" (130). The fact of Hagar's language is certainly the central feature of *The Stone Angel*; we become interested in Hagar's character and thus informed about the much-touted themes of the novel — aging, survival, or whatever — because her voice is a unique and living reality. The art of Margaret Laurence centres in this novel upon her capacity to reproduce this voice in all its forcefulness, variety, and linguistic complexity.

Clearly, then, *The Stone Angel* had to be told in the first person, since Hagar's idiom and cadences are integral to the effect. Here is a representative example of her speech:

> I remember a quarrel I had with Bram, once. Sometimes he used to blow his nose with his fingers, a not unskilled performance. He'd grasp the bridge between thumb and forefinger, lean over, snort heftily, and there it'd be, bubbling down the couchgrass like snake spit, and he'd wipe his fingers on his overalls, just above the rump, the same spot always, as I saw when I did the week's wash. I spoke my disgust in no uncertain terms, not for the first time. It had gone on for years, but my words never altered him. He'd only say "Quit yapping, Hagar — what makes me want to puke is a nagging woman." He couldn't string two words together without some crudity, that man. He knew it riled me. That's why he kept it up so.
>
> And yet — here's the joker in the pack — we'd each married for those qualities we later found we couldn't bear — he for my manners and speech, I for his flouting of them. (79–80)

We notice the emphatic quality of her reminiscing (the deliberately separated "once"), her sarcastic formality ("a not unskilled performance"), her vivid precision of word-choice ("snorted heftily"), her richness of figurative expressions ("bubbling . . . like snake spit"), the vocabulary and phraseology of a particular generation ("rump," "in no uncertain terms," "riled"), and the contrast in style with Bram's equally vivid but different reported speech. It is not an exaggeration to say that in *The Stone Angel* our fascination with the language takes precedence over our interest in the plot — or, rather, that language, character, and plot are inextricably combined in the fact of Hagar.

But the inevitable decision to narrate *The Stone Angel* through Hagar has certain consequences. If the ninety-year-old Hagar is to tell the story of her own life, then she will necessarily be shown as ordering her own life. The concern for tidiness and the "orderly" is prominent from the start, Hagar claiming that these were aspects of her young self, imaged in the trim walks of the cemetery, while as an old woman she sides with the "tough-rooted" wild flowers that threaten to invade them (5). But we are aware of her ordering principles throughout the book. Furthermore, Laurence must herself make decisions about the book's form that will radically affect the order that Hagar brings to her story. And it is this matter of ordering that has caused controversy not only on the part of certain commentators but on Laurence's part as well.

"The form of the novel," she writes, "gave me more trouble than the voice," and, after discussing the pros and cons of flashbacks, she continues:

> But should episodes from the past, in novels, be in any kind of chronological order? That is *not*, after all, the way people actually remember. In some ways I would have liked Hagar's memories to be haphazard. But I felt that, considering the great number of years those memories spanned, the result of such a method would be to make the novel too confusing for the reader. I am still not sure that I decided the right way when I decided to place Hagar's memories in chronological order. This is a very tricky point. One can say that the method I chose diminishes the novel's resemblance to life, but on the other hand writing — however consciously unordered its method — is never as disorderly as life....
>
> All Hagar's memories are touched off by something which occurs in her present, and I think this is legitimate and the way it really happens. However, the coincidence of present happenings touching off — conveniently — memories in sequence is

probably straining credulity. I feel now that the novel is probably too orderly. ("Gadgetry" 83)

I have quoted at some length because the problem Laurence wrestles with here, rather like a dog worrying a bone, is central to her art. When she laments that the method she chose "diminishes the novel's resemblance to life," she is invoking an extraordinarily rigid and at the same time naïve view of literary realism. She knows that literature "is never as disorderly as life," yet she has an uneasy feeling that, as novelist, she should subordinate the "consciously unordered" (odd phrase!) to a method that, by the very fact of its being a method, implies order. While she vacillates from one point of view to another (later in her career, in *The Diviners*, she significantly employs a similar chronological ordering for Morag's memories), she tends towards the conclusion that "the novel is probably too orderly."

I am convinced that Laurence is right in her practice, wrong in her theory. The aesthetic pleasure that we experience in *The Stone Angel* surely originates in the tension generated from the subtle blend of realistic illusion (Hagar's remembering voice) and formal artifice (the ordering of present meditation and past action into a balanced structure). We appreciate the skill with which Laurence manipulates the transitions from now to then and back to now. A few instances must suffice. The glimpse of a nurse during the visit to Silverthreads, the strangeness of the place, and the heat of the day "all bring to mind the time I was first in a hospital, when Marvin was born" (99). Sometimes a mere word, like "waiting," is enough to set off the train of reminiscence:

[I] can only lean here mutely, waiting for whatever they'll perform upon me.

And then, after a section space:

I've waited like this for things to get better or worse many and many a time. (112)

Especially poignant is the moment when Hagar's reliving a sexual encounter with Bram is interrupted by the click of an X-ray machine: "all at once I'm standing in a glare of light. I feel I must be naked, exposed to the core of my head. What is it? Where?" (116). And when Hagar is planning her escape to Shadow Point, and is anxious to allay

125

suspicion, it is particularly apt that her thoughts should turn to an earlier time when she violently broke the pattern of her life, the day she left Bram and took John with her. Careful readers recognize the artistry here, which in no way interferes with the imaginative assent they give to the convincing realism of Hagar's story. The narrative is recognized as art, not as documentary. The skillful control of form in *The Stone Angel* invites admiration rather than apology.[1]

But there are some episodes in the novel where we become aware of an awkward contrivance, an artifice that clashes with the realistic illusion instead of enhancing it. There are, for example the two overhearing scenes — one in the opening chapter where Hagar, concealed behind a chokecherry bush, witnesses her father's frustrated assignation with Lottie Dreiser's mother; the other in the fifth chapter where, on the veranda of Mr. Oatley's house, she hears her son John making love to one of his girl friends. The incidents are trivial in themselves, but belong to an earlier tradition of novel-writing that seems out of place here. Laurence, one suspects, was uneasy about these effects, since in each case she makes Hagar excuse herself rather conspicuously: "At first I didn't realize anyone was there, and when I did, it was too late to get away" (18); "I didn't mean to eavesdrop, but for a moment I couldn't move" (159). We may be forgiven for suspecting that the lady doth protest too much. The problem is not the moral dubiety of eavesdropping but the over-intrusive fabrication that interferes with the realistic illusion.

A related difficulty is raised by the scene where Hagar first realizes that Marvin and Doris plan to put her into a nursing home:

> It is then that I see the newspaper, and the dreadful words. Spread out on the kitchen table, it has been left open at the classified ads. Someone's hand has marked a place in pen. I bend, and peer, and read. (53)

The plot surely creaks here. It is clear that Doris has not deliberately left the newspaper so that Hagar will see it. That would be an uncharacteristic example of planned cruelty, and her surprise and embarrassment on entering the room shortly afterwards sufficiently absolve her from this charge. But it is difficult to believe that she would accidentally leave lying about the evidence that she wants to be kept secret. The incident leads into an excellent passage (properly praised by John Baxter as a supreme instance of Laurence's

"Shakespearian" style), but the manipulation is awkward. It would fit comfortably into a Hardy novel but seems out of place in the kind of fiction to which *The Stone Angel* clearly belongs. I have placed greater emphasis on these minor blemishes than they may seem to warrant because Laurence has a habit of using overhearing scenes to offset the limitations of first-person narration (*A Bird in the House* is full of jolting instances), and a tendency to rely on conventional twists of plot is also a recurring irritant.

The special triumph of *A Jest of God* consists of Laurence's ability to create a totally different character, and yet to retain a comparable sense of linguistic sharpness and complexity. Of course, she has for the most part avoided the problem of flashbacks and their ordering. Rachel's story takes place in an embattled present tense; flashbacks are occasional, brief, and their ordering not especially significant. Whereas Hagar's weakness lay in a lack of self-knowledge, Rachel's manifests itself as an excess of self-analysis and self-criticism. Perhaps it is her obsession with finding fault in herself that enables her to present other characters more compellingly than Hagar. Mrs. Cameron, for example, comes across as a wonderfully vivid, rounded character (any exaggeration is readily accounted for by Rachel's viewpoint), very different from Jason Currie in *The Stone Angel*, who is revealed through the contrivances of the plot as little more than a straw man.

A Jest of God is, I believe, the most technically sophisticated of all Laurence's novels. As readers we become fascinated by her clarity of vision and especially by her sharpness of mind. George Bowering, in an article that originally appeared in 1971 and is by far the best treatment of this novel to date, was the first to recognize that "Rachel has a mind, that is more important than any reviewer has noticed," and properly observed that in *A Jest of God* we are offered "a rare privilege in our fiction, the enjoyment of hearing the mind moving" (211). At the same time, of course, we recognize her neurotic weaknesses, but admire her sense of responsibility and her capacity for endurance. The tension between her sexual timidity and her frank realization of a sexual need is poignant, and is expressed with an extraordinary directness and maturity. Here again readers' responses should be divided between empathy at the level of realism and admiration for the artistry that makes it possible. The art is (or should be) conspicuous in the language, the clipped rhythms, and above all perhaps in the economy of the whole. This is the shortest of Laurence's novels, yet it may well be the most complex.

There is, however, one episode in the novel that displays a slight sense of strain. This is the crucial scene where Nick shows Rachel a photograph of himself as a child, and Rachel misinterprets it as representing a son. The scene is skillfully constructed, and becomes the climax to a series of incidents in which Rachel, in her lack of confidence, comes to erroneous conclusions. At the same time, the chances of misunderstanding seem remote. Rachel's simple "Yours?" (149) is ambiguous, and an unlikely phrasing, given the circumstances. Nick's reply fits Rachel's unspoken question, "Your son?," rather than the one she actually asks. We cannot help feeling, once again, that Laurence has contrived the misunderstanding, that plot requirements are taking precedence over probability. There are two possible explanations that can be offered in defence: the first, argued by Kenneth Hughes (45, 50), that Nick deliberately exploits an opportunity to deceive her; the second, that this is one more "jest of God." Both may be considered plausible, yet both contain difficulties. If Nick is being ruthlessly enigmatic here, we have no way of establishing the fact from Rachel's first-person text, though she does consider the possibility later: "I don't know whether he meant to lie to me or not" (190). The "jest of God" explanation merely passes the responsibility for contrivance from Laurence to a higher authority. There is an inevitable vagueness here, part of the small price that Laurence plays for the otherwise overwhelming benefits of first-person narration.

I began with a detailed analysis of the order-disorder problem as it appears in *A Bird in the House*, so further discussion of this book can be brief. Vanessa MacLeod's story admirably combines two themes: the portrait of the artist, and coming to terms with the burden of one's ancestors. Vanessa's verbal sensitivity makes possible a precise yet emotionally authentic eloquence that makes much of the book intimately moving. Yet once again there is a clash between the first-person techniques and the demands of the plot. The "portrait of the artist" aspect can suitably be presented from Vanessa's exclusive viewpoint, but the larger question of ancestors, especially the way in which Grandfather Connor's personality impinges on other members of the family, is less readily debated in this way. Laurence's solution to this difficulty must, I think, be considered clumsy. She contrives a conspicuously large number of overhearing scenes, including the hoary device of listening through an air-register to conversations taking place in other parts of the house (56).[2] At other times, the child merely sits quietly in a corner, her presence unnoticed. Such scenes are by no means implausible, but Laurence both overuses them and nervously exaggerates their contrivance by drawing attention to them. "I was a professional listener," Vanessa announces at an early stage (11), and later: "I went into the back bedroom to one of my listening posts" (75). Linked to this contrivance is the convention of Vanessa's powers of total recall. She can produce the subtle intricacies of adult conversations twenty years after the event. I am not objecting to this convention in itself; after all, novelists continually employ it, and we generally accept the pretence. I am merely pointing out that it does not mix easily with the illusion of intense realism that is created in so much of the book. It is difficult to escape the conclusion that Laurence has partly failed to mould her technique to the demands of her form.

The problem is magnified in *The Fire-Dwellers*, since here Laurence encounters difficulties in language as well as in plot. The language difficulty stems from the fact that Stacey, unlike Hagar, Rachel, and Vanessa, lacks the gift of precise speech. She has a vigorous idiom, to be sure, but it is derived from the journalese of newspapers and TV, and is an inadequate instrument for recording the complex emotions that she undoubtedly feels. We may admire her resilience but we do not find ourselves admiring the exactness of her speech; in consequence, a dimension of artistic subtlety is lost.

But the plot difficulty is ultimately more troubling. From the beginning of the novel, Stacey is almost paranoiacally sensitive to the fact of violence in the modern world, mainly because her experience is confined to the sensationalism of newspaper headlines and the newscasts of fighting in Vietnam which are dominating her TV screen. She lives in constant fear of accidents happening to her children. It is interesting to compare this fear with the incidence of disaster and sensation written by Laurence into the fabric of the novel itself. We find mention of three suicides (admittedly at side-stage), two attempted suicides (both heard about on the same day), two fatal traffic accidents (and one near miss), one drowning (and one near-drowning), a multiple death by fire, one blinding by vitriol and one by glaucoma, two adulteries, and two examples of perversion (one psychological, one sexual). All this in the ambience of a middle-class Vancouver housewife during the six months or so of the novel's time-span. By the standards of realism (even for a novel set in the rebellious late sixties), this is surely excessive. One gets the uneasy suspicion that Laurence has contrived the plot to justify her heroine's fears. An interpretation of the age is being demonstrated by distortingly selective means. Again, there is nothing against a novelist painting a dark canvas; we need our Kafkas and our Becketts. It is the intrusion of such a selective viewpoint upon the domain of realism that raises disturbing questions.

There are other related instances of plot contrivance in this novel. When Stacey, with characteristic qualms, twice commits adultery with Joe Venturi, on both occasions she returns to find a crisis in her home: first, Katie's discovery of Tess Fogle showing Jen the cannibalistic goldfish; second, Mac's hearing the news of Buckle's death. Two more jests of God? Perhaps, but the plot manipulation that ensures Stacey's moral punishment rings false; it seems intrusive, whether invoked to validate Stacey's paranoia or to provide, in the tradition of a righteous God, the standard punishment for sin.[3] Finally, there is the ending in which Thor Thorlakson is revealed as Vernon Winkler from Manawaka in disguise, Mac is promoted just at the moment when he is planning to resign, and Jen offers her first words after an unnatural period of silence; all these are, to make the point bluntly, the staples of Hollywood B situation-comedy. One is conscious here of an artifice out of keeping with the realistic tone that the rest of the novel has established. I am not denying the emotional force of much of *The Fire-Dwellers*; Laurence is grappling with important issues here, and her attempt to explore the instincts and yearnings of a character in Stacey's situation is admirable. But it seems clear that, in this instance, she has not succeeded in matching her artistic technique to her emotional sympathy.

A more complex kind of contrivance is at work in Laurence's final novel. Most commentators on *The Diviners* describe it as an ambitious culmination to the Manawaka series that ties the loose strands of the earlier novels together. This, I agree, was Laurence's intention, and it is an intention central to my concerns in this discussion. The important point is that, despite the fact that she had written novels offering intimately realistic portrayals of individual women leading separate lives, she felt the need to provide some unifying effect to round off the cycle. We can see her attempting this in particular in two segments of the novel, both of which deserve detailed attention.

The first, which has received surprisingly little comment from critics, is Morag's determination to have a child by Jules Tonnerre (whom she met up with again by convenient novelistic coincidence — "at the psychological moment," as one used to say). That she should feel the need to separate from her unsatisfactory husband is understandable enough; that she should desire a sexual liaison with Jules, the immediate cause of the separation, is similarly acceptable. We may also concede the fact that Brooke's reluctance to have a child is responsible for the break-up of their marriage. But that she should deliberately get pregnant by Jules is another matter. He behaves boorishly throughout her childhood, and she has consistently regarded him with a combination of fascination and suspicious fear. I suspect that the real reason is that Laurence wants to make a political and structural point. Morag is from "the wrong side of the tracks" herself and acutely conscious of social stratifications; Jules, as a Métis, is virtually ostracized by the respectable Anglo-Scot Manawakans. The union of the two makes a social and ideological point (one is reminded of Helen Schlegel's child by Leonard Bast in Forster's *Howards End*). Moreover, the product of the liaison — Pique Gunn Tonnerre, as she is called at the novel's close — is a symbolic figure uniting native peoples and immigrants, a new Canadian woman emerging out of the ancestral past to represent a revivified, more democratic Canada. (I find myself recalling the strained ending of Hugh MacLennan's *Two Solitudes* with the marriage between French- and English-Canadian, another political statement emanating from plot contrivance.) Pique is offered, as Coral Ann Howells has noted, as "the inheritor of both traditions," indicative of a "reconciliation across the gap of history and social custom" (*Private* 36). Yet Pique, as presented, cannot bear the burden of this meaning — to quote Howells again, she "suffers from the weight of too much thematic relevance" (51) — but that this was Laurence's intention seems inescapable.

The second segment involves the revelation of the fortunes of the plaid pin, a unifying device generally mentioned as a structural triumph on Laurence's part. In my view, it is aesthetically problematic. In *The Stone Angel*, John Shipley exchanges the plaid pin of the

Curries, entrusted to him by Hagar, for a knife belonging to Lazarus Tonnerre. When Jules produces it in Morag's cottage just before his death, she is able to produce the knife which John had sold to Christie Logan, Morag's stepfather, and another "fair trade" follows (432). Once again, the lives of Indian-Métis and Anglo-Scot are symbolically interwoven. The structure is neat; my point is that it is *too* neat. This unified conclusion, appropriate to comedies of manners or novels of unabashed artifice like those of Robertson Davies, hardly fits the chronicles of tangled lives that the Manawaka series presents. What has happened, surely, is that Laurence has worked her way through to a new kind of novel capable of presenting human character with an unparalleled depth, immediacy, and poignancy, but has retained the structural principles of an earlier form to which it cannot easily be assimilated. This is a structural variant on the intellectual problem involving conflicting views of order and disorder, with which I began. Laurence suspects that the world in which we live is unordered, but feels an artistic instinct to impose order upon it. This may well be the germ, the irritant, the challenge that leads to artistic creation. But for an artist who has strong predilections towards realism, it can lead to formal and logical difficulties. In my view, Laurence encountered these problems in more extreme form as she sensed the individual novels forming themselves into a larger series that presumably implied further formal demands. *The Diviners* is certainly Laurence's most ambitious book, but, as J.M. Kertzer has recently reminded us, "[t]his does not mean it is her best novel" (293).[4]

I must insist, in conclusion, that the literary-critical observations that I have been making here are in no way intended to detract from Laurence's achievement as a novelist. All I am maintaining is that, like all writers, she belonged to a particular moment in history with all its attendant advantages and disadvantages. As she remarked in a passage already quoted, she was able to start from a particular place because earlier Canadian novelists, including MacLennan, had written before her. I extract MacLennan from her list because the analogy is peculiarly apt. He performed an admirable service in his time by showing how popular forms of fiction could be adapted to become vehicles for the serious exploration of Canadian history, life, and attitudes. Nowadays, we may find many of his novels structured in a rather intrusive manner, but they still retain much of their effectiveness, despite the technical advances that Canadian fiction has made in the last quarter of a century. Laurence is one generation further along the road. The roundedness of characters like Hagar or Rachel was completely beyond the scope of MacLennan and his generation (though in later years he came close in what I take to be his masterpiece, *The Watch That Ends the Night*). But Laurence maintained some of the artificial conventions that seem curiously outmoded when her more contemporary characters are contained within them. She was the first to tackle head-on many of the technical problems that later Canadian novelists take more elegantly in their stride (in part, no doubt, because they have had the benefit of her experience). The time has come when we need to acknowledge some of her limitations, but this should only set in greater relief the impressive magnitude of her achievement.

CHAPTER 8

Hugh Hood

Super-realism . . . that's how I think of my fiction. (*Governor's Bridge* 127)

Everything I write is allegory, there's no question about that. (Hale 37)

[S]ince I am *both* a realist and a *transcendentalist allegorist* . . . I cannot be bound by the forms of ordinary realism. ("Hugh Hood" 145)

These three quotations conveniently sum up the main literary-critical problem represented by Hugh Hood's work. Allegory and realism are generally seen as occupying extreme ends on a spectrum of literary modes; how, then, can the two be reconciled, let alone amalgamated? Before even attempting an answer to this question, however, we are faced immediately with an odd situation: while it would be fair to classify "Recollections of the Works Department" in *Flying a Red Kite* as Hood at his most realistic, and "An Allegory of Man's Fate" in *Dark Glasses* as living up to its name, readers of these two short stories are not likely to become aware of any violent contrast in approach and effect. Herein, I suspect, lies the secret of Hood's elusive skill as a writer. Of course, both "realism" and "allegory" are unusually slippery terms not conducive to clear-cut and unambiguous definition, but, whereas modern readers are well acquainted with varieties of realism, allegory (however widespread the term may be) denotes a much less familiar mode. Since Hood lays so much stress upon the latter term, a brief discussion of allegory, its characteristics and possibilities, is necessary as a preliminary to a study of Hood's "style."

Yet defining allegory is rather like trying to catch the proverbial chicken by putting salt on its tail. Although some scholars have endeavoured to impose their own limited meanings, more flexible inquirers acknowledge that the term is virtually impossible to pin down. As Marius Buning has written, "we almost have to practice critical legerdemain when attempting to describe that special form of literary communication we like to call allegory" (40). In the case of Hood's allegorical practice, problems arise at an early stage. Thus Angus Fletcher, in one of the most comprehensive discussions of the subject, sets out by asserting: "In the simplest terms, allegory says one thing and means another" (2). But for Hood this principle is anathema. Writing of his detestation of irony (categorized in medieval rhetoric, be it noted, as a species of allegory), he remarks: "It seems to me basically dishonest in all its modes, saying one thing, meaning another, that is, lying" ("Hugh Hood" 145). Hood, then, can hardly be a "simple" allegorist. From here we may return to Buning for a comment that brings to a head the critical dilemma so far as Hood is concerned. In the medieval period, he observes, allegory was "essentially *affirmative*, celebrating a structured view of reality"; in the twentieth century, however, it can only be "essentially *ironic* . . . and therefore suspicious of any cosmic or collective system of thought and values" (36).

Hood's Catholic convictions represent, of course, the complicating factor here, despite his determination to separate himself from what he calls "doctrinaire Catholicism" (Hale 35). To be sure, with Hood there is no harking back to an eternally fixed medieval world-view. In *A New Athens* he makes Matt Goderich remark: "The Protestant insistence on freedom of conscience and witness is the best thing that ever happened to Roman Catholicism" (123). At the same time, Hood believes in "the heavenly city, the immortal soul and the whole Christian bag of tricks" (Cloutier 49), a sentiment that is no less genuine for being flippantly expressed. The necessary point to be made here is that his Catholic viewpoint does *not* accept as a kind of secular gospel the historically determined assumption among the theorists that only an ironical version of allegory is possible in the modern world. In his doctoral dissertation, "Theories of Imagination in English Thinkers, 1650-1790," completed in 1955, he explored resemblances between the medieval view of modes of knowing and the poetic psychology represented by Wordsworth and Coleridge, and argued that Thomist attitudes were "life-enhancing and vitalistic" in contrast to the "life-denying" thought of Montaigne and Descartes. He is against rationalistic-scientific notions of the world as "simply a mechanical device," and recognizes the presence of the spiritual within the material as achieved — allegorically, if you will — by the figure of Jesus Christ, who "unites what is the most universal and the most particular" (Struthers "Interview" 22–23).

Far from acknowledging an unbridgeable gap between the Catholic world-view and that of the late twentieth century, then, Hood insists on the possibility of union between the two. His profoundly religious position is far removed from that kind of Christian dualism which separates spirit from flesh or sacred from profane. His emphasis is always on interconnection between the temporal and eternal worlds, a preoccupation that can be illustrated with equal ease from his fiction and non-fiction alike. In his essay on "super-realism" (and it is important to realize that the prefix in this word implies not merely an enhanced realism but a vision and method that go *beyond* realism in the quotidian sense) Hood remarks: "I love most in painting an art that exhibits the transcendental element dwelling in living things" (*Governor's Bridge* 130). The comment is fully applicable to his own literary work. Similarly, Matt Goderich is surely a spokesman for Hood when in *The Swing in the Garden* he admires in a sixteenth-century Dutch set of panels the "image of the holy in the daily" (100), and recognizes in May-Beth Codrington's inspired paintings in *A New Athens* "the vision of the heavenly and eternal rising from the things of this world" (211).

At the same time, despite his insistence on a philosophical and spiritual continuity between the medieval world, romanticism, and our own day, Hood must be aware that his own attitude is very different from that of Coleridge, who unequivocally favoured symbol over allegory, claiming for symbol the very quality that Hood seeks: the "translucence of the eternal through and in the temporal" (qtd.

in Buning 18). Some light may be cast on all this terminological fog if we turn to Hood's brilliantly lucid and self-analytic article "Before the Flood" in *Trusting the Tale*. There he describes the attraction he felt as a boy for the coloured plates of radiator badges in *The Wonder Book of Motors*. These were loved in part because they were "a dynamic blend of the exotic and the quotidian," but also because, though almost blatantly contemporary, their "bright, unambiguous, specific" colours and their formality of design suggested the heraldic and the liturgical: "I found in those enamelled and ornamented designs a kind of exactitude, a poised, rather stiff formality which insistently recalled the Mass and the priestly vestments. . . . They were neither images nor symbols. They were emblems" (18–19). In this context, he remarks that he hates symbols "because they propose an other-worldly truth which they never deliver" (he sees vagueness and imprecision where Coleridge saw spontaneity and universality), and relegates a preoccupation with images to an approach suitable only for "the artist without an idea in his head." But emblems "evoke the world with rich colour and clear definite line, and they name, sign, indicate, point to, formal abstract codes of behaviour, class, worship" (19). He is well aware that such emblems can be used all too often in the interests of class and hierarchy to which he is firmly opposed, yet he feels the need to acknowledge "much earlier, deeper allegiances which are rootedly conservative in a conservatism of the affections" (22). For Hood, allegory and emblem keep us in contact with our human origins.

At this point, we may return to his seemingly idiosyncratic linking of allegory to realism. As many scholars have pointed out, notably Maureen Quilligan, allegorical texts are always "predicated on the existence of other texts" (156), which in any Christian context usually means the Bible. Intertextuality and allegory are thus closely interrelated. But the rise of the realistic novel severed this connection, at least in terms of Christian application, since fidelity to the terms of everyday life replaced any links with eternally sanctioned patterns of behaviour, and thus, in Buning's words, "gave the *coup de grâce* to allegory" (39). Once again, however, a convinced Christian like Hood will regard everyday life in terms of, rather than in opposition to, the traditional patterns. This is not just a matter of seeing human behaviour as reflecting incidents in the life of Christ. A further dimension, in more immediate terms, is illustrated by Hood's account of reading one of his Montreal stories, "Socks" in *Dark Glasses*, in a school close to the area in which the story was set. He detected in his listeners "the unmistakeable signs of the fundamental pleasure of recognition given by literary realism, not simply the naïve pleasure of identifying one's neighbourhood, district or quarter, but the additional, much more complex pleasure of seeing one's place worked into the balance and design of the narration" (*Trusting* 127). The last phrase is crucial, and needs to be acknowledged as a prime end in Hood's fiction. A problem arises, however, with contemporary readers of realistic fiction, many of whom, while responding to the shock of recognition Hood describes, may be confined to the superficial level that realism makes so explicit. Others may feel their way towards a moral level (on the Dantesque scale of interpretation that Hood favours) but without recognizing even the existence of subtler spiritual correspondences. Hood, as we shall see, emphasizes — perhaps over-emphasizes — these levels of interpretation. All this would seem to suggest that his challenge is not so much to write in the allegorical mode in the twentieth century but rather to educate his readers into the allegorical possibilities of what he has written.

An examination of his fiction will bear out this surmise. Of all the writers considered in this book, Hood is perhaps the least interested in the tightly ordered sequence of events that script-writers call the "story-line." His plots show a greater interest in patterns (especially of ascent and descent), in physical journeys that are also spiritual, and in Wordsworthian "spots of time" that lead to moments of vision — or, in other words, in patterns that lead inevitably to some kind of super-literal or allegorical reading. Realizing only too well that the traditional novel "eschews the methods of allegory" ("Hugh Hood" 140), he looks elsewhere for literary models that can be grafted on to an ostensibly realistic presentation of modern living. In consequence, he finds himself doubting if the words "novel" and even "fiction" properly describe the books he writes, and prefers to categorize them himself as "long narrative pieces" (140). He is, however, unambiguous about his ultimate aim: "I am trying to assimilate the mode of the novel to the mode of fully-developed Christian allegory" (145).

We are now in a better position, I believe, to approach Hood's work with an understanding of his basic attitudes and principles. Before we do so, however, one caveat needs to be entered. Keith Garebian has recently asserted: "Hood has spoken so frequently about his allegorical method that a critic who does not read his fiction as allegory is either inordinately perverse or helplessly naïve" (11). This, I would argue, puts the case too strongly. While I agree, as the foregoing discussion clearly indicates, that Hood's work cannot properly be scrutinized without an awareness of its allegorical superstructure, I also believe that we need to be on our guard against accepting Hood's own discussions and assessments of his work as definitive. The writer who has borrowed for a book-title a phrase from D.H. Lawrence's famous dictum, "Never trust the artist. Trust the tale," can hardly claim full authority for the interpretation and appreciation of his own writings. The fact is that, because Hood is such a committed and accomplished technician in fiction, and because he is so articulate in communicating the artistic intentions and decisions involved in the act of literary creation, some commentators — Susan Copoloff-Mechanic, for instance, as well as Garebian — have taken over his emphases and enthusiasms as if they constituted the only satisfactory way of interpreting his fiction.[1] Some of his insights, especially those relating to numerological structure, may well be more important for the author in the process of writing than for the reader responding to the finished product. While the presence of allegorical levels beneath the surface of any Hood narrative must always be considered, I would question the desirability of a constant, rigidly consistent, and exclu-sive allegorical approach. Different stories contain, in my view, differ-ent ingredients of allegorical material at different strengths. Some-times, indeed, Hood can assert an allegorical meaning to the detriment of the fiction as a successful work of art. It will be wise, therefore, to proceed with caution. Certainly, the allegorical approach should not be emphasized at the expense of Hood's subtle verbal effects; it is only one ingredient of his "sense of style." The next step is to trace the course of Hood's development as a literary artist and to map out the main lines of his stylistic evolution.

Hood's mastery of the art of fiction has depended upon his finding satisfactory ways to express his unified vision in artistically valid terms. He admits to an initial uncertainty: "When I started to write novels and stories in 1956, I had no clear idea of what I was doing" (*Governor's Bridge* 127). As late as 1973, in the passage where he asserted his belief in "the whole Christian bag of tricks," he confessed to Pierre Cloutier: "I don't know how to make a literary image out of it yet" (49). The date here is crucial, since he appears to be in the very throes of solving the problem with the composition of *The Swing in the Garden*, that appeared two years later. Dennis Duffy sees Hood's fiction as "a series of experiments in narrative structure through which he searches for a literary form, a structure resembling that of realistic fiction, within which his characteristic way of seeing things can happen" (132). I agree, though I would wish to emphasize stylistic experimentation as well as the trying-out of various narrative structures. The best way of approaching the essential qualities of Hood's writing is, I believe, to trace this development chronologically (but perforce selectively) through his work.

The first challenge was to evolve a flexible narrative style. Although John Metcalf, probably with certain passages from *White Figure, White Ground* in mind, has referred to "the flash and filigree of his earliest rhetoric" before he became a master of mature "austerity" (*Kicking* 152), Hood was in fact experimenting with the colloquial from the outset of his career as a writer. It would be surprising if an author who has acknowledged Wordsworth as his "greatest literary influence" (Hale 36) did not employ the language really used by men. Indeed, the first sentence of his first published story, "The Isolation Booth," reads: "This was a nice little guy — no, I'm not being funny — he was a sweet kid when he first made the program" (5). The narrator, host of a TV quiz-show, is too crude a vehicle for Hood's purpose — the story seems thin because the speaker is incapable of conveying meanings beyond the surface detail — but even here one detects the characteristic Hugh Hood idiom in the act of emerging from the shadow of imitation Morley Callaghan. An attempt, worthy if a little over-ostentatious, is being made to reproduce the language and rhythms of modern Canadian speech; the intention, quite clearly, is to avoid the formal and the aloof.

In "Silver Bugles, Cymbals, Golden Silks" and the frequently reprinted "Recollections of the Works Department," both collected in *Flying a Red Kite* (1962), Hood has extended his experiment in ways that are ultimately going to have considerable repercussions for his mature work. We find here not only a systematic attempt to combine the qualities of sophisticated journalism with those of realistic fiction but also an equivalent blurring of the usual distinction between author and first-person narrator. The two experiments are, of course, clearly interconnected, since the virtual identification of author and speaker creates an illusion of journalistic documentary. "Silver Bugles" begins, "When I was a child of six, in the summer of 1934 . . . " (40), biographical information that fits Hood himself; in "Recollections," the narrator goes so far as to give his name as "Hood" (67). It would, of course, be unwise to take all the information at face-value as "lived" experience, but the illusion of credibility is very strong. This may be seen as a development of the authentic tale of personal experience, Canadian examples of which I have discussed in earlier chapters (O'Hagan and his wilderness men, Wilson and family tradition); this is a form that certainly influenced the practice of later writers exploiting the possible relation between fiction and memoir, including Alice Munro. Furthermore, Hood has created a persona capable of discussing ideas and following through arguments that allows him to encompass a wide intellectual range. Our understanding of the more characteristic members of the Toronto Works Department could not have been expressed and communicated by themselves.

Hood's allegorical leanings may be quickly discerned in *Flying a Red Kite*, since we are confronted in the second line of the opening story, "Fallings From Us, Vanishings," with a protagonist by the name of Arthur Merlin. Here only an unusually imperceptive reader could fail to pick up a clue to larger meanings. We soon notice that the character in question is involved in a modern equivalent of a Grail quest; above all, he is referred to as "Arthur Merlin in captivity" (14) when in the company of a heroine who eventually leaves him "alone in a sandy place" while shouting, "you won't come out, oh, you'll never come out" (17). This is the Merlin/Vivien story in modern guise. Ultimately, we recognize in him many of the hallowed qualities of "courtly love," especially a self-defeating love of the state of being in love. An allegorical emphasis is also underlined by the name of the girl's father, Adam Vere (one recalls Keats on Adam's dream: "he awoke and found it truth"). Commentators have registered the allegory, of course, but none that I know has made the necessary literary-critical point that this *insistent* stress on a larger meaning seriously weakens the effectiveness of the story. Arthur Merlin is so weighed down by the allegorical baggage associated with his name that it is difficult to accept him as an individual human being. The realistic level of the story is in this case severely compromised by the super-realistic stress. The young Hood had a penchant for this kind of effect. Even in *Around the Mountain*, where the two levels are in general deftly balanced, and the cast of characters includes some of Hood's friends and relatives presented under their own names, there is a daunting reference to a "Professor Bonbourgeois" (66).

Hood makes a notable advance in reconciling allegory and realism in the name story of his first volume. The story has been discussed from the allegorical viewpoint by Garebian and in even more detail by John Mills. I would merely observe that the allegorical aspect is hinted at with a remarkable delicacy. Here, and continually in his later work, Hood exploits the fact that allegory, in the words of Maureen Quilligan, "presupposed a potential sacralizing power of language" (156). I'm not fully convinced that Fred Calvert's surname is necessarily chosen to echo Calvary (Garebian 14), but the linkage is available for those who like that kind of thing. The implications only become fully explicit when Fred notices how kite-flying is regarded as "somehow holy," as a "natural symbol" (178); Hood is therefore employing this image (or, rather, emblem) in much the same way (though to very different effect) as Mitchell in *The Kite*, which appeared within a month or so of Hood's collection. Later, though there are few elements that could be unequivocally designated "super-realistic," a sufficient number of references indicate that the simple story is continually impinging on a sacramental dimension. These include Fred's eventually finding "the right sign" (177) at which to wait for his bus; passing a cemetery; mention of obligations and a promise; the physical act of going up the mountain; the emphasis on the colour red (suggesting blood, wine, life) in the raspberry-juice on the daughter's lips and the colour of the kite rising on invisible currents of air. As a result, we are inclined as readers to side with Fred against the "spoiled priest" (183) who sees all as a "sham" (181). The psychological movement on Fred's part from depression to exaltation is recognized as valid and significant without any undue insistence on symbolic meanings.

In his first published novel, *White Figure, White Ground* (1964), Hood attempts to master similar problems on a larger scale. He has consistently discussed the novel in terms of allegory (Struthers "Interview" 57, Mills "Anagogical" 102), and critics have often followed his cue and emphasized allegorical meaning and its quite rigid formal qualities (three sections of eight chapters each, of which the fourth is always contemplative, a total of twenty-four like the "Flawed Crystals" sequence painted by his artist-hero). Moreover, it is easy to become absorbed by the colour symbolism, by the obviously meaningful names of the aunts Blanche and Claire, and so on. Garebian begins his allegorically oriented discussion by complaining of other critics who regard the novel as "a story about an artist's aesthetic problems" (54). But the fact is that, whatever Hood's intentions may have been, the enduring interest in the book is indeed to be found in Alex's agonized wrestling with the demands of his art. *White Figure, White Ground* is an absorbing and intriguing novel, but the artistic theme is never successfully integrated with the plot of Gothic mystery in Nova Scotia which constantly threatens to collapse into the banal. Hood defends the relation between theme and plot at one point with the interesting argument that the book is about Alex's search for a father on the plot level and the sun as father or "light-source" in his painting (Cloutier 51). This, however, is an "intellectual" connection (not unlike Mitchell's defence of the unity of *The Vanishing Point*) that may be applied to the book but does not arise readily or naturally out of it. Similarly, although it is divided so neatly into three named sections — "Barringford," "Toronto," and "Montreal" — the narrative refuses to fit comfortably into these divisions (the "Toronto" section is especially forced); in addition, while it is true that each section contains eight chapters, one does not feel a structural logic here — the pattern seems imposed by the novelist rather than required by the terms of the story. It is clear that Hood has not solved his technical and formal problems at this early stage.

He is much more successful in *Around the Mountain*, a collection of linked short stories set in Montreal. Here the formal strategies are obvious and readily accessible. The book is offered as a celebration of Montreal life, and is suitably divided in terms of time and space: the twelve stories move through the calendar from winter to winter, and each is set in a different section of the city so that, in the course of reading, we encircle Mount Royal as the title suggests. Whether one can trace allegorical or structural patterns further is open to doubt. Personally, I do not find it useful to view the spatial movement as a purgatorial process, and although Monsieur Bourbonnais' cancer in the June story suggests a zodiacal allusion it is difficult to see how such an approach could be applied consistently. That surely is a false trail. More important is the fact that the topographical patterning provides a convenient setting for each individual tale that can develop its own subject, tone, and form. Above all, Hood provides a flexible narrator, close to his own character and attitudes but not dependent upon them, whose voice (all but one of the stories is in the first person) ensures a stylistic unity. Often, as in "Le Grand Déménagement," the speaker and his meditations (compare the later *New Age* series) are more important than the story itself.

Especially significant are the first signs of another practice that will become central in *The New Age*: a technique whereby the narrative movement follows the protagonist's mind rather than his actions in time. An excellent example occurs in the opening story "The Sportive Centre of Saint Vincent de Paul." Driving to a hockey-rink with a friend (the painter and amateur hockey-player Seymour Segal, subject of Hood's *Scoring*, so a clear indication of the closeness of author and speaker), the narrator makes a right turn "onto Pie-IX" (5). There follow two paragraphs in which he meditates about the immediate area, the first Vatican Council, Papal Infallibility, the influence of Catholicism, and the process of naming, before we return to the drive through the city. Such a technique is not, of course, unprecedented; behind it, as so often in Hood, lies the shadow of Marcel Proust (whose protagonist, Marcel but not Proust, doubtless contributed to Hood's author-narrator connection). Similar substitutions of psychological for clock time are to be found in writers like Joyce and Woolf, not to mention Wordsworth and his "spots of time." But Hood adapts the technique to contain his own brand of intellectual appreciation and analysis of the things of this world, that can extend in range from theories of art through geographical speculations to car designs and women's fashions. This strategy, seen in a short and simple instance here and repeated from time to time in *Around the Mountain*, becomes central and often structurally complex in *The Swing in the Garden* and later novels.

Yet another stylistic feature becomes noticeable here. As early as "O Happy Melodist!" in *Flying a Red Kite* Hood had experimented with the intimate, insinuating second-person construction ("... that damned inconvenient floor-lamp shaped like a spear, the kind of thing that you might see in a production of *Macbeth* in Central Park" [19]); in *Around the Mountain* it becomes habitual as the narrator regularly becomes a tour-guide personally and colloquially drawing attention to the features of his city:

144

Going east past Christophe-Colomb towards de Lanaudière, Fabre, past des Érables and Parthenais, you discover small enclaves which are clearly the homes of comfortable older citizens. . . .

Ah, but Henri-Julien, Drôlet, that's the real thing. (21)

That passage is from the opening page of "Light Shining Out of Darkness," which provides an excellent instance of Hood's stylistic flexibility. After a relaxed, conversational chat about the social and architectural features of a particular part of the city, there follows a tavern scene full of colloquial dialogue, and then another narrative sequence with many of Hood's characteristic verbal contractions — "Where Tom lives you can't park" (28), "On the third-floor platform, right at the top, you're apt to feel slightly dizzy" (29). But as soon as the narrator enters Tom's apartment and experiences a moving Wordsworthian spot of time when confronted by the collection of model ships, the mood and style change. The contracted verb-forms and vernacular expressions vanish, and are replaced by a much more formal, elevated tone appropriate to the occasion. The story has moved on to a higher level of significance, but Hood does not enforce an "allegorical" meaning. The references are exalted — "a calm scene like this, a rounded period in the life of the imagination" (30), "I was mysteriously overwhelmed by this various and splendid sight . . . . my suspicions of the possibility of goodness . . . " (31). Like the biblical allusion in the title, these are not forcefully aligned with a dogmatic or sectarian value-system. We are left with the flexible resonances of a scene that implies a deeper meaning without asserting its particular nature.

A full examination of Hood's allegorical and stylistic procedures would require a book-length study. I must confine myself henceforth to some of the more notable instances. In the novel *The Camera Always Lies* (1967), Hood takes as his "pre-text" both the conventions of Hollywood romance and what he sees as the representative behaviour of the purveyors of this form of popular entertainment; his allegorical method takes the form of telling the story according to the sanctioned principles of traditional Romance. Rose Leclair, a no longer young film star, finds her marriage destroyed and her reputation as an actress compromised by the corrupt politics of the filmmakers, and attempts suicide. Her "drift towards death" (Hood quotes D.H. Lawrence's well-known phrase about *Sons and Lovers* as his epigraph) is interrupted by the appearance of Jean-Pierre Fauré, a genuine artist within the medium, who acts Orpheus to Rose's Eurydice, and improves upon that particular pre-text by successfully restoring her to life and happiness. Many of the reviewers, however, proved incapable of distinguishing between true and false romance, or of recognizing Hood's setting-up of the one against the other, and accused him of writing in an outdated and simplistic genre. While this was clearly unfair, Hood just as clearly experienced difficulties in controlling his intricate scheme. His ironic naming of the "good" heroine Rose (an obvious anagram of Eros) and the sexpot Charity sets up a confusing binary opposition which militates against complexity, just as his coat-trailing title stacks the cards against acceptance of his genuine film-maker hero. Moreover, the allegorical level blends imperfectly with the minimal realistic requirements of the basic plot. The morally upright Fauré, with his orthodox Catholicism, appears as an unlikely figure at even the "artistic" extreme of the film-industry, while the theological escape-hatch that eventually enables him to marry Rose despite her previous divorce, like the resolution to the "incest-theme" in *White Figure, White Ground*, is offered too easily. Once again, we find Hood entangled in the problem of combining his realistic and allegorical modes.

This reconciliation is found more readily, at least in his earlier years, within the short-story form. Even here, however, he is sometimes impelled to assert a meaning that is far from obvious. An especially blatant instance occurs in the name-story of *The Fruit Man, the Meat Man & the Manager*. A "simple" reading reveals a touching "human" narrative about relations between store-keepers and customers in a poor district of Montreal, and the commercial rivalry between small businesses and chain-stores. But Hood asserts a larger meaning:

> The Fruit Man is God proffering the apple, and the Meat Man is Christ incarnate, and the Manager is the Holy Spirit moving the world. The Manager manages the world, the Meat Man offers himself to us to eat, and the Fruit Man places the knowledge of good and evil in the middle of paradise and tells us not to strive too high for it. (Struthers "Interview" 38)

This seems awkwardly at odds with a "straight" meaning. Why, for

146

example, should the representative of the Holy Spirit take care of the beer and be "a shrewd judge of credit" (188)? Mendel Greenspon the meat man does *not* "offer himself for us to eat" in the story. I do not see how the Fruit Man's giving Mrs. Cummings's child two pears makes him an emblem of God the Father. (Susan Copoloff-Mechanic's reference to an erudite symbolism in which "pears symbolize Christ's love for mankind" [91] may or may not be alluded to, but it isn't "realized" in the text.) Moreover, the fact that the Meat Man and the Fruit Man take on jobs in more prosperous stores without telling the Manager might suggest a strained analogue to the war in Heaven but represents a bothersome split within the Trinity. Hood's superimposed allegory here confuses the story more than it elucidates it. In much the same way, he insists in his "prefatory note" to the collection that the first three stories ("Getting to Williams-town," "The Tolstoy Pitch," and "A Solitary Ewe") constitute "a deliberately-related triptych. Human art and love are models of immortality" (6). But this is forced. It seems a weak insight to be drawn from stories that, in themselves and by themselves, have so much to offer.[2]

Hood is much more successful in the final story of *Dark Glasses* (1976) with the appropriate title "An Allegory of Man's Fate" — appropriate because the title itself, and not an extrinsic commentary, signals his allegorical intention and warns us against confining our reading to a literal level. We must, however, start there. Bronson, about whom all we know is that he has a wife and family and is rich enough to live in a city but maintain a lakeside summer cottage, decides on impulse to buy a boat-building kit. He intends to assemble it over the winter in town, but the task proves more complex and time-consuming. In fact, it takes his wife and himself most of the summer, and causes physical aches and pains as well as a good deal of mental irritation and ill-temper. After a number of misadventures they succeed, but not until another season has gone by. The story ends with one of Hood's succinct one-sentence paragraphs: "The next summer, reaching and running on his blue lake, Bronson remembered nothing of what had passed" (143). Whether the memories of the rest of the family were keener is not recorded.

If we take up the hint of the title, Dante's fourfold level of interpretation can readily be applied to the story. While the literal meaning is merely an account of building a boat somewhere in eastern Canada, the moral meaning clearly concerns the virtues of doggedness and endurance. "There is no difficulty that cannot be overcome," as Bronson says several times in the course of the action, its tone varying in context from the banal to something approaching the triumphant. In a morally oriented commentary directed to students, Hood simplified to the extent of maintaining that the story is "about hanging in there and finishing what you've started" (*Trusting* 35). The allegorical level is a little more elusive, though here I find it easy enough to accept Hood's extra-textual hint and to associate the story with Noah's building of the ark (Bronson's tiffs with his wife recall the traditional marital discord between Noah and Mrs. Noah in the medieval mystery-plays). A little further from the obvious are other archetypal analogues that Hood lists (Struthers "Interview" 32), including Christ and his disciples on the Sea of Galilee; the Ulysses of Homer, Dante, and Tennyson; the Anglo-Saxon *Seafarer*; Pound's first canto, etc. So far as the anagogical level is concerned, the phrase "Man's Fate" offers a clue to its ultimate representativeness, as does Bronson's seeing the whole building process as a "rude parody of the conditions of human existence" (141). All these potential correspondences may not be necessary for understanding, but they enhance the richness of the story's structure and place it within an appropriate intellectual context.

Hood also emphasizes his stylistic flexibility in this story. "An Allegory of Man's Fate" is communicated for the most part in a clear, compact, dignified prose, but at various points it opens up to embrace other effects. When the delivery van arrives, we catch a hint of the moving-men's language: "the driver and his helper were inclined to bugger off at once" (130). A little later, Bronson "hove into view — the nautical expression seems appropriate" (130–31), where the suggestion of self-conscious pomposity is also apt. At other points, as we might expect from Hood, the prose is transmuted by words that carry a religious application ("they covered the tabernacle. . . . The actual unveiling took place . . . " [136]) or even a biblical tone ("an exceeding great multitude" [138]). More importantly, in terms of this particular story, the narrative takes over a technical vocabulary as the Bronsons gradually master the jargon of boat-building. Much fun is derived from the strange words — "Boom-kicking-strap-chock" (139), etc. — but by the end the technical words come naturally: "Screwed on oarlocks, pintles, eyes, varnished, varnished, sanded, painted, sanded,

painted, painted, painted, painted . . . rigged. Hoisted their burgee"
(143). Much of the aesthetic effect, then, derives from levels of language as well as levels of meaning.

"An Allegory of Man's Fate" first appeared in the *Journal of Canadian Fiction* in 1974, a year before the publication of *The Swing in the Garden*, the opening volume of *The New Age/Le nouveau siècle*. This is Hood's overall name for the twelve-book series which is due to close in the year 2000 (possibly with a volume entitled *The Canadian Style*), and promises to provide a social and mythic panorama of Canada in the twentieth century. "My book," he told Cloutier, "will try to define the mythos of Canadian life" (52). Hood is reported to have sketched out the series as early as 1968, and by 1976 the dates of publication as well as most of the titles of the volumes had been announced. It is clearly a monumental undertaking. Some critics are confident that this will represent the peak of Hood's achievement, while others persist in preferring his short stories. His plan to intersperse volumes of the *New Age* series with collections of shorter fiction may or may not satisfy both groups. Although it would be premature at this stage to judge the success (or even to chart the progress) of the series as a whole, it is fair to regard Hood's early experimentation, both in fiction and non-fiction, as a preparation for this vast work. Certainly the increasing formal and stylistic flexibility that I have been documenting becomes an essential factor here.

The New Age is frequently and accurately described as a *roman fleuve*, a loosely organized, flowing series that allows many varieties of literary effect to co-exist within it. Hood's challenge was to combine this with his devotion to allegory, one of the least flexible of literary modes. He needed to find a way of writing in which something close to Dante's levels of interpretation might be achieved so that the various levels could be appreciated simultaneously rather than representing separate alternatives. Ideally, if he is to be both "realist" and "transcendentalist allegorist," the garden in *The Swing in the Garden* should be an actual Toronto backyard as well as an image of Eden; the swing should suggest a real swing but also, in Hood's words, "the cyclical movement of the fall from the original One into individuation and the return from the fall to the original unity" (Cloutier 52). Matt Goderich's childhood, fully realized in an identifiable time and place, should be able to communicate the essence of *all* childhood. The incidents that contribute to his growth should be equally specific and representative.

Hood is able to succeed in this, at least in part, by introducing the concept of levels as an image within the writing itself. This imagery is touched on only faintly in *The Swing in the Garden*. We register a hint of it in the following passage: "The government of the day, that is, Mr. King, invited the King [to Canada], the sort of confusion of names and of *levels of existence* that can tease the mind for generations" (134; my emphases). In *A New Athens*, levels of existence are presented both literally and metaphorically as conspicuous facts of life. Thus Matt detects the traces of an earlier period (the course of the railway) still visible under the "layers of resurfacing" on the highway (7). This constitutes a sign of the continual impinging of past upon present. As he comments later in *The Motor Boys in Ottawa*, "History is the great example of the residence of earlier things in later things" (203). In *A New Athens* itself, where the literal raising of the ghost-ship from the riverbed is an intriguing example of the process, analogues are found in the surviving Forthton station and even in the history of changing names (the Victorian Macadamized Road, displaced but still retrievable by antiquarians as the original designation of Highway 29, and returning us ultimately to the inhabitant of that first garden; the human sense of continuity symbolized by the historical change of placename from Farmersville to Athens). It is all summed up in an eloquent evocation of human strata: "layer on layer on layer on less discernible layer on faint mark on mere suspected prehistoric spume of cross-hatched human purposes" (11).

Similarly, at the end of *Reservoir Ravine*, where the reservoir still exists beneath the recent man-made surface of the park, Matt is jolted into recalling his childhood in the place that is now literally under his feet. He is shocked by this change in the landscape, but as readers we are gratified to note that the concealed springs of memory can still be tapped. Matt himself realizes that "a reservoir is a form of memory" (221). Other levels of reality are evoked in the curious space-time divisions in *Black and White Keys*, where the wrestling sequence is eventually seen as a bizarre displaced allegory of World War II that heightens the impact of the German scenes involving Matt's father. The list could be extended.

Just as meaning, for Hood, is to be found beneath the surface of story, so form is not confined to the mere shaping of plot. It may be found in recurrent imagery, in the regular introduction of related ideas, and even, more subtly, in recognizing the patterns endemic to human life, patterns that are revealed within the subject-matter, not imposed arbitrarily upon it. Early in *The Swing in the Garden*, for instance, Matt refers to "[f]ilaments of connection" (36) that linked him with neighbourhood families even before he was born, and later, in one of his discourses on art, he argues that "pieces of art serve as ligatures to tie discrete experiences together through time and place" (100) — an apt description of Hood's own artistic procedures. In *Reservoir Ravine* this becomes "a tough network of analogies and nerves, . . . binding all of being together in a continually sliding, self-adjusting set of relations" (204). Throughout his work, Hood imitates not only "ordinary life" but the way things connect within the human mind. He is concerned, in Matt's words from *The Swing in the Garden*, with the "directly experienced *structure* of an individually lived life" (67; my emphasis). This "structure" is, as it were, provided by the human condition and, through God's grace, by the human imagination. Hood sees imagination — especially the artistic imagination — as "synthesizing" (Struthers "Interview" 29).

Ultimately, of course, it is Matt's mind that unifies the series. The invention of Matt Goderich is obviously crucial to the whole scheme. While Hood himself possessed a number of characteristics that made him capable of forming the central consciousness for such a work — notably his bilingualism as the product of an English-Canadian father and French-Canadian mother, his family connections with Nova Scotia, and his Catholicism that facilitates a unified world-view — he saw the need to augment these circumstances in the interests of greater comprehensiveness. Thus Hood's own father was involved in banking (and was the source for much of the financial background to *Reservoir Ravine*); but in making Matt's father a philosopher, a university teacher, and later a member of parliament, Hood creates a decidedly broader social and intellectual background. In *The Scenic Art*, Matt realized that his performance in small parts while acting at university gave him "the status of onlooker" (59), and this role — his version of Davies's "fifth business" — is assigned to him in the series as a whole. In addition, Hood makes Matt an art-historian, thus rendering more credible his understanding of the earlier years of the century and also providing him with both the excuse and the ability to think about and explain the age in which he finds himself.

Most important of all, perhaps, is the conception that links Matt's personal story with the history of Canada, and enables Hood to introduce into his text material that has normally been considered beyond the bounds of fiction. By concentrating the interest, at least initially, on Matt Goderich, Hood is able to make Matt's interests the central subject. Fictional content is thus expanded to take in material usually associated with philosophy, history, politics, theology, and aesthetic theory. Commentators have often been curiously narrow in failing to realize that these ostensibly "non-fiction" elements, so easily dismissed as irrelevant or didactic, are in fact the central experience of a daringly new literary form.[3] Hood's innovative contribution to fiction is in fact most prominent here. In *The Swing in the Garden*, fiction takes over from autobiographical memoir to provide an unparalleled recreation of social history in the Depression era; in *A New Athens* the form of the novel is not the standard fictional structure but an essentially visionary form (comparable to "Mrs. Codrington's twelve wonderful works" [*Scenic Art* 178], themselves analogues to the projected whole of the *New Age* series); *The Motor Boys in Ottawa* becomes an intricate *mélange* of fictional story and high-class political journalism. These novels are not so much the stories of individual lives as "lived history" (*Swing* 75), and an imaginative demonstration of how concepts, attitudes, and experiences come together in a perceptive individual mind.

Commentators have tended to criticize Matt as a pompous prig, though this is probably no more than a reflection of the prejudice against the thoughtful bourgeois which is one of the more tiresome fashions of our time. He is, of course, a semi-allegorical figure, as his name suggests. Matthew, we should remember, is the most allegorically inclined of the evangelists (Sam Solecki has wittily broken down the name into "Matt-Hugh" ["Gospel" 38], but this need not perhaps be taken too seriously). His namesake provides a suitable middle-class middle-view of "God's kingdom." Part of the critics' impatience with him stems, I suspect, from a basic philosophical disagreement. Like Davies, Hood needs a protagonist who is passionately concerned with ideas; moreover, as he told Victoria Hale before initiating the series, he was "interested in the hero as a virtuous person," believing that "virtue, good conduct, is the most important focus of our activities" (36). Hood has an inalienable right to this viewpoint, but it raises an important complication. As Solecki has pointed out, it is possible that "in this period of Canadian history readers will simply not respond to a writer with an explicitly Catholic world-view" ("Songs" 30). There is no resolution possible here. I had better state, however, as a non-Catholic, that although I am frequently in disagreement with Matt's opinionated stances on subjects ranging from art through politics to religious issues, I find him an engaging figure whose genuine intellectual concern is impressive, credible, and even endearing. We are intended, surely, to be amused at Matt, as we are amused at ourselves in our more clear-sighted moments, but his good-natured, earnest decency makes him a companionable guide to a significant part of the Canadian psyche.

It is clear, however, that Hood has had misgivings about Matt's critical reception. Increasingly, he has tended to mitigate Matt's earnestness by making him perceive, and react against, his own pretensions. He is therefore "poor silly Matthew Goderich" in *A New Athens* (159), a "tedious old bore" in *Reservoir Ravine* (205), and subject to a whole string of epithets in *The Motor Boys in Ottawa*: "a bit of a fuddy-duddy" (29), "dull and stupid and out of things" (150), "confused, vacillating" (222). In *Tony's Book* the break-up of his marriage, obscurely hinted at as early as the end of *Reservoir Ravine*, may be interpreted as a drastic way of distinguishing Matt from his creator. As early as the 1975 interview with Robert Fulford Hood had threatened to "shift" away from him if, half-way, "people are getting tired of Matt" (70). I for one hope that this doesn't happen, because *The New Age* is not merely an anatomy of Canada in the twentieth century but an extraordinarily ambitious demonstration of how a human being develops in physical, moral, intellectual, and spiritual or religious terms.

Perhaps that is as far as anyone can safely venture at the present time. As I write, *The New Age* is barely more than half-complete, but already we can see that generalizations about its scope and intention can be quickly outdated. Thus, a number of reviewers complained that Hood was incapable of facing up to the problem of evil in our time, only to be confronted with the Dachau sections of *Black and White Keys*. As yet we have seen little of French Canada, but Hood is uniquely qualified to present the other solitude to English-speaking readers, and there are definite signs (including the Goderiches' move to Montreal in *The Motor Boys in Ottawa*) to suggest that this desideratum will indeed be provided. It is true that western Canadians have reason for doubting if the series will be as comprehensive in its coverage as is sometimes claimed, though Hood may yet surprise us. But even if he doesn't, even if the series remains a vision of Canada from the viewpoint of a middle-class resident of Ontario and Québec, that in itself will be no mean achievement. After all, even Proust did not encompass the whole of France and French society.

Perhaps the best approach to *The New Age* is a determination to avoid reading it with preconceived ideas about what kind of fiction it is — even, indeed, to avoid the assumption that it can be subsumed under one category of fiction at all. Hood himself is at pains to discourage us — rightly, I think — from seeing him as a novelist in any traditional sense. As he told Mills, "I am writing things that look like novels but are only tenuously related to the form" ("Hugh Hood" 140). Ideally, perhaps, *The New Age* should be teaching us how to read it even as it proceeds, teaching us above all to be flexible in our aesthetic responses. *The Swing in the Garden*, for instance, creates the illusion of autobiography rather than fiction; it does not have the feel of a novel, and suggests recollection rather than creation. But in fact Matt Goderich is a genuine fictional construct, a point to be insisted on even if we acknowledge that Hood's emphasis on a separation between himself and Matt may be exaggerated. And *A New Athens*, with its Proustian shifts and uniquely Hoodian colloquial meditations, is different again, as are the subsequent books. It is tempting, indeed, to approach the series as if it were *Around the Mountain* extended to epic scale, with each story expanded to the size of a novel, the time sequence enlarged from a year to a century, and the geographical setting encircling not just a city but a large segment (if not the whole) of Canada. It already seems likely that it will comprise, as Hood promised Fulford, "an enormous image, an enormous social mythology, an enormous prism to rotate, to see yourself and your neighbours and friends and your grandparents" (68). It may even, though this is less clear, ultimately add up to "one huge novel . . . , the one bright book of the redemption and atonement" ("Hugh Hood" 137). But for that we must wait expectantly until AD 2000.

CHAPTER 9

Alice Munro

There is now general agreement about Alice Munro's chief characteristics as a writer. Most often discussed are her fascination with what
she has called "the surface of life" and her need to "get at the exact
tone or texture of how things are" (Gibson 241). This particular form
of realism, however, is concerned not with photographical fidelity
but with communicating her sense of the mysteriousness and complexity of so-called "ordinary life." Helen Hoy has written perceptively of Munro's "matter-of-fact union of incompatible tendencies"
and her sense of reality as "inherently contradictory" (103, 107). This
in turn leads to a consideration of her prose-style, especially with its
way of communicating a jolting surprise by paradoxically establishing precision through oxymoron, the startling juxtaposition of words
with apparently contradictory meanings. Other important aspects of
her work, now well documented, include her blending of the Gothic
with the humdrum; her continuing impulsion to recreate and reinter-
pret the constraining rural world of south-west Ontario; her balancing of "then" against "nowadays," generally an oppressive but
ordered past against a permissive but chaotic present; her psychological penetration (Hood has called her "[t]he great psychological
novelist in Canada" [Struthers "Interview" 58]).

This consensus about what is central in Munro's work does not
mean, however, that it presents no literary-critical difficulties. On the
contrary, because she delves so deeply into the contradictory and

paradoxical, considerable problems relating to interpretation and evaluation tend to arise. A reading of the ever-increasing literary commentary shows not merely that different readers respond to her work in radically different ways but that disagreement exists over the basic meaning of what she writes. While praise is generally expressed concerning the skillful precision and subtle nuances of her prose, this does not apparently prevent the confident assertion by critics of totally opposed interpretations of her fiction. An obvious starting-point for a discussion of the unique qualities of her art is to ask why this should be so.

A climactic moment in Geoff Hancock's 1982 interview with Munro occurs at the point where Hancock asks — rather naïvely, we may think — if Munro embeds lessons into her stories. She replies: "Ahhhh! No lessons. No lessons *ever*" (222–23). Similar responses are found in other interviews. To Alan Twigg she agreed that there is "no preaching for any particular morality or politics" in her books (15); when Harold Horwood asked if she wrote with the intention of conveying any kind of message, she replied simply "No" (134); and in the 1986 interview conducted by *What* magazine, she remarks at one point: ". . . here I sound as if I'm moralizing, and I've always said that there's no morality at all about writing" (Connolly n. pag.). The earlier remarks could be construed as implying merely that she avoids the conspicuously didactic, but to argue that "there's no morality at all about writing" is a very different matter. Can she mean this literally? Some comments elsewhere seem to suggest so. Most notable is an extraordinary remark to Hancock about the "Royal Beatings" section of *Who Do You Think You Are?*: ". . . in the story about the child being beaten, I didn't make any judgments about whether beating children was a horrifying thing" (213). Perhaps not, but she cannot expect readers to approach the scene without certain entrenched moral preconceptions that will either be challenged or reaffirmed by the vividness of the incident. Indeed, she could hardly have chosen a less appropriate scene to cite in an argument (however doomed) for moral neutrality.

It is true, of course, that Munro's stories rarely depend upon a direct and unequivocal moral commitment. "The Shining Houses," an early story from *Dance of the Happy Shades*, is the only clear instance. Here a moral polarity is set up between Mrs. Fullerton, the long-term resident living in an old, shabby, broken-down house, and the new inhabitants of a modern subdivision who want her home demolished as a blot on the landscape that detracts from their property-values. The story centres on Mary, a new inhabitant with an acute but possibly sentimental moral conscience who cannot accept her neighbours' lobbying and refuses to sign their petition. A moral problem is raised and debated, but no resolution is possible in human (as distinct from legal) terms. Our emotions favour Mary and Mrs. Fullerton yet, because we are familiar with the ways of our world, we know what the outcome will be. This is an effective story in its own right, but within Munro's work it is a decided anomaly.

For a more typical and immeasurably more complex instance, we may turn to a speech in Munro's second book which is probably the best-known passage in all her writing:

"'There's a change coming I think in the lives of girls and women. Yes. But it is up to us to make it come. All women have had up till now has been their connection with men. All we have had. No more lives of our own, really, than domestic animals." (*Lives* 146–47)

Superficially, this sounds like a feminist "lesson" and is continually being quoted as such. Yet in context the passage is surrounded with entangling factors that qualify any considered response. Most obviously, the speech is given to Del Jordan's mother, who is presented throughout the book in terms that verge on the ludicrous. Within a few lines of this passage Del "places" her mother's reliability with the deflating comment, "That was how much she knew me" (147), and later in the novel she remarks: "my attitude towards everything my mother said became one of skepticism and disdain" (202). In this case, moreover, Munro has been quite specific about her intentions: "I meant that to be ironic . . . I didn't mean to make fun of her. But I meant her vision to be quite inadequate" (Hancock 214–15). On the other hand, she has enshrined the phrase in the title of both section and book, and has thereby given it prominence and an implied authority.

In this instance, the complexity created around the passage proves rich in resonances, ambiguity adding to the overall subtlety. A moral question is certainly raised, even if it needs to be distinguished from the straightforward feminist viewpoint that Mrs. Jordan expresses. A trickier instance occurs right at the end of the "Lives of Girls and

157

Women" section, where Del objects to the underlying assumption beneath her mother's attitude that "being female made you damage-able." Del resents this: ". . . men were supposed to be able to go out and take on all kinds of experiences and shuck off what they didn't want and come back proud. Without even thinking about it, I had decided to do the same" (147). Many readers, I suspect, accept that statement at face-value because it chimes with their own views (or wishes) and they want it to be true. But is it true? Do men — can men — "shuck off" what is undesirable so easily? As Nancy I. Bailey has noted, "the males in the novel do not correspond to Del's des-cription" (113), and I have grave doubts whether the generalization would pass muster in what Del calls "real life." Moreover, if one reads the passage carefully, one finds indications that Munro has inserted qualifications into Del's statement: "men *were supposed to be able . . . Without even thinking about it*, I had decided to do the same." Munro is surely detached from Del here; indeed, the older narrating Del seems detached from her own adolescent self. We are certainly free, as readers, to register some irony at this point; later, at the end of "Baptizing," when Del tries to "shuck off" her failure to gain a scholarship and her ultimately frustrating experience with Garnet French, a similarly ironic reading is available. But, whether we read it "straight" or at an ironic remove, a moral attitude is equally involved in our exercise of aesthetic judgement.

In some cases, the conspicuous refusal to hint at any moral comment can be deeply troubling. The most disturbing instance in Munro's work to date is certainly the notorious closing page of "Mischief" in *Who Do You Think You Are?*. Rose has for some time been conduct-ing a covert love-affair with the husband of her friend Jocelyn, but adultery has not taken place. Suddenly, after a drunken party, the two have sexual intercourse with Jocelyn looking on, almost cheering from the side-lines. What are we to make of this? One suspects a touch of *épater le bourgeois* here, though my own response (for what it's worth) is to find the scene vulgarly crass rather than shocking. The next morning, Rose is disgusted, and decides to cut connections with both of them. Laurence Mathews, who has written maturely and intelligently about this scene, comments that the reader "feels entitled to ruminate complacently about Rose's moral education" (188), though I see nothing complacent about a firm moral judgement at this point. But then, as Mathews notes, Munro adds a final, disorienting sentence: "Sometime later she decided to go on being friends with Clifford and Jocelyn, because she needed such friends occasionally, at that stage of her life" (132). What do we make of *that*?

Mathews writes well about Rose's selfishness, her advocating "a sort of consumerism with respect to personal relationships," her apparent lack of awareness of the similarities between herself and her two "friends" (189). For my part, however, I cannot stop there. The last sentence *is* shocking. That Rose should get herself into such a situation in the first place is disturbing; that she should just shuck it off like the adolescent Del seems unforgivable. Commentators appear reluctant to face up to the implications here. Gerald Noonan argues that the whole story "shows how life contradicts the expectations of art" (165), but, however realistically convincing Munro may be, the story remains art and not life. Mathews himself is content to categorize this art as "rooted in skepticism about, even hostility towards, the kind of 'truth' which most literature claims to deliver" (190), and then moves on to other things. W.R. Martin (who sidesteps the crucial last sentence) argues that in the final stories Rose "is now clearly . . . a whole and mature person" (119), a judgement I cannot accept since this scene, and others like it, imply the opposite. The final sentence reads to me like a superficially clever but ultimately unsatisfying technical trick (I shall return to the subject of "tricks" later), a way of creating a shock ending that is unpredictable, jolting, and intellectually defiant. But moral and aesthetic judgements cannot be separated here. To attempt a non-committal stance is to be damagingly evasive. It is not merely that we suspect Munro of covertly defending (or at the very least refusing openly to condemn) an action that seems irresponsible and even repellant; there is also the moral element that exists within her decision to employ such an ending. We find ourselves judging three contentious issues: a fictional character's actions, a writer's presentation of that action in moral terms; and that same writer's artistic success (or failure). Individual readers must make up their own minds on these points, and there is obviously room for differences of opinion. But what cannot, I think, be denied is the fact that moral discrimination and artistic success are inextricably interwoven here, and that we cannot offer a judgement on the one without committing ourselves to a judgement about the other.

Although I do not consider it possible to present an action, especially a highly controversial action, without any moral purpose,

Munro's apparent attempt to do so has an extremely important artistic consequence. If she wants us to respond to such a scene without any more judgement, or refuses to accept that her own attitudes are of any concern to her readers, one wonders how she can object to or deny *any* interpretation of her work, however perverse. Is misreading even possible in a morally neutral universe? Suppose, for example, that one chose to interpret a story as dead-pan satire and argued that it was in fact upholding the old-fashioned bourgeois virtues, could Munro legitimately complain? As a matter of fact she has, wittingly or unwittingly, answered this question in the negative. In "The Colonel's Hash Resettled," she allows herself the following sweeping statement: "What you write is an offering; anybody can come and take what they like from it" (181). The implications here are as inescapable as they are staggering.

At this point, however, we may need to consider the possibility that this represents a shrewd artistic strategy on Munro's part. If individuals are indeed free to take what they like from any fictional offering, the chances of pleasing a wide range of readership are thereby enhanced. In such a case, feminist readers may take Mrs. Jordan's speech about the lives of girls and women at face-value, while those who are open to irony may indulge their preference. There is something decidedly troubling about this suggestion, but it may well explain the unusual breadth of Munro's readership. Let us take as a test-case the closing pages of *Lives of Girls and Women*, the end of "Baptizing" and the short "Epilogue." What is the range of "reader-response" available here? First, of course, there are always readers like Naomi looking for "a part in the book where they do it" (100); the scene in which Del loses her virginity among the blood-red peonies will, to some extent, satisfy them. (Others will doubtless latch on to it in the interests of censorship.) Some will respond to the "escape to the big city" theme; others will appreciate the defiance of conventional moral and religious restraints. Close readers will be able to congratulate themselves on their subtlety in recognizing Del's continuing naïveté as expressed in her charming but pathetic faith that "the future could be furnished without love or scholarships" and her callow vision of "getting on a bus, like girls in movies leaving home" and so entering into "real life" (200–01). Finally, of course, the post-modernists can have a field-day with the metafictional possibilities of the "Epilogue." Munro can thus be seen as all things to all men

160

— and, needless to say, to all women. However, although this range of response may explain Munro's prestige at the present time, her permanent position with Canadian fiction will be established by other criteria.

If Munro's attitude to moral judgement is decidedly ambivalent, so is her attitude to the fictive aspects of story, a subject best explored by way of the metafictional epilogue just mentioned. At the close of her adolescence, circumstances cause Del to recall the novel she had planned in her early teens, based on the local Sherriff family. This family had, in the created "reality" of *Lives of Girls and Women* itself, experienced more than its share of sensational events: the elder brother had become an alcoholic, the younger was in an insane asylum, the sister had committed suicide. Interestingly enough, when Del begins to adapt this reality for her own fictional purposes, she feels the need to simplify the plot-line, since "three tragic destinies were too much even for a book" (204). But she makes other alterations as well, seemingly in the opposite direction of heightened melodrama, which as discriminating readers we can recognize as belonging to the conventions of Gothic fiction in which she is writing. Thus the head of the family is changed from a storekeeper to a judge because Del knows from her reading "that in the families of judges, as of great landowners, degeneracy and madness were things to be counted on"; for comparable reasons, their house is transformed from a "mustard-coloured stucco bungalow" to "a towered brick house with long narrow windows and a *porte cochère*," surrounded by Gothic-style topiary (203). Jubilee, the local community, is similarly Gothicized: "It became an older, darker, more decaying town" (205). The daughter becomes, of course, the central figure and represents an adolescent's sexual fantasy:

> She bestowed her gifts capriciously on men. . . . But her generosity mocked them, her *bittersweet flesh, the colour of peeled almonds*, burned men down quickly and left a taste of death. She was a sacrifice, spread for sex on moldy uncomfortable tombstones, pushed against the cruel bark of trees, her frail body squashed into the mud and hen dirt of barnyards . . . (204)

When Del actually makes the acquaintance of one of the Sherriff family, the second son now home from the mental institution, she is jolted into a more genuine imaginative perception by what she calls the "ordinariness of everything" (208). The Gothic family collapses when she enters the "reality" of the Sherriff house. She remembers her novel, and realizes how its "whole mysterious and, as it turned out, unreliable structure" had arisen "from this house, the Sherriffs, a few poor facts, and everything that was not told" (208). She also remembers, however, that her adolescent novel had "seemed true to me, not real but true, as if I had discovered, not made up, such people and such a story, as if that town was lying close behind the one I walked through every day" (206). At this point we need to step back and consider the complex Chinese-box effect that Munro has created. Del is herself a fictional, "made up" character; when Munro makes her write about her "reality," an essentially fictive reality is evoked. Jubilee exists only in an imaginative realm; or, to put it another way, Munro creates Jubilee out of Wingham, the Ontario town in which she grew up, and then creates Del (based in part, but only in part, upon herself), who in turn creates another fictional town at two removes from what we know as reality. *Lives of Girls and Women*, then, is a fiction but, like Del's unfinished novel though on a much more profound level, it is "not real but true"; Munro has "discovered, not made up" the characters; and Jubilee itself lies "close behind" the Wingham that the teenage Munro "walked through every day." As she remarks in a prefatory note: "This novel is autobiographical in form, but not in fact"; this is in line with her "standard" answer duly repeated for John Metcalf to the question about how autobiographical her writings are: "in incident — no . . . in emotion — completely" ("Conversation" 58).

The Epilogue to *Lives of Girls and Women* is a brilliant comment on the complexity of fiction and its relation to "real life," a problematic relation that has exercised Munro throughout her writing career. One thinks of Albert's comment in "Visitors" on an anecdote he has just recounted about earlier days in Hallett Township: "It isn't a story. It's something that happened" (*Moons* 215). How can "story" and "something that happened" be reconciled? The fact that Munro drew upon her childhood memories of Wingham for incidents that could be transformed into fiction is ultimately less significant, I suggest, than the fact that she drew on such memories for her concept of story itself.

It cannot be stressed too emphatically that her art emerges from a social situation in which gossip and anecdote play an unusually large part in local life. Like O'Hagan, though in a very different way, she is concerned with the problem of transforming oral story into written literature. Recently, speaking of the small Ontario town where she now lives, though the remark would be just as applicable to her native Wingham, she has observed how, "in places like Clinton, memory is always preserved in funny anecdotes. Even terrible things are presented as funny, because people have to live with it this way" (Connolly n. pag.). Such anecdotes litter her pages. We have already encountered W.O. Mitchell making a virtually identical point about the tall-tale oral humour of the Prairies during the Depression years. The important point is that Munro so often derives her initial inspiration from such sources and also introduces story-telling figures into her fiction. So Henry Crofton, a typical character in her fine uncollected story "Home," "knows and always has known every story, rumour, disgrace and possible paternity within a range of many miles" (138). In "The Ferguson Girls Must Never Marry" we meet Auntie Kit, a "stubborn, loud-voiced old woman who could hardly open her mouth without . . . spreading an old, bad, piece of gossip" (32), but also Nola, one of the central figures, who is presented as an authority on local gossip: "She had been following many Devlin lives from school right up until the present time. She told of bizarre and untimely deaths as well as preposterous and discommoding longevity" (36). One thinks also of the scandalous lore of West Hanratty preserved and passed on by Flo in *Who Do You Think You Are?*. In one interview, Munro even seems to see the community as creating a corporate story-telling function when she discusses her interest in "the whole business of how life is made into a story by the people who live it, and then the whole town sort of makes its own story" (Struthers "Alice Munro" 103–04).

Numerous examples of, and allusions to, story-telling run through the best-known Munro stories and need be no more than listed here. They include the stories centred on Uncle Benny in *Lives of Girls and Women*, which range from tall tales like that of Sandy Stevenson and the poltergeist, through the sensational accounts recorded in his gutter-press newspapers, to the more immediate stories that gather around his wife after his disastrous marriage. Of greater significance are the stories told by Aunt Elspeth and Auntie Grace, representing rich veins of local lore: "It did not seem as if they were telling them to me, to entertain me, but as if they would have told them anyway, for their own pleasure, even if they had been alone" (28). In context these contrast, of course, with the dully factual history of Wawanish County that their brother spends a lifetime compiling. Also well-known are the anecdotes recalled by the narrator's mother and aunt in "The Ottawa Valley," the concluding story in *Something I've Been Meaning to Tell You*, a title that itself conjures up the anecdotal urgency at the centre of village life.

Yet Munro displays at one and the same time a fascination with story and a distrust of story. The fascination can take the form of trying to persuade us — as in the "Epilogue" to *Lives of Girls and Women* — that her own fictional fabrications are real by comparing or contrasting them with other fictions. In the early story "An Ounce of Cure," after the narrator has recounted her own teen-age "disaster" with alcohol, she insists that she "had had a glimpse of the shameless, marvellous, shattering absurdity with which the plots of life, *though not of fiction*, are improvised" (*Dance* 87–88; my emphases). And in one of her most intricately constructed stories, "Something I've Been Meaning to Tell You," we are told, following the account of Char's death: "There was no fuss about the cause of death as there is in stories" (*Something* 18). Alternatively, she will reverse the process, resist the convention of the string-tying neat ending and so give what is clearly a story the illusion of an authentic memoir. Occasionally, indeed, she will write something so close to the expectations of non-fiction that we may have difficulty in accepting it as fiction at all. The best example of this is "Working for a Living," which Munro has at least twice described as a "story" (Hancock 208; Struthers "Real Material" 10) but which, in its studied avoidance of anything remotely resembling story-telling conventions, seems indistinguishable from non-fiction reminiscence.

Sometimes she will flaunt the artifice of fiction by specifically telling what is not to be told. In the second section of *Who Do You Think You Are?* we find Rose

> building up the first store of things she could never tell.
> She could never tell about Mr. Burns. . . . (24)

Naturally, she *does* go on to tell about Mr. Burns. The point here may perhaps be that she couldn't tell Flo, but a similar instance at the end of the book is unequivocal. Rose has been telling her half-brother and sister-in-law about the village simpleton Milton Homer, basing her information on Ralph Gillespie's unnervingly exact imitation (an image, one assumes, for the intensely realistic recreation at which Munro herself excels). But, after a curiously disturbing conversation with Gillespie just before his death, she becomes ashamed of her gossiping and play-acting: "Rose didn't tell this to anybody, glad that there was one thing at least she wouldn't spoil by telling" (206). Yet, unless she did tell, we would have no means of knowing about it. Munro, we might say, here employs the conventions of omniscient narration to deconstruct its pretensions. She is consciously undermining the art of story-telling.

Munro's distrust of story arises from a suspicion that any adaptation or heightening of an authentic incident that might form the basis for a fiction constitutes a potential betrayal. She has discussed the dilemma in "The Colonel's Hash Resettled" with special reference to the composition of "Images." The account of Joe Phippen and his underground house is, she claims, based on a genuine memory from her Wingham childhood: "there was a man living in a house exactly like that — the roofed-over cellar of a house that had been burned down" (181). This, then, is Munro in intensely realist mood, creating story out of local incident, employing fiction to attain a heightened sense of the actual, an effect paradoxically more real than reality — or, in Del Jordan's words already quoted, "not real but true." Yet — and this is supremely characteristic of Munro as an artist — as soon as she comes close to achieving this effect, she has second thoughts about its legitimacy, believing that she has "betrayed" the reality by "putting it in a story to be extracted this way, as a bloodless symbol." And she continues: "There is a sort of treachery to innocent objects . . . which a writer removes from their natural, dignified obscurity, and sets down in print" (181–82). These contradictory impulses, to attempt an almost surrealistic authenticity and then to question the result, create the tension behind some of her subtlest and best-known stories.

One finds this tension, for example, in "Winter Wind," which begins as a straightforward story drawing upon personal material. But the texture of the narrative is shattered when the narrator, who has just recounted a family anecdote about her grandmother, interrupts to question her own authority to speculate about the actions and motives of others, and even to challenge her right to tell the story at all:

> And how is anybody to know, I think as I put this down, how am I to know what I claim to know? I have used these people, not all of them, but some of them, before. I have tricked them out and altered them and shaped them any way at all, to suit my purposes. I am not doing that now, I am being as careful as I can, but I stop and wonder, I feel compunction. Though I am only doing in a large and public way what has always been done, what my mother did, and other people did, who mentioned to me my grandmother's story. Even in that close-mouthed place, stories were being made. (*Something* 161)

Once more, Munro (the distinction between author and narrator is here broken down by the writer herself) is acknowledging the traditional origins of her art: she is telling stories about her neighbours and relatives as rural people have always done. But she is also conscious of alteration and distortion "to suit my purposes." "I am not doing that now," she maintains, yet in a sense, of course, she is — and as an artist she knows it. This is an example of that most sophisticated (and tricky) of all fictional forms, the fiction that assures us of its non-fictional authority.

Later, she carries her argument still further. Even if she has remained faithful to facts, she has had to invent motives, to imagine the inner thoughts of others. She believes that these were accurate, yet she can never prove it: "Without any proof I believe it, and so I must believe that we get messages another way, that we have connections that cannot be investigated, but have to be relied on" (161). The vocabulary implies an almost religious act of faith, yet Munro is skeptical of such religious assertions, and as her career develops we see this faith (along with many others) steadily and relentlessly eroded. Even here we can detect radical doubts about the legitimacy of fiction.

This technique of questioning story within the story itself is developed in many of Munro's writings in the 1970s. In the well-known story "The Ottawa Valley," the narrator interrupts at the end to admit failure. If she had been "making a proper story out of this," she observes, she would have created a more suitable, presumably more climactic ending. But if this isn't "a proper story," we ask, what is it?

For the narrator, and presumably for Munro, the important thing is to portray the mother adequately, out of motives that range from celebration to exorcism, but "it did not work" (*Something* 197). Similarly, the uncollected story "Home" veers between straight narrative, in which the speaker returns home for the weekend to find her father ill, and italicized passages in which she meditates upon the writing of the story. She is particularly dissatisfied with the conclusion: "*I don't know how to end this. What actually happened was* . . ." (151) — yet another instance of fiction persuading us of its genuineness. She even admits that the final, supposedly clinching sentence had been written in advance, an indication of the transforming (distorting) quality that seems inseparable from artistic creation. And the actual ending — the last words in the story as we have it — is suitably enigmatic: "*I don't want any more effects, I tell you, lying. I don't know what I want. I want to do this with honour, if I possibly can*" (153). She denies "effects" but admits to "lying" when she does so; she does not know what she wants but the next sentence begins: "*I want* . . ." The story ends with the story-teller in an apparently insoluble dilemma.

Although the narrator of "Home" is herself a fiction, the story nonetheless reflects a writer's psychological situation not dissimilar to Munro's own. In recent years, she has expressed increasing reservations about what is desirable and possible in art. It might be said, indeed, that her whole development as a writer has proceeded in tandem with a series of strategic withdrawals and radical qualifications. Her first recorded change of direction led to a renunciation of extreme Gothic effects. In his 1972 interview, John Metcalf reminded Munro how she had once told him that a lot of her earliest work "was concerned with the most violent and romantic of events . . . abortions, rapes . . . ." Munro replied: "Yes. It was all *very* sordid. I only became commonplace later on" ("Conversation" 54). This phase is, of course, fictionalized in the Epilogue to *Lives of Girls and Women* already discussed. That it should be expressed at the conclusion of a book is itself appropriate, since Munro's next retreat involved a dissatisfaction with the endings of her earlier stories, especially with "an awful lot of meaningful final sentences" and "very important words in each last little paragraph" of the stories in *Dance of the Happy Shades*. If she could rewrite these stories, she told Struthers, "I would chop out a lot of those words and final sentences. And I would just let each story stand without bothering to do the summing up" ("Real Material" 9).

It is hardly surprising that artistic doubts should arise as stories reach their conclusions. For any writer troubled with the relation between fiction and realism, endings are likely to be especially problematic, as we have seen in the case of Margaret Laurence. Any attempt to "shape" a conclusion implies an artifice that, from a strictly realist viewpoint, imposes a false order upon the inevitable loose strands that characterize everyday experience. This is implied by the narrative intrusions towards the end of "Winter Wind," "The Ottawa Valley," and "Home." Ironically, however, Munro has more recently cast doubt upon these very challenges of story within story. What she calls "backing off and reflecting on the story" is "a kind of trick I wouldn't use now" (Connolly n. pag.). What was once a warning against "tricks" (forms of the word recur again and again in her discussions of fiction both outside and inside the stories themselves) is now seen as a trick itself. Even the rhetorical use of words themselves, the sense of "style," is viewed with suspicion. As early as "The Colonel's Hash Resettled" she had written: "I am a little afraid that the work with words may turn out to be a questionable trick, an evasion (and never more so than when it is most dazzling, apt and striking), an unavoidable lie" (182).

In turn, this leads to a more general mistrust of art (the narrator of "Home" sees her work as *parody, self-parody, . . . something that is . . . not lovable, not delightful*" [142]), and even, it seems, to a loss of faith in all artistic endeavour. There are few more poignant moments in her interviews than the occasion when she admits: "writers, it seems, have an enormous faith in the importance of art, and then you lose it, like your faith in religion. . . . I did lose it. Now I go on writing because that is what I can do" (Connolly n. pag.). Even the subsequent remark that "it still goes on making life more bearable" does little to mitigate the pathos. And the presumably ultimate position is reached a little later in the same interview: "my disillusionment was always there. And now I think I'm disillusioned with the disillusionment." However, despite her renunciation of techniques and effects which commentators have generally admired, she has not returned to the "simple story" which she advocates in this interview. Instead, we encounter in *The Progress of Love* a number of stories, especially

168

"Circle of Prayer," "White Dump," and the title story, where the temporal structure is deliberately scrambled, and readers find themselves faced with a curious, intriguing, but sometimes infuriating series of jigsaw-pieces. The reason for this is by no means obvious, and it is strange that, as yet, Munro has not displayed mistrust of an effect that is surely as artificial — or "tricky" — as any she has employed in the past. Indeed, in commenting on these stories in the Connolly interview, she specifically insists: "I don't think it's the latest trick." But one wonders.

Alongside this increased skepticism is to be found a notable shift of emphasis in Munro's subject-matter. In the Connolly interview she maintains that "there's just two areas that I know: I know Huron County, I know the lives of middle-aged women, women of my generation who have been through a few marriages and love affairs, who have children." The two are not, of course, mutually exclusive, but the division makes sense to alert readers of her work. Hitherto I have concentrated for the most part on the Huron County stories, which dominated the earlier writing. In *Something I've Been Meaning to Tell You* she attempts to extend her range to include her British Columbia experience, but it is in *The Moons of Jupiter* and *The Progress of Love* that the balance changes in the direction that Munro indicates. The former is framed by Huron County material, but the intervening stories, even when set in Logan or Hanratty, find their centre of interest in what she calls in the Connolly interview "that whole young adult through to middle age kind of life." In *The Progress of Love*, most of the stories are still set in southwest Ontario, but the focus is generally on love, marriage, and the complexities of sexual relationships; moreover, as she has been at pains to point out, she is "not dealing with personal material at all" (Connolly n. pag.). The question remains: what effect does this change in subject-matter have upon the literary quality of her work?

I would suggest here that the crucial distinction is not so much between "Huron County" and "the lives of middle-aged women" as between stories in which the participants are presented within a rich historical and social context and those which lack that dimension. A distinct difference in the much-touted Munrovian texture is surely discernible here. George Woodcock, one of the few commentators to discriminate critically within Munro's writings, has written as follows: "she has always written best when her stories or the episodes in her novels are close to her own experience in a world she knew" (*Northern* 134). I would offer a refinement on this statement. In my view it does not matter whether the story is based on Munro's experience or is derived from elsewhere. In her first collection "An Ounce of Cure" and "Dance of the Happy Shades" originated from anecdotes heard by Munro rather than from her own experience, but they are no less immediate and successful for that. The former fits smoothly and convincingly into a series of stories based on childhood and adolescence in which narrators recreate and evaluate incidents from their early lives; the latter derives much of its effectiveness from the delicate presentation of temporal change, the deterioration in the fortunes of the Marsalles sisters, and their inability to cope with a changed world. In both cases, the way in which "now" has developed out of "then" is subtly and even movingly evoked.

When this dimension is lacking, a vital element in the Munrovian texture is also absent. Whenever the characters try to suppress their past, or are portrayed within a rootless present, a shallowness — even what Woodcock calls "psychological hollowness" (*Northern* 146) — becomes evident. This is the reason, I am convinced, why I find myself agreeing with both Martin and Woodcock when they lament the decline in effectiveness of the *Who Do You Think You Are?* stories that show Rose outside West Hanratty. The chronicle of sexual liaisons that characterizes "Mischief," "Providence," and "Simon's Luck" ultimately grows wearisome; West Vancouver, the small town in the Kootenays, the environs of Kingston, fail to provide Rose with a context in which her most admirable and original qualities reveal themselves. Interest revives again as soon as we return to Hanratty — and to Flo, whose function as a contrasting and stimulating foil to Rose becomes especially clear at this point.

Munro described herself to Metcalf in 1972 as "kind of an anachronism . . . because I write about places where your roots are and most people don't live that kind of life anymore" ("Conversation" 56). In her later stories, she deliberately lays her emphasis on those who are "amputated from [their] past" (*Moons* 13), on the deracinated and the declassed who have broken ties (of family or marriage or both), have attempted like Del to shuck off previous misadventures, and are endeavouring to live exclusively in the rootless present. The process leads to a noticeable narrowing of range; we miss the subtle social gradations that were a source of complexity in the early work. It also

170

leads to an almost oppressive emphasis on sex. One does not have to go to the extreme of Rudy Wiebe's blanket condemnation of stories about "the kinds of petty bedroom-bathroom problems that small people have" (Mandel 154) to detect a palpable lowering of sights here. In *The Moons of Jupiter* I confess to getting bored with the recurrent characters and situations in stories like "Bardon Bus," "Labor Day Dinner," and "Hard Luck Stories" — the divorcees, the casual and trivialized infidelities, the rather desperate philandering. Sexual high-jinks among the liberated bourgeois can prove a dull subject. By contrast, a story like "Visitors" is refreshingly effective in context not merely because the subject-matter is less predictable but because the search for Wilfred and Albert's birthplace allows Munro to revert to a richly textured time-scale. Similarly, in *The Progress of Love*, the most memorable stories — including "Miles City, Montana" (an account of a return journey from Vancouver to Ontario), "Jesse and Meribeth," and "A Queer Streak" — all exploit the subtleties (and often pathos) of temporal change.

This exploration of rootless and essentially temporary life-styles — "the shopping-mall culture," as Munro has described it (Macfarlane 54–56) — coincided with the paring-down of style already noted. This has exacerbated the difference in texture and resonance between the two areas of subject. Often Munro seems intent on limiting her vocabulary to basic and essential words linked by the verb "to be." For instance:

There I met an anthropologist whom I had known slightly, years before, in Vancouver. He was then married to his first wife (he is now married to his third) and I was married to my first husband (I am now divorced). (*Moons* 111)

The house is of pale-red brick, and around the doors and windows there is a decorative outline of lighter-colored bricks, originally white. This style is often found in Grey County; perhaps it was a specialty of one of the early builders. (*Moons* 134)

Magda is in the kitchen making the salad. She is humming a tune from an opera. "Home to Our Mountains." Denise is in the dining room setting the table. (*Progress* 288)

Realism or parody? Or can Munro be suggesting that in this culture the two are indistinguishable? Here, of course, we are forced back once again on Munro's attempted refusal to judge her characters and their actions. But such cases go beyond the question of "freedom of interpretation." At what point, one finds oneself asking, does representativeness cross the border into cliché? It is possible that an aesthetic law of diminishing returns begins to operate here; after the third broken marriage in succession, can the traumas of adaptation and retrenchment seem either fresh or compelling?

This leads to what may well be the most troubling of all questions relating to Munro's work: do not the stories at times seem uncomfortably close to updated versions of the material that used to be called (in pre-feminist days) "women's fiction" — fiction about love and passion and the difficulties of getting a man (especially the right man)? The suggestion is not as preposterous as it may at first appear. The circumstances have, of course, changed. The old conventions — chastity, the romance of love, proper womanly behavior — have been replaced by new preoccupations — the *frisson* of sexual liberation, getting out of love-relationships as well as into them, new strategies for new challenges (relations with the offspring of former marriages, etc.). An ideal of sex may have replaced an ideal of love, but the dominant emphasis is still on passionate feelings and emotions, on something closer to "romance" than may seem evident at first glance. There are even, whatever Munro may claim, hints of "lessons." The message — "love is not kind or honest and does not contribute to happiness in any reliable way" (*Moons* 140) — may have changed drastically, but the over-riding subject remains the same (love, even "the progress of love," explored within very circumscribed boundaries). To be sure, these are supreme examples of the genre, and it should not be forgotten that they share many elements with the greatest classics of literature; but the possibility exists that the genre itself, like most genres, has its limits and its limitations.

These suspicions are enhanced by Munro's curious tendency to exploit what she calls a "preoccupation with fashion" (*Moons* 229). Time and time again, especially in *The Progress of Love*, we find an excessive emphasis on details of dress and adornment: "Beryl slept in a peach-colored rayon nightgown trimmed with écru lace. She had a robe to match" (16); ". . . her dress has a full skirt and long, billowy sleeves. It's a dress of cobwebby cotton, shading from pink to rose, with scores of tiny, irregular pleats that look like wrinkles" (33). This is, in a sense, a variant of an earlier narrative tendency to which Munro often refers: the temptation to describe all the furniture in a room before any human action can take place within it. All this contributes to her deserved reputation for meticulous realism, but there are distinct signs of its becoming a distracting mannerism, especially when it plays no part in enhancing the intellectual texture of the story. At the same time, the combination of a sophisticated presentation of contemporary mores with an updated version of a traditionally popular form may provide another explanation for the impressively broad range of her reputation at the present time.

No didactic lessons (at least, no traditional ones), a simple story, an uncluttered style, an avoidance of artistic pretension, a translucent directness: these are the distinguishing features of Munro's work as it has developed over the past thirty years. They are admirable qualities, and it is not my intention to undervalue them. I cannot, however, totally suppress an uneasy impression that the apparently "value-free" openness conceals a hidden message welcome to many contemporary readers. This goes beyond the ambiguous freedom of interpretation mentioned earlier. The life-styles of her main characters presuppose a "liberal" and "liberated" society whose standards are covertly upheld; religious (especially puritan) values are invariably suspect; the emphasis on a political, somewhat reductive egalitarianism (who do you think you are?) seems pervasive. "Old-fashioned" attitudes are regularly put into the mouths of unsympathetic characters like Patrick and Rose's half-brother Brian in *Who Do You Think You Are?* or elderly figures of fun like the reactionary fathers in "The Progress of Love" ("a real old sweetheart, a real old religious gentleman" [*Progress* 6]) and "White Dump." Divorce and adultery seemingly represent the behavioural norm; a social round of parties ending in drunkenness and sexual assignation appears the general rule. When offered without comment, this can easily be seen as advocacy rather than neutrality; to retort that such actions have been the subject of art from time immemorial is not a satisfactory answer since Munro's supreme capacity for realistic illusion is designed to break down a distinction between art and life. My point is not to offer a moral critique of Munro's work but merely to suggest that, when social attitudes change (and the current AIDS scare has already given some of her tales of carefree sexual liberation a decidedly outmoded look), what now seems excitingly contemporary may become disturbingly dated.

When this happens, however, the best of Munro's stories will undoubtedly be saved from oblivion by the art of which she was so ironically suspicious. Despite her mistrust of artifice, we can recognize in her finest work, late as well as early, a practical achievement that endures at the expense of her theory. Her masterly control of the varied narrative threads in stories like "Circle of Prayer" is one example; her impeccable sense of place and of distinctive temporal detail is another. While her recent endings are generally indecisive, this indecisiveness is as much contrived and controlled through art as the neater endings in *Dance of the Happy Shades*. Sometimes, as in the final paragraph of "The Progress of Love," a moral query is raised which seems indistinguishable from the pattern of her earliest effective work. Even the prose style regularly transcends the simple to become eloquent and even sonorous. The last phrases of "Miles City, Montana" — "whatever was flippant, arbitrary, careless, callous — all our natural, and particular, mistakes" (*Progress* 105) — have all the adjectival richness and paradoxical complexity that Munro has officially renounced as "tricks." We are left, then, with a final paradox. Just as W.H. Auden maintained that Time would pardon Yeats for political opinions Auden himself found objectionable, so Munro, who has displayed an extraordinary mistrust of the art and language that are her great glory, will similarly be vindicated, pardoned for the supreme literary quality that really matters — "for writing well."

CHAPTER 10

Margaret Atwood

When Joan Foster in *Lady Oracle* publishes her book of poems (also entitled *Lady Oracle*), the image of the poet presented to the public by the media bears little resemblance to the woman herself. Margaret Atwood is commenting here on a notable aspect of our publicity-ridden age, and she writes with particular authority because she has herself been a notable victim of the process. She has characterized this process in her interview with Linda Sandler: "a political image is invented by other people for their own convenience. They need a figurehead or they need a straw person to shoot down. It's that simple" (8). A little later, she admits to having been "quite unprepared" for the experience, "and rather horrified by some of the results" (9). It is only too easy to read into her work attitudes expected of the false media creation. Perhaps the greatest challenge in coming to terms with her writings involves getting behind both public mask and public misconception in order to find what is there in the text rather than what is assumed to be there.

Because Atwood is now a public figure, it is generally assumed that she must be extreme, controversial, and radical in her attitudes, that she moves in the vanguard of contemporary causes. That she is radical in the root (or "radical") sense of the word I would be the last to deny, and her progressive stances on many contemporary public issues should not be underestimated; if one turns to her work with an open mind, however, one is struck first by the traditional nature of her concerns. Her most withering satire — and I take satire to be her dominant literary mode — is generally directed against current fads, contemporary abuses, what Trollope called "the way we live now." Her deepest instincts rebel not so much (as the media image tends to suggest) against the strait-laced middle-class assumptions of our time as against the trendiness, superficiality, and irresponsibility of the "with it" generation. To be sure, she paints some witheringly critical portraits of respectable fuddy-duddies like the landlady in *The Edible Woman* or Aunt Muriel in *Life Before Man*, but these are outnumbered by such wickedly destructive caricatures as Ainsley in *The Edible Woman*, David in *Surfacing*, the Royal Porcupine in *Lady Oracle*, Jake in *Bodily Harm*, and the feminist painters in *Cat's Eye*. Her books are full of individuals who have broken away from conventional life-styles, but these characters are almost invariably the butts of her satire. Ainsley is perhaps the most conspicuous example. Beginning as an extreme, albeit unorthodox feminist (she wants a child without the inconvenience of a husband), she ends as a pregnant bride finding a bridegroom (not the father) at all costs and departing for that most conventional of rituals for a North American bride, a honeymoon at Niagara Falls.

Ainsley acts as a comic foil to Marian McAlpin,[1] who is committed throughout *The Edible Woman* to a quest for normalcy. Indeed, all Atwood's heroines to date, up to Offred in *The Handmaid's Tale* and Elaine Risley in *Cat's Eye*, are seeking normality or decency or both in a world presented as either absurd or evil or both. A strong didactic element is present from the beginning, though it becomes more explicit in *Bodily Harm* and *The Handmaid's Tale*. Atwood — and this is borne out dramatically by her poetry — is preoccupied with the threat and terror of existence in a world apparently lacking in all moral standards and respect for basic human values. In order to insinuate her relatively traditional position, she has resorted to the full resources of art and artifice, with particular reliance on satirical presentation and the employment of a number of variants on the Swiftian satiric trap designed to shock readers out of their numbed passivity. In this respect, though it sounds at first odd, she is remarkably close in her artistic strategies to Robertson Davies, and at the furthest extreme from Alice Munro, since she exploits and even revels in the dazzling technical effects which Munro increasingly mistrusts as "trickery."

All this creates severe challenges for any commentator on her work. The mixture of thematically serious with generically comic or even farcical elements can be unsettling, and Atwood's own emphasis on thematics in her critical writings has exacerbated the problem. Too often commentators concentrate on tracing thematic or intellectual consistency in her work to the neglect of the artistic variety at the heart of her achievement as a novelist. That there are links between, say, *The Edible Woman* and *Surfacing* may be granted, but any reading that makes the two novels sound similar in their ultimate effect is doomed to absurdity. It is time to focus on what distinguishes Atwood's novels from each other, on the impressive variety of her formal and tonal approaches — in a word, on her (generally satiric) artistry.

The Edible Woman (1969) is best approached by way of its literary conventions. We immediately recognize — or should recognize — the deliberate artifice traditionally associated with the comedy of manners. Examples include the type-characters (Leonard Slank, the single-minded seducer; Clara, the always pregnant housewife), the conspicuous formal symmetry (the three-part structure, three office-virgins, three graduate students), the set comic scenes (most notably, the virtually slapstick climax to Trevor's dinner-party), the comic reversals (Leonard as the seducer who is seduced; Ainsley's transformation already mentioned). Also conspicuous is the "well-made" quality of the book, especially the tendency of so many chapters to end on a punch-line (Marian's turning on the cold tap at the end of the sex-scene in the bathtub; Len's tie hanging like a trophy on the door-knob of Marian's room; the proposal scene that reads like a parody of its equivalent in *Jane Eyre*). What is to be appreciated here is the sheer skill of the novelist. It would be ridiculous to criticize the novel because the characters lack depth, or because Ainsley's transformation is unlikely from a realistic viewpoint. This is the art of caricature, partaking of all the exaggerations and artfulness that we are accustomed to in, say, Restoration comedy or the plays of George Bernard Shaw.

At the same time, of course, there are complications. Despite the artificiality of the structure, the background is rendered with an extraordinarily vivid realism. The absurd comedy-situations are played out against an authentic Toronto of the 1960s. Moreover, and this is to become an Atwood trade-mark, comic scenes can suddenly turn serious and sinister. The most obvious instance is the episode in which Marian breaks away from her companions at the Park Plaza and begins to run. The traditional love-chase suddenly takes on a mythic dimension and turns into a macabre, almost Gothic battle of the sexes. As Marian says: "All at once it was no longer a game. . . . It was threatening" (73). As readers we are jolted from one literary convention to another, and forced to reconsider our assumptions. Here we find the beginnings of what is to develop into the satiric trap. The enforced shift of perspective (reflected later in the novel by the abrupt switch from first- to third-person narration) shocks us into realizing that a set of comic routines played out by unreal characters from whom we are detached becomes identified with forces with which we have to contend in our own lives.

Similarly, the hunting-talk between Peter and Len (ch. 8) changes disturbingly from exaggerated caricature to a serious satire on what we would now call male-chauvinist domination. But (and this is an excellent example of Atwood's procedures) feminist critics emphasize this aspect of the book at their peril, since the satiric trap is waiting for them also. Marian's visit to the hair-dresser's is riotously comic ("her head resembled a mutant hedgehog with a covering of rounded hairy appendages instead of spikes" [209]; "After one of the nurses had pronounced her dry she was returned to the doctor's chair to have the stitches taken out" [210]), yet at the same time it offers a devastating account of the processes of feminine fashion. What begins as light-hearted comedy has turned into a bitter criticism of contemporary life and values.

Marian McAlpin, the central figure, represents the means by which the farcical comedy merges into satire, since she is inevitably a deeper, more rounded character than the others. But she is by no means the standard rebel against society. When her body starts rejecting food, we are told quite specifically that "what was essentially bothering her was the thought that she might not be normal" (203), and she immediately goes to the people she knows best — Ainsley, Clara, and Peter — and asks them the same basic question: "do you think I'm normal?" (204–07). Only her idiosyncratic mentor Duncan, later in the novel, questions the desirability of normalcy. He advises her not to seek psychiatric help because "they'd only want to adjust you" — to which Marian replies significantly: "I want to be adjusted" (263). Attempts have been made by some commentators to see this novel as promoting feminism or representing the rebellious challenges of the 1960s, but this is valid only insofar as these movements were similarly questioning the absurdities of contemporary assumptions. Whenever such movements become themselves extreme, Atwood is in the vanguard in exposing their excesses. Marian, a thoroughly conventional girl, only begins to go against the grain of her society when she recognizes it as profoundly abnormal. Her dismissal of Peter at the end of the book is not a rejection of marriage itself but a refusal to continue a relationship with someone whose "up-to-date" values have been judged inadequate.

The Edible Woman is clearly a satire on consumerism and packaging, to which we all in varying degrees comply. (It can be seen, ultimately, as a massive attack on the danger of peer-group pressure.) But this is merely to extract the theme; it is Atwood's treatment of the theme that matters. First, consumerism is attacked in punning fashion through the image of literal consuming, a motif that runs through the book from the epigraph quoting *The Joys of Cooking* to the half-symbolic baking of the woman-cake, from getting breakfast on the opening page to the final consumption of the cake on the last. Marian is both consumer (she must eat to live) and consumed (she sees Peter as wanting to devour and absorb her). But the image of packaging — Marian dressed up for presentation to Peter's party friends, etc. — is in a more complicated way reflected in the form of the book which draws attention to Atwood's own packaging of her theme. Marian begins by conducting a consumer survey into the packaging and marketing of Moose Beer; Atwood, we might say, packages her message about the state of contemporary society in a deceptively humorous but ultimately effective guise. Formally, the novel is conventional while at the same time playing with convention, parodying conventional expectations. It has a happy ending (of sorts) because the "heroine" escapes from the convention and doesn't marry the "hero" at the end. Intellectually, the ending is a necessary compromise. Marian establishes a reasonable equilibrium. From being someone uncritically accepting her society's mores, she becomes in the course of the story excessively defiant of them (the symptoms being physical and psychological as well as instinctive and basic). At the end she finds some kind of balance between consumer and consumed, accepts the realities of modern living while clearly recognizing their frequent absurdities.[2]

The change from *The Edible Woman* to *Surfacing* is extreme in tone though not in theme. While the unnamed protagonist of the latter novel (who, following the example of my colleague Russell Brown, I shall call the surfacer) resembles Marian in finding herself totally alienated from her society, the style and form of the two novels could hardly be more different. The artistic dexterity with which Atwood moves so expertly from one fictional mode to another is a token of her mastery of her craft. She has herself described *The Edible Woman* as "anti-comedy" (Gibson 20), though parody-comedy might be a more accurate term. By the same token, *Surfacing* can be described as a disorienting version of pastoral. It uses the traditional patterns of pastoral (retreat from city to pastoral place, the working out of personal problems within that place, and — presumably — return to the city) for an exploration of self which, though it may seem far removed in tone from pastoral norms, ends in a position decidedly more compatible with the traditional morality that pastoral generally upheld than with contemporary modes of behaviour. Like Marian, the surfacer is hardly the rebel she may first seem. Of David, Anna, and Joe she comments: "They all disowned their parents long ago, the way you are supposed to" (17), yet she is herself returning to her father and at a significant moment is represented as acting out one of her mother's characteristic gestures (93). She is outraged when she discovers that "the old road" (12) has been replaced by a new one; the response encapsulates her own "conservative" instincts. Throughout the book she is with her modern companions but not of them. Where Marian comes to regard her society as abnormal, the surfacer sees hers as positively deranged. In the course of the book she journeys through madness in quest of an unfashionable sanity.

The central fact in her emotional crisis is, of course, her abortion, the reality of which she is not initially prepared to acknowledge. In a society reluctant to admit either shame or guilt in reference to the subject, she is at last strong enough to admit her complicity: "Whatever it is, part of myself or a different creature, I killed it. . . . I could have said no but I didn't; that made me one of them too, a killer" (143, 145). Neither the surfacer nor Atwood minces her words here — words which have relevance far beyond the controversial abortion issue, since they raise the whole question of social and personal responsibility ("I could have said no but I didn't"). Moreover, it is interesting to note, given the concern with normality I have examined in *The Edible Woman*, that this recognition, in an Indian sacred place, is followed by an instinctive urge to do what is customary, sanctioned, expected, accepted as traditional proper behaviour: "I had to go onto the shore and leave something: *that was what you were supposed to do*, leave a piece of your clothing as an offering" (145; my emphases).

Without getting into theoretical arguments about intentionality and the necessary distinction between a character's view and those of the author, we can, I would think, agree that Atwood is treading on decidedly contentious ground here. *Surfacing* was published in 1972, at a time when all sorts of extreme attitudes, from both ends of the political spectrum, were being loudly proclaimed. It seems clear to me that Atwood was trying to express imaginatively a viewpoint which was not receiving much attention and which would not be likely to gain a sympathetic hearing if it were presented directly. (The issue, I take it, is the psychological effects of abortion as an instance of the larger topic of responsibility for what we do.) Atwood's tactic is to wrap this theme in a plot which provides connections with traditional forms, like the detective story and even the ghost story, and also, through the device of the satiric trap, to jolt her readers' passivity and detachment with a series of narrative deceptions.

The first of these is the incident involving the supposed Americans. Not only do they turn out, on closer acquaintance, to be Canadians after all, but as Canadians they had originally assumed that the surfacer and her party were Americans. The result is unsettling (especially for Canadian nationalists!). Subsequently, in what is openly offered as a desperate but no less cogent manoeuvre, the terms are transformed from political and national to moral and behavioural categories: "It doesn't matter what country they're from, my head said, they're still Americans, they're what's in store for us, what we are turning into" (129). Canadian readers respond to this with the uneasy suspicion that they may have turned already. In narrative terms, all this is a comparatively innocent deception. It is not all that far removed from Dickens's technique in *Great Expectations* where, unless we are very canny readers indeed, we initially err with Pip in assuming that the change in his material fortunes takes its origin from Miss Havisham. But Atwood's second trap is more extreme. She now reveals that, earlier in the story, the surfacer had lied about her past and so deceived her readers as well as herself. Here Atwood defies a conventional rule of story-telling — the principle, for example, that in Elizabethan drama the protagonist will always tell the truth in a soliloquy; she does this in order to shock readers into confronting a complicated question that they had not expected to encounter.

But the satiric trap, as employed here, involves more than the revelation of earlier duplicities or the moral questioning that it provokes. At the moment the trap is sprung, the mythic and the detached collapse into the human and the immediate. The climactic seventeenth chapter is, above all else, deeply moving as a personal statement. I risk the charge of murdering to dissect when attempting to analyse this confession to a kind of murder. As we read the chapter, we are simultaneously puzzled, shocked, morally challenged, and finally — if we are responding properly — overwhelmed by the control of Atwood's art. The prose style, with its deadened rhythms, its clipped vocabulary, its spliced sentences that embody a failure to connect nothing with nothing, suddenly assumes a stark directness which enables it to become a vehicle for the emotion that has previously been suppressed: "feeling was beginning to seep back into me" (146). Nowhere, perhaps, in all Atwood's fictional writing (with the possible exception of certain passages in *Life Before Man*) do human feelings flow so genuinely and immediately as here, an interesting effect since the surfacer is at the opening of the book the most tight-lipped of all Atwood's tight-lipped protagonists. And the surfacer becomes a literal protagonist (the word is cognate with *agon* and agony), torn apart emotionally by the conflicting pressures of a morally confused world. A profoundly disturbing fable, *Surfacing* draws upon all Atwood's resources — her story-telling skills, her mythopoeic imagination, her command of an appropriate minimalist prose, and what I can only call an intense moral vision. In some respects, it is a rough, angular novel, but the well-made smoothness of *The Edible Woman* would be hopelessly incongruous here. The linguistic complexity can best be indicated, perhaps, by the suggestion that this is the novel closest in tone to Atwood's characteristic tone in her poetry.

Jerome Rosenberg has revealed that, in a private letter written in the year of publication (1976), Atwood described *Lady Oracle* as "a kind of antithesis to *Surfacing*" (112). Certainly, any commentator seeking for connections between the two novels will soon notice that Joan's fake suicide by drowning, the event that sets off the narrative, apparently parodies the pattern of mythic descent treated seriously in the previous book. Similarly, *Lady Oracle*'s comic analysis of the artist as liar throws curious echoes back upon *Surfacing*. Moreover, if links with *The Edible Woman* are sought, one can contrast not only Marian's anorexia with Joan's perpetual eating but, more subtly, Joan's attraction to the odd and the extreme with Marian's desire to be normal; it is significant, for instance, that Joan loses all interest in the grotesque Royal Porcupine when he metamorphoses himself into plain Chuck Brewer. In addition, of course, she is always liable to the temptation of transforming ordinary reality into the stuff of Gothic. Atwood seems determined, indeed, to undermine, overturn, even deconstruct the narrative effects and thematic preoccupations established in her earlier work.

Although some sharp implications are contained in the various types of intellectual and verbal play that characterize *Lady Oracle*, it is clearly the most light-hearted of her books. Here paranoia is firmly controlled by comedy; exuberant parody takes precedence over any darker satire, and the novel becomes a *tour de force* of parodic virtuosity. Rosenberg has offered a by no means exhaustive list when he describes it as "at once a parody of the gothic romance, a spoof on the quest myth developed in *Surfacing*, a satire on activist politics and the Canadian nationalism of the 1960s and early 1970s, a poignant anatomy of childhood terror and alienation of the late 1940s and 1950s, a meta-fictional narrative" (112). I would add the parody of excess in all aspects of life: fashion, art, politics, communications, religion, feminism. Above all, it is essential to point out that Atwood is continually making fun of herself (especially the "violent duality" so often associated with her work) and of her readers. *Lady Oracle*, indeed, parodies every subject that comes within its orbit.

In particular, *Lady Oracle* parodies literature and the *literati*. Although Atwood has denied elements of the *roman à clef* suggested by some of the early reviewers (Letter 3), there are clearly a number of in-jokes smuggled into the text. Some of the more obvious include Columbine Books (for Harlequin), Black Widow Press (for Anansi), and the initials of Joan's publishers, Morton and Sturgess. More speculatively, certain passages seem to throw playful light on well-known scenes from recent Canadian fiction. Can the encounter with the exhibitionist daffodil man (ch. 6) be an amused and amusing reference to a memorable scene in *Lives of Girls and Women*, or the incident where her mother pricks her with a paring knife (ch. 11) a sly allusion to the mother of Dunstan Ramsay chasing him round the kitchen table with a knife in *Fifth Business*? Certainly, more generalized literary parody confronts us on virtually every page. The continual coincidences (the reappearances of Marlene the Brownie, the restaurant owner, and Leda Sprott) obviously make fun of the contrivances of traditional fiction. The hoary question of the artist as liar recurs throughout a novel in which, to quote Robert Lecker, "every 'I' is a lie" ("Janus" 194). As Joan says herself, "I fabricated my life time after time; the truth was not convincing" (150). We realize ultimately that this can apply to the whole book, which means that it becomes a parody of the *Bildungsroman* as a genre. Again, Joan's increasing inability to distinguish between the events in her own life and the inventions of her costume Gothics develops into a shrewd if light-hearted investigation of the relation between literature and life.

Problems of narrative also become material for parody. The sequence in which Joan and her cronies embark on the crazy project of blowing up the Peace Bridge involves a complex pun on "plot" in what might be called its terrorist and literary senses. The humorous possibilities here are exploited to the full in the scene where Joan, after numerous subterfuges, meets Sam and Marlene where they cannot be overheard (itself a spoof on contemporary spy novels and movies) and reveals her plans for the false suicide. Her motive as given to Sam and Marlene is, of course, a fabrication ("The truth was out of the question, as usual" [296]), and the plan itself is based on one of several newspaper-clippings kept by Joan because "they might come in handy as plot elements" in her writing (299). What we have here, then, is a plot-line involving "plot elements" being used for the basis of a "real" plot-conspiracy! This is but one example among many of the intricate comic effects that Atwood introduces into this deceptively complex novel.

Nothing, then, is exempt from parody in *Lady Oracle*, which might be described, in its own imagery, as a gigantic mothball scattering the diaphonous graceful dancers representing art and literature. Nor, of course, is literary criticism exempt. This is most obvious in the scenes following the publication of Joan's poetry, where Sam (a biographical critic) sees the book in terms of her relationship with Arthur, and (a subtle comment on art as fabrication) no one believes her genuine confession that it represents automatic writing. Warnings against the dangers — even absurdities — of interpretation are to be found throughout the novel: one discusses the book at one's peril. But a final point needs to be made. Joan herself is at least as much the butt of this satirical comedy as any interpreting reader. She is the character most obviously caught in her own trap. She sees herself as an escape artist (which also implies "escapist artist"), yet, if she learns anything in the course of the novel, she learns (like Rennie Wilford in very different circumstances in the later *Bodily Harm*) that no escape is possible. "Why," she asks herself, "did every one of my fantasies turn into a trap?" (335). But the biggest trap, of which the reader is the (generally amused) victim, is *Lady Oracle* as a whole. Perhaps the ultimate irony resides in the fact that the novel which offers so sustained a parody of the absurdities and pretensions of art should itself be a supreme example of sophisticated artistry.

As usual, in her next novel, *Life Before Man* (1979), Atwood displays a radical change in style and tone though not, I think, in basic approach. When the book first appeared, it was generally categorized as pessimistic and as Atwood's most sustained writing in a relentlessly realistic mode. Both judgements seem to me questionable, though they are certainly not surprising in view of the extreme tonal contrast with the high-spirited intellectual play of *Lady Oracle*. There is no technical satiric trap here, but a hermeneutical trap is involved in the temptation to see the characters in *Life Before Man* as themselves trapped in a Sartrean "no exit."

Life Before Man is only depressing if readers share the values, or lack of them, displayed — at least at the opening — by the principal characters. The first sentences (spoken by Elizabeth) are immediately striking: "I don't know how I should live. I don't know how anyone should live. All I know is how I do live" (3). Not "can" but "should." And this is followed by Elizabeth's cynical diagnosis: "that's no way to make money." Atwood's implicit diagnosis is very different. The novel can be seen, indeed, as basically conventional in moral terms, illustrating the appalling price that can be paid for violating traditional norms; it constitutes a virtual anthology of the painful problems encountered by individuals who accept the standards of "modern living." Atwood presents a domestic waste land of disillusion and frustration, interspersed with casual adulteries that only exacerbate the sense of monotony. Any sense of fulfillment is lacking. Traditional religious values and practices have been abandoned but nothing of equivalent spiritual quality has taken their place. Of the three main protagonists, Lesje, because she retains an imaginative capacity, is still open to flashes of insight, and in one of these she sees "an adult world where choices had consequences, significant, irreversible" (203). She is clearly, as Frank Davey has called her, "the most redeemable character of the novel" (92), though I cannot accept his reading of the climactic scene in which she flushes the birth-control pills down the loo. To Davey this is an act of rebellion — "to reject good taste, to reject rationalism, and assert her protean reality" (92). I would lay emphasis on the decision as a moral act on the side of "nature," conventional almost to a reactionary extent. The important point, surely, is that she has made her "choice," and is prepared to accept the "consequences." (It is instructive to compare *Life Before Man* with Munro's later work; the societal values presented are similar, but the implied moral tone is very different.)

"[U]nder the novel's realistic surface," writes Ildikó de Papp Carrington, "lies a non-realistic structure" (68). The relation between realism and artistry in this novel seems to me crucial. Ostensibly, Atwood offers a dourly realistic transcription of modern living, and certainly portrays the central characters with a depth and understanding that are comparatively rare in her work. We feel with these characters, experiencing their anguish and uncertainty through the numbed cadences of their speech-rhythms. Atwood's strategy, however, of dividing the story between three viewpoints continually interrupts any sense of realistic illusion and draws attention to her own artistry as it moulds the narrative events into a conscious structure. As in *The Edible Woman*, we are constantly made aware of the well-made quality of the book. To take one example, the entry on p. 53 begins: "Lesje is having lunch with Elizabeth's husband . . . "; that on p. 160 begins: "Elizabeth is sitting at the black-topped table in Fran's. Opposite her is William." William is Lesje's companion. The parallel lunch-scenes, with each woman meeting the other's partner, deliberately balance each other and emphasize the structure of sexual musical chairs that characterizes the whole book. Furthermore, Atwood takes care to show how Elizabeth is tempted to enforce the parallel so as to impose an artificial human order on what she regards as chaos: she considers seducing William "to create some balance in the universe, a tit for a tat" (161).

This artificial structuring is to be found all through the novel. In the three sections dated "Saturday, October 30, 1976," for instance, each of the protagonists is seen involved with a love-companion — Elizabeth reliving her affair with Chris, Lesje with William, Nate with Martha. Each scene is realistically presented; the selective juxtaposition turns the sequence into carefully crafted art. Similarly, Nate's jogging around Queen's Park in an early section is specifically recalled when he is engaged in a similar circle-game at the close (39, 287), just as his watching the results of the Québec election in the Selby Hotel is parallelled by a similar scene in the same place a year later (59, 250). The two flashbacks involving Chris create a related effect (154, 211). We become increasingly aware that Atwood is creating an artistic structure, and we respond to the sculpture-like proportions of her making.[3]

Bodily Harm, like *The Handmaid's Tale* to follow, is much more explicitly didactic and so may justify what might otherwise be considered an excessively moralistic emphasis in my discussion to date. In both novels the satiric trap is much in evidence. In *Bodily Harm* we meet it first in the scene where Rennie researches an article on pornography. The gross irresponsibility of her world is indicated when her managing editor "thought it would be sort of fun to do a piece on pornography as an art form" (207). Rennie's ultimate shock at the obscenities recorded in the police exhibit may be likened to the surfacer's response to abortion or Lesje's rejection of the birth-control pills. In all three instances, her heroines react to a controversial issue in a way calculated to surprise any readers expecting an "enlightened" or "modern" response. Here the trap works both ways. If readers veer towards Rennie's trendy superficiality, they will undergo a process of shocked adjustment similar to her own; if they do not, they will be surprised (perhaps even gratified) to see her at last confronting the seriousness and complexity of the subject. The incident represents in miniature the larger changes in literary perspective required of readers in the course of the novel.[4]

At first, despite certain troubling facts (the unidentified man with the rope, her mastectomy), the brittle tone seems to prepare us for a novel not far removed from *Lady Oracle*. Rennie shares with Joan a basically irresponsible attitude to life and a capacity to get into absurd and potentially dangerous situations. But whereas the Gothic elements in *Lady Oracle* are treated in a comic, even at times farcical manner, in *Bodily Harm*, as Coral Ann Howells has demonstrated so well, they become frighteningly immediate ("Worlds" 131–36). At one point Rennie observes poignantly, "it's too grotesque not to be true" (132), a sentiment echoed by Dr. Minnow: "Here, nothing is inconceivable" (133). Nonetheless, the shift of conventions threatens to split the novel apart; the change from witty satire to didactic earnestness is impressive morally and politically but hard to acknowledge artistically. An additional difficulty is involved, since astute readers are likely to begin the novel with the attitudes to violence and political tyranny that Rennie only discovers at the end. That we should experience the sufferings through Rennie is, of course, appropriate and important, but a sense of moral anti-climax, I think, remains.

The most audacious, and controversial, trap occurs at the end of the novel, where Rennie, despite her wish-fulfillment dreams, is still apparently imprisoned in her cell, the tourist-resort turned torture-chamber — and we as readers are trapped with her. The text is ambiguous, but the verb-tenses give the clue to this entrapment, which itself casts a dark shadow over the insistence on "luck" in the final lines. Rennie has been humanized by an experience of man's inhumanity to man, and especially to woman, and the paradox takes on mythic proportions as we realize how humane insight so often stems from adversity. We are on the brink of a religious truth here; indeed, *Bodily Harm* has been described to me as Atwood's most religious book.[5] I am inclined to agree, but I also share Urjo Kareda's unease about the strained apotheosis involved in Atwood's desperately balanced close (72). In its moral and political concern, this is possibly Atwood's most ambitious novel, but it contains some uncharacteristic snags in terms of artistry (am I the only reader who finds the plot-line at the time of the political coup too confused to follow?).

As before, Atwood is preoccupied in *Bodily Harm* with the concept of normality. The novel could hardly be more different in tone, emphasis, and texture from *The Edible Woman*, yet in this respect the two books are closely linked. "We'll get back to normal, she told herself, though she could not remember any longer what *normal* had been like" (35). This passage occurs close to the beginning, just after Rennie's mastectomy, but the word reverberates throughout the book, taking on bitterly ironic overtones by the end: "The situation is normalizing all over the place, it's getting more and more normal all the time" (296). The implication is that political torture and corruption have become "normal," and this becomes the basic *donnée* of *The Handmaid's Tale*.

Whereas in *Bodily Harm* the radical shift in tone is achieved spatially as Rennie's escapist tourist-trip to the Caribbean becomes a journey into terror, in *The Handmaid's Tale* it is ostensibly temporal as we are transported into a bleak future in which what we like to consider "normal" has become unattainable, almost unimaginable (even a quiet, domestic game of Scrabble is now a subversive political act). Formally, the book offers itself as a satiric dystopia, but the central epigraph from Swift's *Modest Proposal* should put us on our guard. Here the satiric trap operates in characteristically Swiftian fashion. In *Gulliver's Travels*, Gulliver voyages into remote parts of the world only to be confronted by some unpleasant truths about his own country. Lilliput appears at first a fantastic and unfamiliar place, but contemporary readers were soon forced to recognize, in such absurdities as the rivalry between Big-Endians and Little-Endians, mirror images of their own religious and political squabbles; in Brobdingnag Swift extends the process by having Gulliver explain the political system he knows and reveres to the King of that country only to have his people condemned as "the most pernicious Race of little odious Vermin that Nature ever suffered to crawl upon the Surface of the Earth" (108). And in *A Modest Proposal* the reader begins with a proposed philanthropic solution to Ireland's problems only to be shocked at the actual proposal — the eating of surplus infants — and then forced to recognize the solution as little more than a logical extension, from metaphor to *Realpolitik*, of existing practices.

Atwood's strategy in *The Handmaid's Tale*, I suggest, is remarkably similar. At first we are appalled by the police-state of Gilead and shocked that such a set-up could possibly emerge in North America in the near future. But we soon realize, if we read carefully, that this is not just a warning about the possibly consequences of a rightist, religious-fundamentalist takeover. An early passage is crucial:

189

> There is more than one kind of freedom, said Aunt Lydia.
> Freedom to and freedom from. In the days of anarchy, it was
> freedom to. Now you are being given freedom from. Don't
> underrate it. (34)

Aunt Lydia, one of the instructors training the handmaidens for their submissive sexual role in the new society, is hardly a sympathetic character, but her words nonetheless have the effect of shocking us out of our complacency. A connection, however tenuous, is established between our civilization and the one presented in the novel. This is buttressed by later references. "You see what things used to be like?" Aunt Lydia asks after the compulsory showing of a pornographic movie "from the seventies or eighties" (128), and we realize how a future age could judge us by our own evidence. The handmaidens are offered constant reminders of the "old days of no safety" (129). The powers that be in Gilead do not, like Orwell's Party in *Nineteen Eighty-Four*, rewrite the past; they merely have to refer to it in terms that sound sickeningly familiar.

Atwood manages, therefore, to manipulate her satire on two fronts. The past (our now) was terrible; the present (our future) is terrible in a different way. The very suggestion that Gilead represents a possible evolution from the North America of the 1980s has to be acknowledged as a crushing indictment of our own times. Some embarrassing questions are raised: for instance, is the killing of deformed babies morally worse than aborting healthy foetuses? Similarly, the novel can backfire on those who talk glibly about women's subjugation in the mid-eighties. And at one horrendous climax, the public slaughter of a supposed criminal, just as we realize that the victim is to be ritually torn to pieces by the handmaidens, the narrator remarks with apparent casualness, "there's a surge forward, like a crowd at a rock concert in the former time" (291), thus recalling images of hysteria and violence relevant to our own day. By the final chapter, a historical analysis of the text of the tale, which takes us further into the future to a post-Gilead age, we are prepared to agree with a historian that "we must be cautious about passing moral judgement upon the Gileadeans" (314), and a little later we are told quite openly that Gilead's "racist policies . . . were firmly rooted in the pre-Gilead period" (317). To read *The Handmaid's Tale* from this perspective can be a chastening experience.

Atwood's manipulation of the satiric trap for didactic purposes seems here to have reached its climax; it is difficult to see how the technique could be developed further. In this respect, despite the apparent novelty of employing the dystopia form, she is perfecting an approach that has been used throughout her fiction. The desire for normalcy, a preoccupation ever since *The Edible Woman*, is again conspicuous and is given its most surprising and at the same time poignant expression in the Commander's desire for a domestic game of Scrabble, perhaps the most memorable of those "flashes of normality" which, Offred tells us, "come at me from the side, like ambushes" (58). But beneath all this is another level, not hitherto prominent in Atwood's work, at which the book casts more than a passing glance towards contemporary interest in the self-reflexive. With the possible exception of *Lady Oracle*, this is the Atwood novel that draws most deliberate attention to its own artifice. The title itself emphasizes the fictive quality of the book — it is specifically presented as a *Tale* — and allusions to the story as story rather than as a direct account of supposed experience accumulate.

As early as the seventh chapter we encounter this:

> I would like to believe this is a story I'm telling. I need to believe it. I must believe it. Those who can believe that such stories are only stories have a better chance.
>
> If it's a story I'm telling, then I have control over the ending. Then there will be an ending, to the story, and real life will come after it. (49)

In the very process of acknowledging that the narrative relates to an actual experience, Offred highlights the artistic conventions that can allow it to be interpreted, paradoxically, as "only" a story yet at the same time as more than a story. If it is merely an account of what has happened, it belongs in Aristotle's definition to history; if it is a story, what may happen, it belongs to Poetry and can therefore contain a larger (potentially didactic) meaning. Of course, we know that it is "a story" because we are reading it before the supposedly historical events have taken place. And by an additional paradox, the "Historical Notes" with which the novel ends take us further into the future, a future which has mercifully replaced the totalitarian horror of Gilead but has unfortunately reverted to some of the flippancy and academic fence-sitting characteristic of our own time; and so, while offering the ostensible illusion of non-fiction discourse, this epilogue further demonstrates that it is "only" a story. Atwood is once again drawing attention to the supremacy of artifice within her work.[6]

In her introduction to *Second Words* (1982), a collection of critical prose, Atwood remarks that, at the outset of her career, she was "a profoundly apolitical writer" but that subsequently she "began to describe the world around [her]" (15). A year earlier she had spoken of the "kinds of stories I wish to tell or think I ought to tell" (335), and *Bodily Harm* and *The Handmaid's Tale* clearly belong to the latter category. She has, of course, been criticized for this — "critics sneer somewhat at anything they consider 'heavy social commentary' or — a worse word — 'message' " (394) — but although what she has to say may have taken on a new urgency, her fidelity to art and artifice is in no way affected. Similarly, if in the early 1980s her fiction became increasingly "political," a word she defines as "who is entitled to do what to whom, with impunity" (394), this is in line with the basic traditionalism I have stressed in the course of this chapter. A lecture entitled "An End to Audience?" given by Atwood at Dalhousie University at the time she was writing *Bodily Harm* is relevant here. Like most of her non-fiction pronouncements, it veers uneasily between the flippant and the thoughtful; at its best, however, it makes some profound assertions about novels and novelists, some of which are worth extracting here:

I believe that fiction writing is the guardian of the moral and ethical sense of the community. (346)

The writer *bears witness*. (348)

Writing, no matter what its subject, is an act of faith; . . . I believe it's also an act of hope, the hope that things can be better than they are. (349)

. . . the writer functions in his or her society as a kind of sooth-sayer, a truth teller; . . . the novel is a moral instrument. (353)

Such remarks, which seem almost Victorian in their earnestness, firmly link Atwood to the "great tradition" of nineteenth-century

British and American fiction with its solid emphasis on moral and social issues. They bear witness themselves not only to her fundamental seriousness but also to her artistic courage.

Atwood is still, one assumes and hopes, in mid-career. Given the extraordinary twists and turns of her writing to date, it would be even more foolhardy than usual to risk any prophecies about future developments. In the early 1980s, after Rennie Wilford encountered real life and *Realpolitik* on Ste. Agathe, her satiric procedures abandoned brittle humour for something closer to apocalyptic warning, though *Cat's Eye* shows signs of returning to her earlier modes with a deepened commitment. Yet the continuing explicit didactic emphasis would seem to confirm my earlier assertion that she represents a position at the opposite extreme from that of Alice Munro. This is true, however, only if one emphasizes her novels at the expense of her short stories. As Barbara Godard has emphasized, the latest collection of these, *Bluebeard's Egg* (1981), "marks a shift in her narrative technique" (57).[7] In the opening story, "Significant Moments in the Life of My Mother," the narrator purports to preserve her mother's oral reminiscences in much the same way that Munro ostensibly draws on authentic family traditions in such stories as "Winter Wind" and "The Ottawa Valley." Two of the anecdotes, those about the poisoned muskrats and the preacher's false teeth (2, 6), Atwood recounts in non-fiction contexts (*Second Words* 110, 336), while others have already been transformed into other fictions.[8]

In the final story, "Unearthing Suite," where the (apparently) same narrator reproduces further anecdotes and incidents involving her parents, even the employment of the framing device recalls Munro and *The Moons of Jupiter*. The opening words, "My parents have something to tell me" (240), conceal a Munro echo; more subtly, the narrator claims, in contrast to the parents' actual conversation, to be "concocting fictions" (242), thus trickily suggesting that the main narrative is *not* fiction (for similar effects in Munro, see   p. 164 above). Moreover, the last paragraph presenting the mother's response to the finding of the marten's dropping on the cottage roof goes so far as to reproduce Munro's characteristic vocabulary and tone: "For her this dropping . . . is a miraculous token, a sign of divine grace; as if their mundane, familiar, much-patched but at times still-leaking roof had been visited and made momentarily radiant by an unknown but by no means minor god" (258). The half-ironic use of "miraculous" and (especially) "radiant," the complex but potentially reductive association of "animal shit" and "divine grace" seem intended to recall Munro, but rather by means of intertextual allusion than through the full-scale if good-natured parody of *Lady Oracle*.

Yet the Munrovian mode suggested here is, of course (and ironically), one that Munro herself has now renounced. Atwood is nowhere more concerned with the fascinations and complexities of words and narrative than she is in this collection (one story is subtitled "The Domestic Life of the Language"; another, "Bluebeard's Egg" itself, centres on an elaborate exercise concerning point-of-view in fiction). At the same time, there is an engaging tenderness, a human immediacy, about the frame-stories which is all too rare in contemporary experiments with self-reflexive fictional forms. "Unearthing Suite," like all Atwood's writing (and all writing) may involve "the translation of the world into words" (248), but it also celebrates and perpetuates through art the best moments in the unusual but ultimately "normal" life she has known. Godard has called the whole collection "a book about origins, about the origins of storytelling and the storytelling of origins" (72). This is undoubtedly true, and it neatly expresses the paradox that Atwood, when at her most innovative technically, remains profoundly traditional in both tone and attitude.

Jack Hodgins

One of the stories in Jack Hodgins's first collection, *Spit Delaney's Island* (1976), is remarkable for its apparent (but, as we shall see, only apparent) generic incongruity so far as the rest of the book is concerned. While the other stories conform to a basic realism, frequently heightened to the extent of suggesting "magic realism," "At the Foot of the Hill, Birdie's School" can only be described as a kind of allegory. A young man by the name of Webster Treherne has been living in a now disbanded commune in the hills with his father, "the Old Man," who "taught that time was meaningless and God was all" (137). Descending to a town in the valley with the "one and certain goal" of joining the McLean gang, a historical group of outlaws in British Columbia active in the late 1870s, he enters a school run by Balk-Eyed Birdie where courses are offered in Truth, Love, and Life. But Birdie assures him: "we don't teach you how to *find* those things, we teach you how to *lose* them" (141). In the valley, Webster continually encounters a small boy who throws chunks of coal at him, and a group of girls who tempt and mock him; in his turn, though he shows clear signs of being too compassionate for a real criminal, he holds up a local storekeeper (with an unloaded gun). The man curses him by invoking the consumption that is killing his wife. Webster indeed falls sick, and appears to be dying; but at the end, when Birdie has gone for a doctor, Webster knows that "when she came back . . .

he wouldn't be there" but would have returned "in his freedom" to the hills from whence he came (151).

Clearly, this story can only be understood if it is interpreted to reveal a hidden meaning. Webster Treherne is obviously a significant name, and Hodgins has observed: "I don't know a character until I know his or her name" (Hancock 74). Allan Pritchard has noted that the name brings together the two greatest English visionaries of the seventeenth century, one seeing corruption, the other goodness (35). His place of origin in the hills suggests a heaven or paradise, and his descent to the town either a Fall or a Christ-like incarnation. The town presumably represents the evil of the world in which Webster, despite his ambition to crime, can never ultimately remain. The syllabus at Birdie's school suggests an image of education in our world seen through a glass darkly, as well as an inversion of an ideal trivium like St. Paul's faith, hope, and charity. Throughout the story are scattered allusions to the apocalyptic poetry of Dylan Thomas, and the final paragraph in which Webster returns "in the pale April sunlight" (151), the time of resurrection as well as the cruellest month, suggests an ultimate divine comedy of redemption. The allegory here is tricky. At first Webster, with his ostensible aim "to pistol-whip Chinese, to shoot Indians right and left, stab policemen, murder strangers" (137), seems closer to Antichrist than to Jesus, but we are invited to consider the difficulty of goodness trying to acclimatize itself to a world of violence and evil. In order to inculcate Truth, Love, and Life, one must go through the way of their opposites. The hold-up of the shopkeeper, a crime in our world, may look different if we can see Webster (remember the ambiguous unloaded pistol) attempting to lure mankind away from material things while remaining within human (fallen) conventions. This is a dark, perhaps dangerous allegory without rigid elucidations, one in which individual elements within the story are open to a series of seemingly traditional but in fact radical and shifting symbolic meanings.

"At the Foot of the Hill, Birdie's School" is not, I think, a successful story within *Spit Delaney's Island*, whatever its (arguable) separate merits, since it breaks the tonal unity of the rest of the volume. Waldemar Zacharasiewicz has compared it to Flannery O'Connor's work and also detects within it "a Kafkaesque touch" (99); in addition, we may feel that it might have been managed more deftly by a consistently explicit modern allegorist like T. F. Powys. One wonders, indeed, why it was included in an otherwise carefully integrated collection. A possible explanation is that it alerts readers to the underlying levels of meaning that exist in the other stories and to the more general tendency towards allegory in Hodgins's approach to the art of story-telling ("I'm writing allegories I suppose," he admitted to Hancock [77]). In his most characteristic work, certainly, he has created for himself a form in which allegorical meanings are available, not always consistently or continually but intermittently and sometimes even to comic effect, beneath the surface of the literal story.

This is true, for example, of the two Spit Delaney stories that frame the book. The first, "Separating," alerts us even in its title to a more generalized significance. Separation is a theme that echoes throughout the story — Spit's separation from "Old Number One," the break-up of his marriage, the continuing image of the "long curving line of sand that separates island from sea and man from whale" (4), and the larger, more philosophical *dividing line* separating *what is and what isn't* (8). It also echoes throughout the volume — the "three women of the country" all separated from each other in the story of that title, the way the Georgia Strait separates island from mainland in "The Trench Dwellers," the lonely deserted woman in "By the River." I am even tempted to extrapolate and suggest that Hodgins himself is here exploring the dividing line that separates what is and what is not possible in fiction. In addition, other words, notably "edge," "real," and "touch," recur in this story and become resonant concepts throughout Hodgins's work. We soon realize that, without in any way undervaluing his regional preoccupation, he is concerned to communicate something far more ambitious than a vivid portrait of the colourful and often idiosyncratic inhabitants of northern Vancouver Island.

When Spit is suddenly confronted with the profound — and ultimately dislocating — question that pops into his mind on the beach ("*Where is the dividing line?*" [7]), he necessarily embarks on a journey that is much more than the standard world-trip of the average tourist. (This sequence is present, I assume, to suggest that the answer to Spit's problem is not to be found among the things of this world.) When, at a moment of spiritual crisis, he goes to the shore and encounters "a naked youth coming up out of waves to greet him" (17), mythological as well as allegorical analogues become available.

Finally, these images converge as he imagines himself going off with the hitch-hikers into an unknown but clearly different future, standing at the edge of the water, himself stripped metaphorically as the youth was physically (an image Hodgins considers again in a climactic scene in *The Honorary Patron*), and then addressing himself to God or, at any rate, to the unknown:

> *Okay you son of a bitch!*
> *I'm stripped now, okay, now where is that god-damned line?* (23)

In "Spit Delaney's Island," at the close of the book, Spit is led up from his symbolic seashore (he is now living in a motel where "tides slosh forward . . . almost to the cabin door" [171]) to an equally symbolic yet at the same time, of course, equally authentic British Columbian mountain. Phemie Porter, the grotesque but liberating poetess who takes him in tow, insists on referring to him as "Mr. Man" (184, 187), thus establishing him as, in part, an Everyman figure. She invites him to follow the pattern of her own father, to disappear into the mountains as a way of "going into yourself" and to come back as "a changed man" (189). Spit only gets part of the way up the symbolic ascent, and eventually turns back; nonetheless, he has obviously learned something from Phemie, and we sense at the close that he is less "a man who is trapped by [his] own limits" (194) than he was at the beginning. Here and elsewhere in the book the stories are embedded far more firmly in realistic conventions, yet like "At the Foot of the Hill, Birdie's School" they respond to interpretation as allegorical fables.

In "Three Women of the Country" the allegorical possibilities are signposted by the choice of names. Pritchard has already written of these, noting the apparent borrowing of the resonant place-name Cut Off from a late Ethel Wilson short story ("A Visit to the Frontier," where she too moves towards allegory), the allusions to *The Tempest*, and the connection with Melville's *Moby Dick* through the name Starbuck, the last two of which, he says, put us in mind of other islands and other isolations (22). This is helpful. It needs to be pointed out, however, that other names in this story are less erudite and certainly less solemn in their implications. Mrs. Wright is appropriately named in view of her incorrigible self-righteousness (Hodgins has remarked how he likes to create a character who thinks he knows "what life is all about" and then to "pull the rug out from under his feet" [Hancock 64]); but she has already been married to a Mr. Left, and the joke warns that allusive interpretation can be carried too far. Is Hodgins here setting an Atwood-like satiric trap for excessively close readers? Certainly the Larkin triplets — Percy, Bysshe, and Shelley — strengthen this possibility, a possibility heightened by the fact that they spend much of their time skylarking around. Hodgins's mischievous humour sets a necessary brake on over-subtle connections and over-ingenious parallels. Within these limits, however, he does encourage us to consider his Vancouver Islanders in the light of previous literature (Canadian and otherwise) and to recognize that they belong not just to their all-important local place but to a world of larger patterns and universal meanings.

The same is true of the more specifically mythic references that underlie some of the stories. When, for example, in "Every Day of His Life" Big Glad Littlestone holds out an apple to Mr. Swingler, we register consciously what we would in any case have sensed implicitly: that a unique variation of the old pattern stretching back to Genesis is being played out in a very different Eden and in a very different key. The latter needs to be stressed; it is not enough to pick the Eve reference out of the myth-kitty. Big Glad is not tempting Swingler to sin — though she has already "fallen" in the popular sense since there is "no sign of a father for that boy of hers" (86) — and Swingler refuses the apple but takes her. The Eden myth is both used and altered, and in this instance, because the myth and its symbolic situation are so well known, Hodgins does not have to underline the connection. In "After the Season," however, since Classical allusion is no longer part of the common store, he has to point up his mythological reference. Hallie Crane, who runs a tourist cabaret in a remote fishing-camp during the summer and spends most of the winter in bed with Morgan the camp owner, is in conversation with Mr. Grey, an unwelcome stormbound visitor:

> She told him about this story she once read, an old-fashioned tale in some book somebody'd given to her when she was a little girl. This girl in the story, this Proser-something, was out running around in a place something like this, ... and up out of that hole came old Pluto, the king of the underworld, riding in a chariot, and hauled her off against her will down into his deep horrible black place. (164)

This passage could also be a trap for a narrowly archetypal critic; the point is not so much an analogy between Proserpina's situation and Hallie's as a contrast between Hallie's version of the pattern and its high classical equivalent. Despite her claim that Morgan is "[p]ulling me down into his hell with him" (165), she ultimately descends of her own free will, and refers in the last word of the story to "us" (169). Once again, the myth is invoked and then adapted. Hodgins's analogies are invariably flexible comparisons, never point-by-point correspondences. They serve to connect his highly localized stories with predominant and recurrent patterned sequences in the larger world. Such connectives indicate the guaranteed presence of the universal within the regional.

Hodgins seems, then, to be interested in an allegorical form that offers insight into a higher reality while remaining within a fundamentally comic mode. This balance receives its most brilliant treatment to date in *The Invention of the World*, and, so far as this novel is concerned, Hodgins has been unequivocal about his intentions. The "different levels of the novel are allegorical," he told Alan Twigg; "the primary concern is the search for the return to the 'created' [as distinct from the 'invented'] world" (192). And to Geoff Hancock he was even more explicit:

> While I was writing *The Invention of the World*, . . . I was aware of seven different levels that the story could be read on. I was aware of a single theme that controlled the imagery on every page and tied all these "layers" together. I had drawn strange charts and diagrams and written volumes of what could be considered literary criticism of the as-yet-invisible novel. (65)

This sounds daunting, as if Hodgins, like Hood, were inviting us to read him as a Dante or a Spenser, but he is really drawing our attention to the serious structure behind the comic surface of the book. He is insisting that comedy, and even farce, can be as profound as more obviously serious forms of literature, that the all-important tone determines how we read but must not blind us to the ultimate significance of what we are reading.

No one can read *The Invention of the World* attentively without becoming aware of the comic variations that are being played on traditional mythic patterns. Most obvious are those drawn from biblical sources (Genesis and the Eden story, Exodus, Revelation) and from Classical tradition (Jove and Europa, Becker as Charon, "The Wolves of Lycaon"), but Hodgins also draws quite extensively on Celtic myth, from the *Táin Bó Cuailnge* onwards.[1] Once again, however, he takes pains to avoid solemnity in these academic matters. While such patterns are seriously intended, and contain profound meanings, they are never exempt from playful parody. Nor are they invariably imported myths (though part of his point is the way human beings tote alien myths in their baggage). Moreover, he is fascinated with the problem of how myths are invented and take on power. In the following (highly concentrated) passage concerning the Irish immigrants' journey to Donal Keneally's colony, Dervit O'Connell sees Ned O'Mahony fabricating a North American myth before his eyes:

> They say the hero of the land we're sailing for had a fine hand at the harpsichord. . . . A fine red-nosed Irishman named Sir Sean A. McDermott. . . . The whole country worships the ground that he walks on and damned if he wasn't born in Macroom. . . . 'Twas his father, pardon me, that was born in Macroom. . . . The man himself was spawned in a log cabin somewhere in the wilds. Did his lessons by the candle light. They called him Honest Sean for refusing to cut down a cherry tree no matter how much the English bastards tried to force him. . . . The boy came out of those wilds wearing a raccoon on his head and shooting up the redskins right and left. . . . He made a fine great hero out of himself for sure and marched himself straight as you please to the big white palace up in Ottawa where he crowned himself the king. (112–13)

Here we are present at the invention (*not* creation) of a mythic world in which Sir John A. Macdonald, George Washington, Abraham Lincoln, and Davey Crockett all combine into a counterfeit hero.

Hodgins may here be indulging in a parody of the mythic process but he is also making fun of his own practice as a novelist. He is continually developing his characters in such a way that they illustrate a particular pattern of behaviour, and so can be interpreted allegorically, and even take on roles that align them with myth. Madmother Thomas provides a conveniently clear example. She is introduced complete with manure-spreader and all her eccentricities at the loggers' sports early in the novel, but she is much more than a merely colourful and idiosyncratic supernumerary. Her allegorical function is in fact made clear from the start: "Madmother Thomas, like someone in an ancient book, was looking for the place where she'd been born" (15). We are also told that she turns up regularly in Maggie Kyle's life two or three times a year (14). In a flashback through which we witness their first encounter, she reveals herself as a sibyl-figure with the ironic habit of giving advice that is the opposite of her own practice: "If you've any sense, child, you'll just stay put" (18), she advises while she is herself continually on the move, and later tells the young Maggie: "the where of a life don't matter at all, it's the how of your life that'll count" (19). If on first acquaintance we see her on a literal level as a comic grotesque, we soon find reason to change our opinion. By the time we come to the section entitled "Pilgrimage," in which Maggie, Becker, and Wade go off to Ireland, we realize that they too are engaged on a quest for origins. So, in a curiously ambiguous way, is Keneally when he burrows down into the earth that originally spewed him up (a variation, incidentally, of the mythic pattern employed in *Tay John*). So is Becker by virtue of his role as historian, since an important aspect of history is the discovery of origins. To return to Madmother Thomas, it is clearly not accidental that, as soon as the three get back from Ireland, they return to Maggie's personal origins, discover the old woman in Maggie's shack, and find that she has abandoned her quest just as theirs is completed. Appropriately, since she is a survivor of Keneally's colony, she is taken back to Maggie's trailer park where she replaces the dead Lily and so provides an element of continuity within Maggie's new dispensation.

Madmother Thomas is a typical Hodgins character because, although her quest may be both futile and absurd, she is herself portrayed as, by turns, grotesque, amusing, pathetic, and sometimes even wise. She is a reminder, if such were needed, that Hodgins is a master of varying tones, and that it is always a mistake to assume that an initial response to a character or a situation can be more than provisional. For example, the final section of the novel, which Hodgins has described as "a mock epic" (Hancock 77), is a veritable literary roller-coaster of shifting responses. It begins with Becker assuring us that what follows is *the true story of what happened* (339), and this prepares us by a Hodginsian law of opposites for the outrageous climactic fantasy. The loggers' riot, "the best damn brawl the island had ever seen" (347), is at once an exaggerated presentation of British Columbian celebratory energy and a parody of the traditional epic games. The list of wedding presents (352–53) begins with standard items ("pillows and sheets"), proceeds through the menacingly unlikely ("a box of matches, a tin of peaches, a promise of peace") and the farcically impossible ("Twin grandchildren. American oil tankers. Bad television programmes"), and ends with the patently allegorical ("Beauty. Grace. Forgiveness") and the genuinely moving ("Passion. Retirement. Neglect. Loneliness. Love"). A little later, the arrival of Horseman initiates a shift to an almost mystical transformation in which "the bride and the bridegroom" become "the new man and the new woman" (353–54) and are led out of the hall into a new dimension.

One would have thought that Hodgins's exuberance made an obvious positive point here; once again, however, we encounter the preference of Canadian critics for rigid categories and their reluctance to follow the clear tonal and stylistic indications provided. In this instance, it is Gaile McGregor who goes to extraordinary lengths to force upon *The Invention of the World* a vision related to Kierkegaardian *Angst*. Despite Hodgins's own assurance that "the novel has a positive ending. . . . It's a story of triumph" (Hancock 70), she is determined to read it as presenting a world with "no redeeming promises to offer at all" (81), a world in which any "possibility of transcendence" is precluded (83). She argues that "Hodgins's Fall into the absurd world is non-reversible and non-transformable" (81), and, in more detail:

> In Hodgins's fictional universe, . . . life is a closed system, a *box*, from which — as from the reception hall that stands as its symbolic correlative at the end of the novel — there is only one exit, under the aegis of the Horseman, death. It is possible (and only human), of course, to euphemize this finale, as Becker does, but the nursery rhyme echo evoked by his choice of closing words quite pointedly undercuts both the redemptive implications of the so-called House of Revelations, . . . and the religious rhetoric that has historically provided man with a kind of consolation. (82–83)

Far from presenting a "closed system," Hodgins takes care to leave the precise details of his ending intriguingly and (from a literary viewpoint) appropriately vague. The stranger "*apparently* drove the new couple all the way back to their home at the House of Revelations" (my emphasis); "*if they're not dead nor gone they're alive there still*" (354). A certain flexibility of interpretation is possible here, within limits, but we can be sure that Maggie and Wade are translated, if at all, into a higher realm of experience, perhaps the world of eternity, but certainly not death or nothingness. McGregor significantly omits Hodgins's reference to "the new man and the new woman" and neglects the fact that the section is entitled, positively, "Second Growth."

Once again, we find the assumption that any playful allusion to myth "undercuts" (McGregor's word) the original to which it refers. McGregor is not alone in this. In an essay on Hodgins's "burlesque," Susan Beckmann maintains that the "mythopoeic trappings" in *The Invention of the World* "are deliberately undercut by the burlesque" (123), and even Robert Lecker says much the same thing: "through parody and burlesque he undercuts the belief, expressed by Morag Gunn near the end of *The Diviners*, that 'The myths are my reality'" (86). This insistence on undercutting is especially notable when we remember that similar arguments were made about O'Hagan's use of myth by Fee and Davidson (see pp. 37–38 above). If a mythological pattern is altered, so the argument seems to run, then the author is thereby exposing the falsity of the original myth. But this does not follow. When O'Hagan has Father Rorty crucify himself on the school-marm tree in *Tay John*, this doesn't mean that the Crucifixion is an exploded myth but rather that human beings can follow Christ too literally and for varied motives. Rorty demonstrates, indeed, that crucifixion is a potent image continually applicable to human dilemmas. Denham's curt comment, "Priestly arrogance could go on farther" (219), represents one view, but another allegorical meaning, equally available in context, implies that Rorty undergoes an agony that symbolizes his betrayal by sexual desire. He thereby becomes an emblematic figure torn between flesh and spirit. Similarly, Tay John himself leads his tribe "into the wilderness" like Moses; like Moses, too, he is prevented from experiencing the Promised Land (which may not be attainable, least of all for Canadian Indians, in the modern world). This does not "undercut" Moses or Exodus or the concept of the Promised Land, but uses them for a new purpose. O'Hagan seems to me neutral in his employment of religious patterns for secular and literary ends. Hodgins, on the other hand, rearranges traditional myth in what can only be called an exhilarating way. The "Eden Swindle," Hodgins's "mock myth" (Hancock 77), is eventually redeemed by Maggie Kyle's community on the same site. A genuine "creation" is always available as an antidote to demonic "invention." Indeed, Hodgins's capacity to alter established myths, his ability to envisage new endings as well as new beginnings, represents a delivery from the tyranny of an inevitable repetition of a predestined Fate.

It would, of course, be possible to continue this examination of Hodgins's secular allegory by tracing it all through his later fiction. Indeed, *The Resurrection of Joseph Bourne* especially encourages this kind of approach, since there the allegorical allusions are not complicated, as they are in *The Invention of the World*, by intricate shifts of narrative and perspective. But the basic point should now be clear, and it will be more useful to proceed a little differently. Now that the fact of Hodgins's allegorical concerns has been documented, it is important to show how the otherwise austere effect of allegory is humanized by means of his congenial narrative voice.

As early as the opening page of *Spit Delaney's Island* we are made aware of the casual, relaxed quality of the narrator's prose: "People driving by don't notice Spit Delaney." The first sentence with its contracted verb sets the tone, and the paragraph ends with Spit muttering "that he'll be damned if he can figure out what it is that is happening to him" (3). A little later, we catch a glimpse of Spit's confidence before his world suddenly fell apart: " 'This here's one bugger you don't catch with his eyes shut' was his way of putting it" (5). The "way of putting it" is essential. As we proceed through the book, we encounter numerous individual ways of putting it, from Mrs. Wright's genteel rationalism in "Three Women of the Country" through Gerry Mack's staccato impatience in "The Trench Dwellers" ("*Macken this, Macken that*. Gerry Mack had had enough" [73]) and Mr. Swingler's laconic conversation in "Every Day of His Life" to the final story in which Spit returns as first-person narrator. Part of the almost Dickensian vitality in Hodgins's work derives from his ability to record faithfully and convincingly an abundance of distinctive speech-rhythms.

205

This gift is developed in *The Invention of the World*, where the verbal variety is an intrinsic part of the richness of the book. It is most obvious in the "Scrapbook" section, where a representative cross-section of local inhabitants talk briefly about their responses to the Keneally colony and are all clearly and immediately differentiated from each other. It is also evident in the confidently established idiolects of Becker and Julius and Lily Hayworth and Maggie and Wade Powers — and even in a minor character like Ned O'Mahony, whose story of "Sir Sean A. McDermott" I have already quoted. But this quality comes into its own in *The Resurrection of Joseph Bourne*. This novel differs from the rest of Hodgins's work because the central protagonist is really the community of Port Annie as a whole; it is made up of the stories — and the language — of an astonishingly large cast of characters. Hodgins has himself described it as a "concert for voices" and has observed how he was able to "float from person to person for reactions to certain events" (Twigg 193).

At this point he has also perfected the art (perhaps under the influence of Ethel Wilson, whose work he has praised [Hancock 54, 60]) of floating from authorial narrative into the words and rhythms of his characters. Here, for example, is Jenny Chambers:

> Three days later she was on the phone again, to Mabel (let Eva wait, the skinny traitor): two days in Nanaimo, it was like a dream, Mabel. She stayed in the Tally-ho, no less, with a view over the swimming pool and under a bridge and out to the harbour where there were sailboats; she hated to leave the room. But she did, because cripes, guess what — it didn't rain a drop the whole time she was there, she could hardly believe air could be so dry, she didn't even wear her fur, just carried it over her arm, and stores stores stores . . . (101–02)

It isn't merely the verisimilitude that impresses here, but Hodgins's capacity to make ordinary chitchat sound warmly human. Moreover, Jenny's accents and emphases are effortlessly absorbed into the omniscient narration.

But more is involved than a capacity for dramatic monologue. Hodgins is also adept at blending and contrasting voices. The scene where the squatters are preparing to resist eviction is an excellent example:

Larry looked at Bourne and lowered his voice. "And you encourage them in this game? A lost cause like this?"

The old man's hands were busy ransacking his pockets. "I don't encourage them. I don't encourage them. . . . I've told them to try sinking their roots into something a little more solid and lasting than a piece of earth, but nobody listens to me down here any better than they do in the town."

Hill Gin grunted. "Babble, babble."

"Solid and lasting like what?" Larry said.

"Like what?" One hand emerged with an apple, which he held up by the stem and examined. "Like those good old invisible things that can't be stolen or disappear." He polished the apple on the front of a sweater. "What our grandparents used to call the things of soul." And bit.

"Babble, babble," Hill Gin said. "People still have to live somewhere. That old fool would have us floating off into space like ghosts."

Bourne accepted the rebuke with a nod. "So you see, Larry Bowman, there's nothing left for me to do but . . . what?" — his hands turned up in a gesture of mock helplessness — "but love them, I guess."

The old woman, recoiling, cracked her skull on the floor. "Crap."

Bourne laughed — and sank his teeth once more into the apple. (228–29)

The control of tone is masterly here. Bourne is offering an old-fashioned and potentially vulnerable positive. Stated baldly, it could easily be dismissed as weak and sentimental. But Hodgins inserts it in a beautifully modulated scene that moves gracefully and with aplomb between the practical, the idealistic, the earthy, the whimsical, the grotesque, the amusing, and even perhaps the sublime. The values of traditional Christian "love" (Bourne, we remember, has returned from the undiscovered country as a resurrected man) are upheld against secular, twentieth-century "crap." And they are upheld by a character who would seem closer to Beckett than to any traditional optimist. (Technically, I am reminded of the scene at the close of Dickens's *Hard Times* where the gin-sodden, lisping Mr. Sleary, proprietor of a shabby circus-ring, announces "that there ith a love in the world, not all Thelf interetht after all"; in both cases a serious moral positive is rendered acceptable by its subtle placing within a crisply humorous context.) Bourne's apple is not a symbolic/allegorical one like Big Glad Littlestone's in "Every Day of His Life," but its homely particularity is essential to the overall effect of the scene — which is dependent, once again, upon a skillfully managed artifice.

Voice — or, rather, voices — may be recognized as the key to Hodgins's art. " 'People have their own way of talking, everybody's different'," says Lily Hayworth (*Invention* 251), and Hodgins demonstrates the truth of this in his fiction. Ironically, he found his own voice by discovering the diversity of other voices. As a beginning writer he had fallen under the stylistic influence of William Faulkner, and, as he was later to realize, "there's nothing worse than imitation Faulkner" (Hancock 54).[2] He emerged from this unfortunate period when, as he told Twigg, he "started listening to the voices of people who live on Vancouver Island" (188–89). This proved to be a revelation. Not only did he discover that "people have different speech patterns, different favourite expressions and different rhythms of speech" (189), but — perhaps unwittingly, since he does not seem at this time to have ventured outside British Columbia — he incorporated into his work many of the distinctive phrases and usages of his region. Pritchard has noted a number of these, including "up-island people," "spat snoose," "gyppo logging camp," "fire season," "watching for sparks" (30). Numerous others could be added: "hightail," "pickup," "logged-off hillsides," "whanging up," "the little scrunch," "second growth," etc. Hodgins displays a remarkable capacity to combine these elements into a style that is indisputably his own. His "concert of voices" depends for its effectiveness on his distinction as a consummately skillful and versatile conductor.

But "style," here as elsewhere, is inseparable from a concern for art and artifice. Writing of *The Barclay Family Theatre*, Waldemar Zacharasiewicz points out that the stories in this collection "deal more clearly with questions of the arts than does Hodgins' early work" (102). This is true, and the subsequent publication of *The Honorary Patron* underlines the point, though it is also true that the experience of reading *The Barclay Family Theatre* leads us to appreciate the extent to which the subject of art, especially within a context of philistine hostility, has been a constant preoccupation in his writings. As early as the opening story in *Spit Delaney's Island* we see Spit employing an artist to create a pictorial record of "Old Number One," and in the final story, while he is puzzled and outraged by Phemie Porter — "You can't trust people who write things on paper, they think they own the whole world and people too" (187) — he is also clearly affected by her artistic life-style. We may also recall Mr. Swingler the artist in "Every Day of His Life." But for the most part the emphasis falls, as in "The Religion of the Country," on "the logger and coalminer mentality of the island" (98), with Halligan the bookseller's admittedly snobbish preference for *Rigoletto* over the loggers' sports very much the exception. This is a society in which "if they have any spare time you'd never catch them reading a book" (99), where Spit's library is "a pile of dog-eared old paperbacks I'll never read" (171).

In *The Invention of the World* the arts are more prominent. Julius is a poet who liked "pushing words around on paper" (55), Wade's girl-friend Virginia Kerr is a serious painter who has her demonic counterpart in Lily Hayworth with her painting-by-numbers, while Becker, the historian who "wants to be God" (x), is seen throughout as an image of the artist. But philistinism is strong. When Wade quotes poetry in his wedding-speech, he prefaces his recitation with the assertion that he "hated the stuff" (351), and Julius sums up what is becoming a familiar view of the Island: "it leaped over civilization, . . . all the way from frontier town to Disneyland. You'll find pornography shops and slot machines and periodic festivals of idiocy, but you'll never find an art gallery" (233). In *The Resurrection of Joseph Bourne* the process is extended still further. Mayor Weins here represents the forces of philistinism: "By cultural centre, he explained, he meant a tourist-information bureau" (207). To Weins a church is "just a piece of real estate . . . unexploited" (210). What he calls "honest-to-goodness culture" means "Hollywood screen-writers and people who wrote television commercials" (216); he is looking for "the most tasteful rows of fast-food outlets and car-dealers and tourist attractions" (265). "Who needs you, you uncooperative old goat?" (7), he asks of the genuine poet Joseph Bourne. Mrs. Barnstone is Bourne's demonic counterpart as bad epic poet, but Jenny Chambers's striptease transforms miraculously into an authentic art-form as she is shown "dancing life back into things" (270).

In *The Barclay Family Theatre*, however, the concern with art is continual. Desmond is pushed by his mother towards the concert-stages of Europe, but instead he becomes a novelist (in "The Lepers' Squint"); a disagreeable poet appears in "Invasions '79"; Eli Waina-moinen is a painter with vision in "More Than Conquerors"; the art of *kabuki* is both celebrated and parodied in "The Sumo Revisions." Of course, the philistine world is still conspicuous. Mr. Pernouski's dream is to convert the natural paradise of Vancouver Island into profitable lots for the Eden Realty Company. Unease about "matters of history and culture" (24) are expressed throughout. Cornelia Hardcastle learns to play the piano on a paper keyboard so that her mother "doesn't even have to miss an episode of *Ma Perkins*" (2); Sparkle Roote is named after a character in a comic strip (104); David Payne "had never pretended to understand what the business of art and artists was all about" (141); Jacob Weins deserts *kabuki* for *sumo*, while Conrad "made it sound as if reading a book was one sure sign of senility" (239). At least two of the imaginative Barclay sisters consider they inhabit a "hickish dump of a place" (282).

In *The Honorary Patron*, Hodgins's most recent novel at the time of writing, an art critic is the main protagonist. That he is an Islander might suggest that the arts are now flourishing, but he left as a young man and has made his reputation in Europe. True, he is invited back for a hitherto unlikely "Pacific Coast Festival of the Arts" (25), but once again the forces of philistinism are supreme. The patrons are regarded as "artsy-fartsy people" (68, 215); a representative response to *Macbeth* is " 'Thought those guys'd never stop talking and get on with it' " (65). And the Festival folds, despite Elizabeth's back-handed confidence "that something so fine just couldn't fail — *not even here*" (243; my emphases). But stock-car racing is invariably popular, and the narrator finds it easy enough to imagine the populace "hurrying towards a scene of promised violence — a public execution or a duel" (296).

I emphasize all this because it seems an appropriate way to conclude a discussion not only of Hodgins but of the representative collection of writers considered in this book. A recurrent complaint voiced, directly or indirectly, by Canadian writers focuses on a basic resistance to their work on the part of a large section of the population. Not just indifference, but positive hostility. A significant number of them have commented on their sense of embarrassment at showing an interest in an activity looked upon as useless if not downright abnormal. Hodgins records the most extreme instance. He makes the point most eloquently in an interview with Jack David:

There has never been a time that I can remember when I didn't write. I kept it a secret of course, because it was a very shameful thing to do. I was very ashamed of it. To let somebody else find out outside my family it would be like declaring to the whole world that I wanted to be a ballet dancer. And in a logging community you can imagine the response there would be to that. (142)

This might be regarded as a typically heightened British Columbian reaction, but other writers have offered similar reports. Mavis Gallant remarks:

I had been determined to write as a way of life in the face of an almost unanimous belief that I was foolish, would fail, would be sorry, and would creep back with defeat as a return ticket. ("Do you still have those nutty ideas of yours?" I was asked, not so many years ago.) (*Home* xxii)

And Alice Munro, who talks about "coming from such a totally unliterary environment" (Hancock 220), told Graeme Gibson: "to most of my relatives the work I do is still a very meaningless, useless type of work" (246).[3] Hodgins's testimony is merely the most extreme account of a situation that seems recurrent in Canadian society. His work is of particular interest because he has made the fact of philistinism a central subject within his fiction.

I shall be returning to the subject of art and philistinism in my brief conclusion to the book as a whole. It would be a mistake, however, to end a discussion of Hodgins's work on this note. *The Honorary Patron* differs from his earlier books in having an elderly protagonist who, though attracted to the vigour of the youth that he encounters, is generally passive, introspective, and retrospective. This novel sounds deeper and more threatening notes than we have heard in Hodgins before, but this should not blind us to the characteristic Hodginsian exuberance that remains prominent. On the one hand, we have Jeffrey Crane realizing that he had "made himself enough of a clown and a sad, sad fool to be taken at last for a genuine specimen of twentieth-century man" (263); on the other, we find him protesting against a world of relativity: "What else was the twentieth century about, if not an attempt to recover from Einstein's blow?" (24). By the end of the novel, a promising young local artist (whom Crane has, to his chagrin, neglected) displays a series of canvases in which the "tunnel walls" of subterranean Nanaimo (which are also the abysses beneath all our crumbling houses) are portrayed with " 'the old guy's [i.e. Einstein's] face just sort of peeking out' " as if in search of something " 'that would sort of balance out what he scared everybody with before' " (317). The phrasing is that of a youthful acquaintance, but it embodies a confidence from which Crane takes hope. Much earlier — in equally hesitant phraseology — Crane had offered his own decidedly traditionalist aesthetic: ". . . the fashion has been to acknowledge little more than excellence of form. Yet beauty, dignity, that sort of old-fashioned thing is what I've gone on looking for — amongst other things, of course" (47).

So, one might add, has Hodgins. "That sort of old-fashioned thing" recalls Joseph Bourne's already quoted "good old invisible things that can't be stolen or disappear" (*Resurrection* 228). (The basic psychological pattern of Crane's life, indeed, will be seen to bear some notable resemblance to Bourne's.) All Hodgins's work seems based on the conviction that there is "lots of room for new ways of looking at things" (*Resurrection* 205). His strategy, ironically in view of what I have said about critical response to his mythologizing, is to "undercut" the now conventional view of a meaningless world with disturbing intimations of mystery and purpose. Hodgins doesn't ignore the disasters and fears of our world — these are represented by the cataclysmic landslide at the end of *The Resurrection of Joseph Bourne*, and the violence typified by Blackie Blackstone and his tribe in *The Honorary Patron* — but he refuses to acquiesce in a numbed helplessness. Jacob Weins ceases to be an absurd grotesque at the end of the former novel and urges the townspeople to "spring back to life from the ashes of disaster" (265). In the latter, Crane's experience on Vancouver Island is ultimately seen as a curious combination of the shaming and the liberating. He knows a little more about "how to live" his remaining years (272) at the end of the book than he did at the beginning. The fact of "growing old" naturally remains, but it is now recognized as a "giant comedy" (293); he learns from his sister about "the great old joke that life is" (73). Even the fatal accident at the stock-car races, involving Blackstone's terrorist son and recounted in the final sentences of the book, includes instinctively heroic self-sacrifice as well as violent absurdity.

Hodgins sets his protagonist in an absurdist plot but, like his creation, refuses to accept an absurdist philosophy. It is difficult to write about this aspect of his work without making it seem didactic and tiresomely uplifting, but within fiction that encompasses the horrendous and the hilarious, that combines the lusty with the tender, the flamboyantly grotesque with the humanly pathetic, this positive stance contributes to a sense of rich complexity. Hodgins's depiction of life seems not only more attractive but more accurate and more "real" than that of the post-modern cynicism which has become the convention of the supposed avant-garde. His distinction consists of an unfashionable but refreshing and sustaining enthusiasm for the miracle of life.

CHAPTER 12

Conclusion

This book has concentrated on the need for intelligent and perceptive *reading* of Canadian fiction, and has done so by drawing attention to the art through which this fiction is achieved. I have ended with Jack Hodgins because he seems to me the latest major talent to have emerged and established himself, but such a concluding emphasis is appropriate for other reasons as well. Hodgins's example, both in his life and in his writings, may be seen as both disturbing and comforting. Disturbing for two reasons: because his autobiographical account gives a dramatic indication of the high odds against a creative talent developing in such unpropitious as well as actively hostile circumstances; and also because it indicates how isolated modern writers are from the vast majority of their contemporaries, who ought to be their readers. Comforting, however, because the determination of such people as Hodgins, and Gallant and Munro, is an indication of the way in which creativity continues to manifest itself against the grain of an age. Moreover, the need of individuals to express themselves creatively suggests a parallel need on the part of a larger section of the population for the imaginative sustenance that can be satisfied by the kind of creative reading I am trying to encourage here.

Unfortunately, this audience has still to be tapped. As John Metcalf has remarked: "The good [Canadian] writers are [now] trusting readers to be able to read. The problem, of course, is that there are so few of them to trust" (*Kicking* 13). Naturally, there has always been a small minority seriously interested in what is best in literary culture, but until recently this has meant, in Canada, the importation of foreign masterpieces that, however profound and illuminating they may be, can never serve as the substitute for an adequate local product. (That we need foreign masterpieces as well goes, I hope, without saying.) As we all know, Canadian literature took a long time to emerge. It is now doing so — it may even be time to say that it has now done so — but it cannot survive without readers. The efforts of a Hodgins, against seemingly insuperable odds, will be in vain if the imaginative vision embodied in his fiction is not communicated to his society which, in his early days, was so resolutely opposed to it. In a sense, that is what *The Honorary Patron* is about. The best of modern Canadian fiction deserves to be read because of its intrinsic merits; but it also *needs* to be read if we are to have a healthy and living culture within the country. One can only hope that the recent increase in attention to Canadian literature in schools and universities will lead to an eventual leavening of the mass, the non-reading majority who can never be adequately fulfilled (whether they know it or not) by the pabulum of spectator sports and TV.

There is, however, an added — and final — complication. Modern Canadian fiction deserves and needs more readers quantitatively. But the very nature of the literature that is now being produced also means that we need readers of better quality. To quote Metcalf again, "[w]e now have *sophisticated* writers who make considerable demands on readers" (*Kicking* 13). This places the onus, then, on an informed, experienced, and discriminating reading public — the kind of "clerisy" that Davies called for at the opening of *A Voice from the Attic*. Such an audience must ultimately, of course, arise out of the nation as a whole. Initially, however, it needs to be fostered by teachers of literature in schools and universities, upon whom falls the duty and responsibility to encourage appropriate and more subtle reading methods. This can only be done, I believe, if literature is offered not as sociology (content, thematics) nor as a patriotic imperative (use, application), but as a literary art that stimulates both understanding and imagination. As Hugh Hood once said: "If you want to have a civilization, you have to have a rather small number of people who can do what I do" (*Trusting* 37). You also, of course, have to have a much larger number of people who can appreciate why he does it, and support him when he does it. It is with the faith that at least a modest advance can be made in this direction that I have written this book.

NOTES

Chapter 2 • *Howard O'Hagan*

1 Montana Pete appears only in the first edition of *Wilderness Men* (1958). A whole chapter, "Montana Pete Goes Courting," was omitted, for reasons explained later in this chapter, from the 1978 reprint. Because the latter is more readily accessible, I quote from it here, unless the 1958 edition is explicitly indicated.

2 The text of the 1958 *Wilderness Men* differs very slightly from the one reproduced here from *The Woman Who Got On at Jasper Station*. The variants do not, however, affect my discussion of O'Hagan's verbal subtlety in this passage.

Chapter 3 • *Ethel Wilson*

1 For a vivid semi-fictional account of the saltier side of Vancouver at the time when Wilson was in her teens, see M. Allerdale Grainger's novel, *Woodsmen of the West*.

2 Parts of *The Innocent Traveller* were certainly written as early as the 1930s, and David Stouck has gone so far as to assert that "*The Innocent Traveller* . . . was the first book she wrote" (49). Apparently a complete manuscript was in existence by 1944, while *Hetty Dorval* was written in a few weeks in 1945. The technical difference between the books is so great, however, that *The Innocent Traveller* must have gone through a drastic and complete revision before taking its final form. This is borne out by the evidence provided by Stouck in his edition, *Stories — Essays — Letters*.

3 A reproduction of this ending is printed as a frontispiece to *The Ethel Wilson Symposium*, edited by Lorraine McMullen.

4 For a more positive view of Hetty, which I find interesting but do not share, see Beverley Mitchell, "Ethel Wilson," 201–08, and her article in McMullen, 73–85.

Chapter 4 • *W.O. Mitchell*

1 For a detailed account of these changes, see Keith, "W.O. Mitchell."

2 For a cogent, positive reading of this novel, however, see Davidson, "Lessons in Perspective."

3 I am indebted on this point to a perceptive comment by an anonymous publisher's reader.

Chapter 5 · *Robertson Davies*

1 In *The Lyre of Orpheus*, the italicized comments on the action from E.T.A. Hoffmann in limbo repeat — rather perfunctorily, it seems to me — the effect employed creatively in *What's Bred in the Bone*.

2 See, for example, "An Elite Exists" (*Voice* 294–95).

3 B.W. Powe's chapter on Davies, "Odd Man Out," in *A Climate Charged* provides a useful complement to Solecki's review-article, since it too offers a healthily skeptical initial approach, but ends with a rather more positive evaluation of Davies's overall achievement. T.D. MacLulich raises the matter — somewhat inconclusively, in my view — in "Colloquial Style and the Tory Mode." The essay has been radically revised and given a more critical emphasis for incorporation into his recent book, *Between Europe and America*. For a more specific defence of Davies as a writer in the tradition of Thomas Love Peacock and Aldous Huxley, see James Mulvihill's excellent article, *"The Rebel Angels*: Robertson Davies and the History of Ideas."

Chapter 6 · *Mavis Gallant*

1 These are "Mavis Gallant: Returning Home" (1978), "The Three Stages of Mavis Gallant's Short Fiction" (1978), and "Mavis Gallant and the Creation of Consciousness" (1985). Neil Besner's *The Light of Imagination*, a solid and welcome full-length study of her work, appeared too late for discussion in this chapter, while Janice Kulyk Keefer's brilliant *Reading Mavis Gallant* was published while the present book was already in proof.

Chapter 7 · *Margaret Laurence*

1 For an excellent treatment of this novel that approaches the matter of life versus fiction from a different angle, see Constance Rooke, "Hagar's Old Age: *The Stone Angel* as *Vollendungsroman*."

2 This device is used more sparingly and adroitly by Robertson Davies in early chapters of *Fifth Business* (12, 24), and is later parodied in Margaret Atwood's *Lady Oracle* (75).

3 Marian Engel puts the necessary critical comment into her protagonist's mouth in *Joanne*: "Remember in those old-fashioned books how the moment the mother sneezed in the direction of another man, the baby died of diptheria?" (54).

4 I have written on the artistic problems involved in *The Diviners* at greater length in "Margaret Laurence's *The Diviners*: The Problems of Close Reading."

Chapter 8 · *Hugh Hood*

1 A good illustration may be found in their discussions of "New Country" (in *None Genuine Without This Signature*). Lester and Molly are driving back from Toronto to Stoverville on Highway 401, and decide on impulse to deviate into the "Highlands of Hastings" country, where they encounter a ghost town. Lester is not used to the road, and has a narrow escape from an accident. The last sentence of the story reads: "He speeded up, heading into a blind curve" (76). For Garebian, the "tenor of death produces a sudden, though not unpredictable, ending" (43); for Copoloff-Mechanic "[t]he couple's blindness finds its counterpart in a blind curve that delivers them into the unanticipated new country of death" (121). Both critics seem to me to overinterpret. The "new country" clearly suggests an awareness of aging and of death, an increased realization of man's mortality. It is equally clear that the couple is entering a sombre, even threatening future, but Hood does *not* finish the story on a violent death. His unspecific ending is decidedly more subtle than the crudely allegorical climax provided by the commentators. This kind of rigid interpretation damages the flexible artistry that Hood is at pains to create.

2 Since this was written, Copoloff-Mechanic has discussed the "triadic" connections between these stories in the third chapter of her *Pilgrim's Progress*. I do not, however, see any reason to change what I have written. The intellectual and structural effects that she discusses (see, especially, 74–75) significantly ignore any more immediately stylistic or literary-critical considerations.

3 A notable exception is Robert Lecker's excellent discussion in "A Spirit of Communion: *The Swing in the Garden*," an article that throws interesting light on more than the first part of the *New Age* series.

Chapter 10 · *Margaret Atwood*

1 There is confusion in the printed texts about the spelling of Marian's surname. On pp. 13 and 20 of the standard editions, it is spelled "MacAlpin"; on pp. 126, 168, and 223, it appears as "McAlpin," and this is also the form in the blurb-digest. (The problem is compounded in the New Canadian Library edition where the current Introduction reads "McAlpine" throughout!) This confusion stems from a change of name made at a late stage in the writing of the novel. In typescripts in the Thomas Fisher Rare Book Library of the University of Toronto, the heroine's name originally appears as Marian Moorhouse or Moorehouse. In the final transcript, some older pages have been incorporated, and "McAlpin" is substituted by hand in the last three instances. Since the form not only enjoys a slight numerical majority but also appears to be Atwood's latest decision about the name, I am employing it here.

2 I have written at greater length on the satiric and artistic complexities of this novel in *Introducing Margaret Atwood's* The Edible Woman.

3 This was written before the appearance of Gayle Greene's "*Life before Man*: 'Can Anything Be Saved?'," an excellent article that confirms much that I have written here about the complex tone of the novel.

4 This point is not, I think, undermined by Atwood's recent public stand against

a new anti-pornography bill (1987–88), since she is clearly drawing attention to the implications for free speech and artistic expression that might result from the new legislation. For further comments on the matter of pornography and censorship, see *Second Words* 353–54.

5 By Fiona Sparrow, in conversation.

6 This chapter was written before the publication of *Cat's Eye*, a challenging novel of considerable complexity. An adequate discussion of this work inserted into the text at the last moment would run the risk of doing less than justice to Atwood's achievement, and might well threaten the proportions of the chapter and perhaps of the whole book. Suffice it to say here that many of the preoccupations I have discussed in the course of this chapter are developed further in *Cat's Eye*. It is a profound novel about Time, and the protagonist's memories of growing up in Toronto in the 1940s are tellingly juxtaposed with her experiences in the contemporary world. Especially interesting to students of Atwood's *oeuvre* is the way in which incidents and images treated almost farcically in *Lady Oracle* are presented seriously, even movingly here. The protagonist is quintessentially Atwoodian, not least in her admission: "I'm aware that my tastes are not fashionable" (327). The reading of Atwood's fiction offered in this chapter will be found to be compatible with her latest novel.

7 Naturally, I dissociate myself from the argument on the same page, attributed to Frank Davey, concerning "Atwood's radical suspicion of narrative art," a phrase that might, however, legitimately be applied Munro.

8 For echoes of the account of the grandfather on the first page, see *Dancing Girls* 188 and *Bodily Harm* 55.

Chapter 11 • *Jack Hodgins*

1 For the Celtic background, see Horner.

2 A specimen of this style is preserved in the brief extract from a novel called "White Smoke Rising" printed in *Beginnings*.

3 Feminist critics often quote such passages as evidence of male hostility to female creativity, but it is clear from Hodgins's example that the problem is by no means confined to women writers.

WORKS CITED

Atwood, Margaret. *Bluebeard's Egg*. 1983. Toronto: Seal-McClelland, 1984.

_____. *Bodily Harm*. Toronto: McClelland, 1981.

_____. *Cat's Eye*. Toronto: McClelland, 1988.

_____. *Dancing Girls*. Toronto: McClelland, 1977.

_____. *The Edible Woman*. 1969. Toronto: McClelland, 1973.

_____. *The Handmaid's Tale*. Toronto: McClelland, 1985.

_____. *Lady Oracle*. 1976. Toronto: Seal-McClelland, 1977.

_____. Letter. *Saturday Night* Jan.–Feb. 1977: 3.

_____. *Life Before Man*. 1979. Toronto: Seal-McClelland, 1980.

_____. *Second Words: Selected Critical Prose*. Toronto: McClelland, 1982.

_____. *Surfacing*. 1972. Toronto: Paperjacks, 1973.

Bailey, Nancy I. "The Masculine Image in *Lives of Girls and Women*." *Canadian Literature* 80 (1979): 113–20.

Barclay, Patricia. "Regionalism and the Writer: A Talk with W.O. Mitchell." *Canadian Literature* 14 (1962): 53–56.

Baxter, John. "*The Stone Angel*: Shakespearian Bearings." *Compass* (U of Alberta) 1 (1977): 13–18.

Beckmann, Susan. "Canadian Burlesque: Jack Hodgins' *The Invention of the World*." *Essays on Canadian Writing* 20 (1980–81): 106–25.

Besner, Neil. *The Light of Imagination: Mavis Gallant's Fiction*. Vancouver: U of British Columbia P, 1988.

Bowering, George. "That Fool of a Fear: Notes on *A Jest of God*." *Canadian Literature* 50 (1971): 41–56. Rpt. in *A Place to Stand On: Essays By and About Margaret Laurence*. Ed. George Woodcock. Edmonton: NeWest, 1983. 210–26.

Buitenhuis, Elspeth. *Robertson Davies*. Toronto: Forum House, 1972.

Buning, Marius. *T.F. Powys: A Modern Allegorist*. *Costerus* 56. Amsterdam: Rodopi, 1986.

Cameron, Donald. *Conversations with Canadian Novelists*. Parts 1 and 2. Toronto: Macmillan, 1973.

Cameron, Elspeth. *Hugh MacLennan: A Writer's Life*. Toronto: U of Toronto P, 1981.

Carrington, Ildikó de Papp. "Demons, Doubles, and Dinosaurs: *Life Before Man*, *The Origin of Consciousness*, and 'The Icicle'." *Essays on Canadian Writing* 33 (1986): 68–88.

Cloutier, Pierre. "An Interview with Hugh Hood." *Journal of Canadian Fiction* 2.1 (1973): 49–52.

Connolly, Kevin, Douglas Freake, and Jason Sherman. "Interview: Alice Munro." *What* (Toronto) Sept.–Oct. 1986: n. pag.

Copoloff-Mechanic, Susan. *Pilgrim's Progress: A Study of the Short Stories of Hugh Hood.* Toronto: ECW, 1988.

Cowan, Hugh, and Gabriel Kampf. "*Acta* Interviews W.O. Mitchell." *Acta Victoriana* (Victoria College, U of Toronto) 98.2 (1974): 15–26.

Cude, Wilfred. "Criticism as Astrology." Rev. of *What's Bred in the Bone* by Robertson Davies. *Antigonish Review* 66–67 (1986): 43–47.

Darling, Michael. " 'Undecipherable Signs': Margaret Laurence's 'To Set Our House in Order'." *Essays on Canadian Writing* 29 (1984): 192–203.

Davey, Frank. *Margaret Atwood: A Feminist Poetics.* Vancouver: Talonbooks, 1984.

David, Jack. "An Interview with Jack Hodgins." *Essays on Canadian Writing* 11 (1978): 142–46.

Davidson, Arnold E. "Being and Definition in *Tay John.*" *Etudes Canadiennes* 15 (1983): 137–47.

_____. "Lessons in Perspective: W.O. Mitchell's *The Vanishing Point.*" *Ariel* 12.1 (1981): 62–78.

_____. "Silencing the Word in Howard O'Hagan's *Tay John.*" *Canadian Literature* 110 (1980): 30–44.

Davies, Robertson. *The Enthusiasms of Robertson Davies.* Ed. Judith Skelton Grant. Toronto: McClelland, 1979.

_____. *Fifth Business.* 1970. Harmondsworth: Penguin, 1977.

_____. "Four Distinguished Novels." *Saturday Night* 20 Dec. 1941: 16.

_____. *Leaven of Malice.* 1954. Toronto: Clarke Irwin, 1964.

_____. *The Lyre of Orpheus.* Toronto: Macmillan, 1988.

_____. *The Manticore.* 1972. Harmondsworth: Penguin, 1977.

_____. *A Mixture of Frailties.* Toronto: Macmillan, 1958.

_____. *One Half of Robertson Davies.* Toronto: Macmillan, 1977.

_____. *The Papers of Samuel Marchbanks.* Toronto: Irwin, 1985.

_____. *The Rebel Angels.* Toronto: Macmillan, 1981.

_____. *Tempest-Tost.* 1951. Toronto: Clarke Irwin, 1955.

_____. *A Voice from the Attic.* 1960. Toronto: McClelland, 1970.

_____. *The Well-Tempered Critic: One Man's View of Theatre and Letters in Canada.* Ed. Judith Skelton Grant. Toronto: McClelland, 1981.

_____. *What's Bred in the Bone.* Toronto: Macmillan, 1985.

_____. *World of Wonders.* 1975. Harmondsworth: Penguin, 1977.

Duffy, Dennis. "Space/Time and the Matter of Form." *Essays on Canadian Writing* 13/14 (1978–79): 131–44.

Eliot, T.S. *Complete Poems and Plays (1909–1950).* New York: Harcourt, 1952.

Engel, Marian. *Joanne: The Last Days of a Modern Marriage.* Don Mills, ON: PaperJacks, 1975.

Fee, Margery. "Howard O'Hagan's *Tay John*: Making New World Myth." *Canadian Literature* 110 (1986): 8–27.

Fletcher, Angus. *Allegory: The Theory of a Symbolic Mode.* Ithaca: Cornell UP, 1964.

Frye, Northrop. *Anatomy of Criticism.* Princeton: Princeton UP, 1957.

Fulford, Robert. "An Interview with Hugh Hood." *Tamarack Review* 66 (1975): 65–77.

Gabriel, Barbara. "Fairly Good Times: An Interview with Mavis Gallant." *Canadian Forum* Feb. 1987: 23–27.

Gallant, Mavis. "The Burgundy Weekend." *Tamarack Review* 76 (1979): 3–39.

_____. *A Fairly Good Time.* 1970. Toronto: Macmillan, 1983.

_____. *From the Fifteenth District.* 1979. Toronto: Macmillan, 1981.

_____. *Green Water, Green Sky.* 1959. Toronto: Macmillan, 1983.

_____. *Home Truths: Selected Canadian Stories.* Toronto: Macmillan, 1981.

_____. *In Transit.* Toronto: Viking (Penguin Group), 1988.

_____. *My Heart Is Broken.* 1964. Toronto: General, 1982.

_____. *The Other Paris: Stories.* 1956. Toronto: Macmillan, 1986.

_____. *Overhead in a Balloon.* Toronto: Macmillan, 1985.

_____. *Paris Notebooks.* Toronto: Macmillan, 1986.

_____. *The Pegnitz Junction.* 1973. Toronto: Macmillan, 1982.

Garebian, Keith. *Hugh Hood.* Boston: Twayne, 1983.

Geddes, Gary. "The Writer that CanLit Forgot." *Saturday Night* Nov. 1977: 84–92.

Gibson, Graeme. *Eleven Canadian Novelists.* Toronto: Anansi, 1973.

Gill, Brendan. "A Lost Lady." Rev. of *A Fairly Good Time* by Mavis Gallant. *Time* (Canada) 8 June 1970: 62.

Godard, Barbara. "Tales Within Tales: Margaret Atwood's Folk Narratives." *Canadian Literature* 109 (1986): 57–84.

Grainger, M. Allerdale. *Woodsmen of the West.* 1908. Toronto: McClelland, 1964.

Gray, John (with Eric Peterson). *Billy Bishop Goes to War.* Vancouver: Talonbooks, 1981.

Greene, Gayle. "*Life before Man*: 'Can Anything Be Saved?' " *Margaret Atwood: Vision and Forms.* Ed. Kathryn VanSpanckeren and Jan Garden Castro. Carbondale: Southern Illinois UP, 1988. 65–84.

Hale, Victoria G. "An Interview with Hugh Hood." *World Literature Written in English* 11 (1972): 35–41.

Hancock, Geoff. *Canadian Writers at Work.* Toronto: Oxford UP, 1987.

Harrison, James. "The Rhythms of Ritual in Margaret Laurence's *The Tomorrow-Tamer.*" *World Literature Written in English* 27 (1987): 245–52.

Hatch, Ronald. "Mavis Gallant and the Creation of Consciousness." *The Canadian Novel: Present Tense.* Ed. John Moss. Toronto: NC, 1985. 46–71.

_____. "Mavis Gallant: Returning Home." *Atlantis* (Acadia U) 4 (1978): 95–102.

_____. "The Three Stages of Mavis Gallant's Short Fiction." *Canadian Fiction Magazine* 28 (1978): 92–114.

Hetherington, Renée, and Gabriel Kampf. "*Acta* Interviews Robertson Davies." *Acta Victoriana* (Victoria College, U of Toronto) 97.2 (1973): 69–87.

Hodgins, Jack. *The Barclay Family Theatre*. Toronto: Macmillan, 1981.

_____. *Beginnings*. Toronto: Grand Union Press, 1983.

_____. *The Honorary Patron*. Toronto: McClelland, 1987.

_____. *The Invention of the World*. Toronto: Macmillan, 1977.

_____. *The Resurrection of Joseph Bourne*. Toronto: Macmillan, 1979.

_____. *Spit Delaney's Island*. Toronto: Macmillan, 1976.

Hood, Hugh. *Around the Mountain: Sketches from Montreal Life*. Toronto: Martin, 1967.

_____. *Black and White Keys*. *The New Age/Le nouveau siècle*, part 4. Downsview: ECW, 1982.

_____. *The Camera Always Lies*. 1967. Toronto: McClelland, [1982].

_____. *Dark Glasses*. Ottawa: Oberon, 1976.

_____. *Flying a Red Kite*. Toronto: Ryerson, 1962.

_____. *The Fruit Man, The Meat Man & The Manager*. Ottawa: Oberon, 1971.

_____. *The Governor's Bridge Is Closed*. Ottawa: Oberon, 1973.

_____. "Hugh Hood and John Mills in Epistolary Conversation." *Fiddlehead* 116 (1978): 133–44.

_____. "The Isolation Booth." *Tamarack Review* 9 (1958): 5–12.

_____. *The Motor Boys in Ottawa*. *The New Age/Le nouveau siècle*, part 6. Toronto: Stoddart, 1986.

_____. *A New Athens*. *The New Age/Le nouveau siècle*, part 2. Ottawa: Oberon, 1977.

_____. *None Genuine Without This Signature*. Downsview: ECW, 1980.

_____. *Reservoir Ravine*. *The New Age/Le nouveau siècle*, part 3. Ottawa: Oberon, 1979.

_____. *The Scenic Art*. *The New Age/Le Nouveau siècle*, part 5. Toronto: Stoddart, 1984.

_____. *Scoring: The Art of Hockey*. Illus. Seymour Segal. Ottawa: Oberon, 1979.

_____. *The Swing in the Garden*. *The New Age/Le nouveau siècle*, part 1. Ottawa: Oberon, 1975.

_____. *Tony's Book*. *The New Age/Le Nouveau siècle*, part 7. Toronto: Stoddart, 1988.

_____. *Trusting the Tale*. Downsview: ECW, 1983.

_____. *White Figure, White Ground*. 1964. Richmond Hill: Simon, 1973.

Horner, Jan C. "Irish and Biblical Myth in Jack Hodgins' *The Invention of the World*." *Canadian Literature* 99 (1983): 6–18.

Horwood, Harold. "Interview with Alice Munro." *The Art of Alice Munro: Saying the Unsayable*. Ed. Judith Miller. Waterloo: U of Waterloo P, 1984. 123–35.

Howells, Coral Ann. *Private and Fictional Worlds: Canadian Women Writers of the 1970s and 1980s*. London: Methuen, 1987.

_____. "Worlds Alongside: Contradictory Discourses in the Fiction of Alice Munro and Margaret Atwood." *Gaining Ground: European Critics on Canadian Literature*. Ed. Robert Kroetsch and Reingard M. Nischik. Edmonton: NeWest, 1985. 131–36.

Hoy, Helen. " 'Dull, Simple, Amazing and Unfathomable': Paradox and Double Vision in Alice Munro's Fiction." *Studies in Canadian Literature* 5.1 (1980): 100–15.

Hughes, Kenneth. "Politics and *A Jest of God*." *Journal of Canadian Studies* 13.3 (1978): 40–54.

James, Henry. *The Art of the Novel*. Ed. R.P. Blackmur. N.Y.: Scribner's, 1962.

Jenness, Diamond. *Indians of Canada*. 1912. Toronto: U of Toronto P, 1977.

Kareda, Urjo. "Atwood on Automatic." Rev. of *Bodily Harm* by Margaret Atwood. *Saturday Night* Nov. 1981: 70, 72.

Keefer, Janice Kulyk. "Criticism and Mavis Gallant." *Dalhousie Review* 64 (1984–85): 721–35.

_____. "Mavis Gallant and the Angel of History." *University of Toronto Quarterly* 55 (1986): 282–301.

_____. *Reading Mavis Gallant*. Toronto: Oxford UP, 1989.

Keith, W.J. *Introducing Margaret Atwood's* The Edible Woman. Toronto: ECW, 1989.

_____. "Margaret Laurence's *The Diviners*: The Problems of Close Reading." *Journal of Canadian Studies* 23.3 (1988): 102–16.

_____. "Overview: Ethel Wilson, Providence, and the Vocabulary of Vision." *The Ethel Wilson Symposium*. Ed. Lorraine McMullen. Ottawa: U of Ottawa P, 1982. 105–17.

_____. "W.O. Mitchell from *The Alien* to *The Vanishing Point*." *World Literature Written in English* 27 (1987): 252–62.

Kertzer, J.M. "Margaret Laurence (1926–87)." *Canadian Writers and Their Works, Fiction Series, Volume Nine*. Ed. Robert Lecker, Jack David, Ellen Quigley. Toronto: ECW, 1987. 253–310.

Kroetsch, Robert. "A Conversation with Margaret Laurence." *Creation*. Ed. Robert Kroetsch. Toronto: new, 1970. 53–63. Rpt. in *A Place to Stand On: Essays By and About Margaret Laurence*. Ed. George Woodcock. Edmonton: NeWest, 1983. 46–55.

Laurence, Margaret. *A Bird in the House*. 1970. Toronto: McClelland, 1974.

_____. *The Diviners*. 1974. Toronto: McClelland, 1978.

_____. *The Fire-Dwellers*. 1969. Toronto: McClelland, 1973.

_____. "Gadgetry or Growing: Form and Voice in the Novel." *Journal of Canadian Fiction* 27 (1980): 54–62. Rpt. in *A Place to Stand On: Essays By and About Margaret Laurence*. Ed. George Woodcock. Edmonton: NeWest, 1983. 80–89.

_____. *Heart of a Stranger*. 1976. Toronto: Seal-McClelland, 1980.

_____. *A Jest of God*. 1966. Toronto: McClelland, 1974.

_____. *The Stone Angel*. 1964. Toronto: McClelland, 1968.

_____. "Ten Years' Sentences." *Canadian Literature* 41 (1969): Rpt. in *A Place to Stand On: Essays By and About Margaret Laurence*. Ed. George Woodcock. Edmonton: NeWest, 1983. 28–34.

_____. *This Side Jordan*. 1960. Toronto: McClelland, 1976.

_____. "Time and the Narrative Voice." *The Narrative Voice*. Ed. John Metcalf. Toronto: McGraw, 1972. 126–30. Rpt. in *A Place to Stand On: Essays By and About Margaret Laurence.* Ed. George Woodcock. Edmonton: NeWest, 1983. 155–59.

——. *The Tomorrow-Tamer.* 1963. Toronto: McClelland, 1970.

Lecker, Robert. "Haunted by a Glut of Ghosts: Jack Hodgins' *The Invention of the World.*" *Essays on Canadian Writing* 20 (1980–81): 86–105.

——. "Janus Through the Looking Glass: Atwood's First Three Novels." *The Art of Margaret Atwood: Essays in Criticism.* Ed. Arnold E. and Cathy N. Davidson. Toronto: Anansi, 1981. 177–203.

——. "A Spirit of Communion: *The Swing in the Garden.*" *Essays on Canadian Writing* 13/14 (1978–79): 187–210.

Macfarlane, David. "Writer in Residence." *Saturday Night* Dec. 1986: 51–54, 56.

MacLulich, T.D. *Between Europe and America: The Canadian Tradition in Fiction.* Toronto: ECW, 1988.

——. "Colloquial Style and the Tory Mode." *Canadian Literature* 89 (1981): 7–21.

Mandel, Eli, and Rudy Wiebe. "Where the Voice Comes From." *Quill & Quire* Dec. 1974: 4, 20. Rpt. in *A Voice in the Land: Essays By and About Rudy Wiebe.* Ed. W.J. Keith. Edmonton: NeWest, 1981. 150–55.

Martin, W.R. *Alice Munro: Paradox and Parallel.* Edmonton: U of Alberta P, 1987.

Mathews, Lawrence. "*Who Do You Think You Are?*: Alice Munro's Art of Disarrangement." *Probable Fictions: Alice Munro's Narrative Acts.* Ed. Louis K. MacKendrick. Downsview: ECW, 1983. 181–93.

McAlpine, Mary. "On Ethel Wilson." *Transitions II: Short Fiction. A Source Book of Canadian Literature.* Ed. Edward Peck. Vancouver: Commcept, 1978. 243–46.

——. *The Other Side of Silence: A Life of Ethel Wilson.* Madeira Park, BC: Harbour, 1988.

McGregor, Gaile. *The Wacousta Syndrome.* Toronto: U of Toronto P, 1985.

McMullen, Lorraine, ed. *The Ethel Wilson Symposium.* Ottawa: U of Ottawa P, 1982.

Metcalf, John. "A Conversation with Alice Munro." *Journal of Canadian Fiction* 1.4 (1972): 54–62.

——. "The Curate's Egg." *Essays on Canadian Writing* 30 (1984–85): 35–59.

——. *Kicking Against the Pricks.* Downsview: ECW, 1982.

Mills, John. "Hugh Hood and John Mills in Epistolary Conversation." *Fiddlehead* 116 (1978): 133–44.

——. "Hugh Hood and the Analogical Method." *Essays on Canadian Writing* 13/14 (1978–9): 94–112.

——. "Robertson Davies (1913–)." *Canadian Writers and Their Works, Fiction Series, Volume Six.* Ed. Robert Lecker, Jack David, Ellen Quigley. Toronto: ECW, 1985. 21–78.

Mitchell, Beverley. "Ethel Wilson (1888–1980)." *Canadian Writers and Their Works, Fiction Series, Volume Six.* Ed. Robert Lecker, Jack David, Ellen Quigley. Toronto: ECW, 1985. 183–238.

——. "The Right Word in the Right Place: Literary Techniques in the Fiction of Ethel Wilson." *The Ethel Wilson Symposium*. Ed. Lorraine McMullen. Ottawa: U of Ottawa P, 1982. 73–85.

Mitchell, W.O. "But as Yesterday." *Queen's Quarterly* 48 (1942). 132–38.

———. "Elbow Room." *Maclean's* 15 Sept. 1942: 18–20, 39.

———. *How I Spent My Summer Holidays*. Toronto: Macmillan, 1981.

———. *Jake and the Kid*. Toronto: Macmillan, 1961.

———. *The Kite*. Toronto: Macmillan, 1962.

———. *Ladybug, Ladybug . . . .* Toronto: McClelland, 1988.

———. *Since Daisy Creek*. Toronto: Macmillan, 1984.

———. *The Vanishing Point*. Toronto: Macmillan, 1973.

———. *Who Has Seen the Wind*. 1947. Toronto: Macmillan, 1972.

Moss, John. *A Reader's Guide to the Canadian Novel*. Toronto: McClelland, 1981.

Mulvihill, James. "*The Rebel Angels*: Robertson Davies and the Novel of Ideas." *English Studies in Canada* 13.2 (1987): 182–94.

Munro, Alice. "The Colonel's Hash Resettled." *The Narrative Voice*. Ed. John Metcalf. Toronto: McGraw, 1972. 181–83.

———. *Dance of the Happy Shades*. Toronto: Ryerson, 1968.

———. "The Ferguson Girls Must Never Marry." *Grand Street* 1.3 (1982): 27–64.

———. "Home." *New Canadian Stories 74*. Ed. David Helwig and Joan Harcourt. Ottawa: Oberon, 1974. 133–53.

———. *Lives of Girls and Women*. 1971. Scarborough: Signet-NAL, 1974.

———. *The Moons of Jupiter*. 1982. Harmondsworth: Penguin, 1983.

———. *The Progress of Love*. Toronto: McClelland, 1986.

———. *Something I've Been Meaning to Tell You*. 1974. Scarborough: Signet-NAL, 1975.

———. *Who Do You Think You Are?* Toronto: Macmillan, 1978.

———. "Working for a Living." *Grand Street* 1.1 (1981): 9–37.

New, W.H. "A Feeling of Completion: Aspects of W.O. Mitchell." *Canadian Literature* 17 (1963): 22–33. Rpt. in *The Canadian Novel in the Twentieth Century*. Ed. George Woodcock. Toronto: McClelland, 1975. 174–85.

Noonan, Gerald. "The Structure of Style in Alice Munro's Fiction." *Probable Fictions: Alice Munro's Narrative Acts*. Ed. Louis K. MacKendrick. Downsview: ECW, 1983. 163–80.

O'Brien, Peter, ed. *So to Speak: Interviews with Contemporary Canadian Authors*. Montréal: Véhicule, 1987.

O'Hagan, Howard. *The School-Marm Tree*. Vancouver: Talonbooks, 1977.

———. *Tay John*. 1939. Toronto: McClelland, 1974.

———. *Wilderness Men*. Garden City, NY: Doubleday, 1958. Rev. ed. Vancouver: Talonbooks, 1978. [References in text are to the revised edition unless otherwise indicated.]

———. *The Woman Who Got On at Jasper Station*. 1963. Rev. ed. Vancouver: Talonbooks, 1977.

O'Rourke, David. "An Interview with W.O. Mitchell." *Essays on Canadian Writing* 20 (1980–81): 149–59.

Peterman, Michael. *Robertson Davies*. Boston: Twayne, 1986.

_____. "W.O. Mitchell." *Profiles in Canadian Literature 2*. Ed. Jeffrey M. Heath. Toronto: Dundurn, 1980. 9–16.

Powe, B.W. *A Climate Charged*. Oakville: Mosaic, 1984.

Pritchard, Allan. "Jack Hodgins's Island: A Big Enough Country." *University of Toronto Quarterly* 55 (1985): 21–44.

Quilligan, Maureen. *The Language of Allegory: Defining the Genre*. Ithaca: Cornell UP, 1979.

Ricou, Laurie. "Notes on Language and Learning in *Who Has Seen the Wind*." *Canadian Children's Literature* 10 (1987–88): 3–17.

Roberts, Kevin. "Talking to Howard O'Hagan." *Event* 5.3 (1976–77): 42–48.

Rooke, Constance. "Hagar's Old Age: *The Stone Angel* as *Vollendungsroman*." *Crossing the River: Essays in Honour of Margaret Laurence*. Ed. Kristjana Gunnars. Winnipeg: Turnstone, 1988. 25–42.

Rosenberg, Jerome. *Margaret Atwood*. Boston: Twayne, 1984.

Sandler, Linda. "Interview with Margaret Atwood." *Malahat Review* 41 (1977): 7–27.

Solecki, Sam. "The Gospel of St. Andrew." Rev. of *Black and White Keys* by Hugh Hood. *Canadian Forum* Dec. 1982–Jan. 1983: 38.

_____. "The Other Half of Robertson Davies." Rev. of *The Rebel Angels* by Robertson Davies. *Canadian Forum* Dec. 1981–Jan. 1982: 30–31, 47.

_____. "Songs of Innocence." Rev. of *A New Athens* by Hugh Hood. *Canadian Forum* Oct. 1979: 29–30.

Stouck, David. "The Ethel Wilson Papers." *The Ethel Wilson Symposium*. Ed. Lorraine McMullen. Ottawa: U of Ottawa P, 1982. 47–59.

Struthers, J.R. (Tim). "Alice Munro's Fictive Imagination." *The Art of Alice Munro: Saying the Unsayable*. Ed. Judith Miller. Waterloo: U of Waterloo P, 1984. 103–12.

_____. "An Interview with Hugh Hood." *Essays on Canadian Writing* 13/14 (1978–79): 21–93.

_____. "The Real Material: An Interview with Alice Munro." *Probable Fictions: Alice Munro's Narrative Acts*. Ed. Louis K. MacKendrick. Downsview: ECW, 1983. 5–36.

Sullivan, Rosemary. "An Interview with Margaret Laurence." *A Place to Stand On: Essays By and About Margaret Laurence*. Ed. George Woodcock. Edmonton: NeWest, 1983. 61–79.

Swift, Jonathan. *Gulliver's Travels*. 1726. Ed. Robert A. Greenfield. New York: Norton, 1970.

Twigg, Alan. *For Openers: Conversations with 24 Canadian Writers*. Madeira Park, BC: Harbour, 1981.

West, Paul. "Canadian Fiction and Its Critics." *Canadian Forum* 41 (1962): 265–66.

_____. "Sluices of Literacy." *Canadian Literature* 14 (1962): 62–64.

Wilson, Ethel. *The Equations of Love: Tuesday and Wednesday [and] Lilly's Story*. 1952. Toronto: Macmillan, 1974.

_____. *Hetty Dorval*. 1947. Toronto: Macmillan, 1967.

_____. *The Innocent Traveller*. 1949. Toronto: Macmillan, 1960.

_____. *Love and Salt Water*. Toronto: Macmillan, 1956.

_____. *Mrs. Golightly and Other Stories*. Toronto: Macmillan, 1961.

_____. "Series of Combination of Events & Where is John Goodwin?" *Tamarack Review* 33 (1964): 3–9.

_____. *Stories — Essays — Letters*. Ed. David Stouck. Vancouver: U of British Columbia P, 1987.

_____. *Swamp Angel*. 1954. Toronto: McClelland, 1962.

Woodcock, George. *Northern Spring: The Flowering of Canadian Literature*. Vancouver: Douglas, 1987.

_____. *The World of Canadian Writing: Critiques & Recollections*. Vancouver: Douglas; Seattle: U of Washington P, 1980.

Zacharasiewicz, Waldemar. "The Development of Jack Hodgins' Narrative Art in his Short Fiction." *Encounters and Explorations: Canadian Writers and European Critics*. Ed. Frank K. Stanzel and Waldemar Zacharasiewicz. Würzburg: Königshausen, 1986. 94–109.

INDEX

231